Leadership Luminaries

CCBS Press

Leadership Luminaries

Cross-cultural empirical analyses of leadership styles and practices

Amsterdam University
of Applied Sciences

CCBS-Press

First edition 2024, ISBN: 978-90-79646-58-6, NUR: 812
Editorial managers: Christopher Higgins, Aynur Doğan, Sander Schroevers
Inner and cover design: SH69T Studio, Amsterdam, Netherlands
Cover graphic: Lifeonwhite, Brussels, Belgium
Text copyright: Abel Fego, Adam Prittie, Alaa Jabaly, Олексій Ставіцький (Oleksii Stavitskyi), Alide-Marie Hovenkamp, Amber Bolte, Amber van Nieuwenhoven, Amir Ait Aicha, Amir Kila, Anass Banani, Anastasia Otabil, Anita Elzinga, Anna Csillag, Anna Spinola, Annabel Kruis, Ansa Mohammad, Артем Любенко (Artem Liubenko), 計良歩夢 (Ayumu Keira), Beaudine Overtoom, Ben Oort, Bianca Motta, Carmen Martínez-Almeida García, Caroline Sweep, Casper de Groot, Casper Dokter, Charlotte Dijkman, Chislaine Andrade Costa, Christopher Chin, Cis den Blanken, Clara Weißenhorn, Daan Groot, Daan Tönjes, Dániel Péter Kádár, Daphne Jansen, Diam Mohammed, Dilara Sepetci, Domenico Testa, Dóra Plébán, Douae Merzouki, Douha Moudou, Dounia Belkas, Douwe Schmitt, Dylan Peeters, Dzenis Kuburović, Екатерина Радева (Ekaterina Radeva), Emma Dijkstra, Ericardo Romeo, Erik Oomen, Erin Hoek, Fleur Huurman, Francisca da Conceição Bôto, Frank Mooijer, Gabriela Castillo De Sales, Gaelle Kenjoian, Georgina Addai, Ghizlane Azzaoui, Gianna van Ommeren , Gijs Dekker, Gina Coronel, Hajar El Yakoubi, Hamza Momand, Hanzalah Latif, 김희준 (Heejun Kim), Isabeau Boender, Isak Douah, Ismail Wafelgha, Jamiro Rozendaal, Janou Dihal, Jari Stumeijer, Jeffrey Dominique de Dood, Jessie Peters, Jiya Anwar, Job Pesch, Joe Gimpel, John van der Bent, Juri Siewert, Kaio Leering, Karen Loth, Katherine Landry, Kemeal Khaddage, Kıvılcım Kafkas, Laila Kool, Lara da Fonseca, Latifa El Aissati, Levente Hargitai, Lisa-Marie Cardoso, Maartje Nauta, Manisha Chand, Mantej Dhaliwal, Margaret Maclellan, Mariana Fernandes Cabral, Marit de Zeeuw, Mark van Heijningen, Marlon Clijd, Martijn Carels, Mauro Knebel, Max Bijenveld, Melisa Demiryürek, Mette Kabo, Mike Smith, Milou van Hengel, Mitchell Mugie, Naomi van der Jagt, Nikki van Pelt, Noa Serra de Kloet, Obed Bonsu-Osei, Omayma Amallou Garnat, Pariya Afshintabar, Paul van den Ende, Pelle Brinkhof, Rafi Al Gareb, Ramy Girgis, Renata Calvelli Fonseca, Renske Hogeboom, Roksana Beyer, Sadaf Hamid, Saram Saddiqui, Savino Every, Scarly Mayi Santos, Selman Muğlu, Sergio Mendez Vilas, Shanna Strube, Sofia Kontaktsiou, Soraya Panoet, Tamara Liefting, Thea Hughes, Tom Remmerswaal, Vanessa Vieira de Sousa, Vlad Milosteanu, Waiz Malik, Warsha Tamang, William Horsford, Zach Saine, Ziad Elwakeel and Zineddine Rhninou.

Table of Contents

Preface

Welcome to the latest edition of our ongoing empirical cross-cultural analyses of global leadership styles and practices. The noun *Luminaries* heads the title of this issue in our Global Leadership series. A luminary is a prominent person who inspires or influences others. We hope this edition may inspire global professionals. This book is the result of collaborative research by 143 students on the 'Cross-Cultural Business Skills' and the 'Global Business Skills' electives (minors), which are hosted by the University of Applied Sciences Amsterdam. Over the course of a single semester, these students have empirically investigated leadership styles and practices across multiple countries, through employing a combination of research methods. More specifically, the students performed desk-based literature reviews of local scholarship, in conjunction with generating both quantitative and qualitative data through conducting a survey and interviews with thousands of local business professionals and cross-cultural scholars and practitioners. The quality of the contributions in this edited collection are thus, above all, a testament to the perseverance and collaborative work ethic of everyone involved, and, moreover, provide rich and colourful insights.

First and foremost, we would like to take this opportunity to thank all the individual co-authors for their determination to complete their respective analyses. Moreover, we also wish to extend our upmost gratitude to all the survey respondents and interviewees for being gracious enough to provide insight into the prevailing leadership styles and practices in their country. To the reader, we hope this book finds you well and perhaps, dare we say it, sitting in a convenient airport lounge waiting to board a flight to one of the countries explored in this book, with locally-informed insights into cross-cultural leadership, eager to apply them in practice.

Christopher Higgins, Sander Schroevers & Aynur Dogan

About CCBS

Since 2010, Cross-Cultural Business Skills (CCBS) has sought to educate bachelor students in both the fundamentals of cross-cultural business skills and specific research methods. CCBS is an elective course ('minor') established and taught by Prof. Dr.Hc. Sander Schroevers, Aynur Doğan MA and Christopher Higgins MA at the Amsterdam University of Applied Sciences (the Netherlands).

Educational approach

At CCBS we believe that effective learning takes place through sharing and engaging with first-hand experiences. For this reason, we challenge our students to produce new knowledge from a localised perspective. Often this involves conducting research in an unknown language, alphabet or cultural milieu, which, in turn, helps out students develop fundamental skills for the contemporary interconnected world. Our main objective is to co-create country-specific bodies of knowledge, which we generate through carrying out both expert-interviews (video and audio) with native professionals and scholars and in-depth analyses of local academic and trade literature. In order to create a truly international classroom experience, we try to host students from across the globe. Moreover, we attempt to connect our students with a broad range of representatives from the business, media and diplomatic sectors, through hosting professional symposia in the school. All CCBS-learning materials (print, digital and video) are 100% bespoke. We are honoured by the fact that we have consistently received the university's highest evaluation scores over the last ten years, and that Sander was elected as teacher of the year at the FBE-faculty.

About CCBS global leadership research

CCBS global leadership is our ongoing academic research project for the Amsterdam University of Applied Sciences, which directly informs the cross-cultural business material taught on the minor. Every six months, CCBS researchers survey C-level executives around the world. Our analytical gaze is focused on five main areas: management, meetings, leadership, recruitment and expatriates. Since conducting the inaugural international poll in 2012, the CCBS global-fact-tank has conducted interviews in 137 trade nations, with more than twenty-three-thousand professionals. Thank you!

Methodological approach

Three modes of data collection were employed to generate the insights published in this book. Firstly, insights into the cultural aspects of leadership were gathered through country-specific literature searches, in both peer-reviewed academic journals and in-country books, which served as the foundation for the subsequent research. Secondly, a global online survey on leadership was conducted with qualified respondents from each country (CCBS Survey, year). Expert sampling was used to identify the survey respondents, in conjunction with snowballing techniques, which were subsequently introduced to target a population who are often difficult to reach. In total, over 24,000 respondents participated in the CCBS survey; however almost one-third of these surveys were not used, because they were not fully completed, or their background or sometimes IP-addresses did not match our target group. The survey was created in English and subsequently translated by competent bilinguals, who were either research collaborators or supervised by them. The present study made use of translations into Arabic, Papiamentu, Hindi, Gujarati, Punjabi, Hungarian, Romanian, German, Nepali, Urdu, French, Ukrainian, Portuguese, Brazilian-Portuguese, Spanish and surely: English. Evaluations of translation accuracy were completed by using back-translation or parallel translations, where possible. The Portuguese, English and Arabic version were rolled out in multiple countries. The questionnaire comprised 27 items, both multiple-choice and open-ended questions, which provided descriptive information on national-based views on leadership.

The respondents answered the psychometric multiple-choice questions on five or six-point Likert scales, which were anchored by terms ranging from 'not at all' to 'a lot'. All the qualitative data provided comprehensive knowledge into the topic of local leadership styles and practices. The multinational survey and interviewing were conducted between 05 March and 20 May 2024. The findings that emerged out of this research have not been presented prior to the publication of this book. Thirdly, in addition to the survey respondents, a selection of 21 leadership experts were also interviewed for the present study. These audio and video recorded interviews lasted between 20-70 minutes on average, and were transcribed verbatim (a selection of these will be published on the YouTube and Spotify channels of the CCBS minor).

Country profiles

Empirical studies have revealed that the relationship between certain kinds of motivating leadership behaviour and work outcomes systematically varies from culture to culture. As noted by the Global Leadership and Organizational Behavior Effectiveness (GLOBE) Research Program: "to date, 90 percent of leadership literature reflects US-based research and theory". The American-centric nature of extant literature is a profound problem, insofar as it fails to account for how leadership theories, styles and practices operate across national frontiers. This is important, because as the number of countries expand, so do the differences. It is for this reason that I have always been fond of Peter Drucker's quote: "Management is doing things right; leadership is doing the right things". That is to say, leadership encompasses the human element of business, whereas management is often about systems and processes. For the purposes of writing this paragraph, I conducted a quick check on Amazon.com for the number of books with the word 'leader' in their title, which produced an incredible 60,000 results. Similarly, a quick search on ProQuest (one of the databases we recommend to students for accessing scholarly journals) resulted in almost a million hits for 'leadership'. Evidently, there is extensive research informing us of how leaders' communication styles are profoundly influenced by the geographical region in which they are operating. Regrettably, some business leaders overlook local managerial and cultural practices, and instead acquiesce to management-styles that are grounded in Western concepts, which, in turn, undermines the performance of their organisation. Given that ineffective managers risk costing organisations notably large sums of money, there is an emergent trend among both human resource professionals and senior executives to adopt more localised leadership styles and practices.

Chapter makeup

This book consists of country-specific chapters, which each describe at length the leadership styles and practices within their respective country. All country profiles have been written in a standard format, in order to allow for a clearer identification of points of similarity and divergence across the different business cultures.

Most of the country profiles in this book contain the following sections:

- Country introduction,
- How the indigene characterise leaders,
- Survey results and what local respondents say,
- An in-country YouTube review,
- A transcribed telephone interview with a local leadership scholar,
- A summarised video interview with a local cross-cultural trainer,
- A description of an in-country best-selling book on leadership,
- Understanding hierarchy in the chapter's country,
- How to achieve leadership empathy in that particular culture.

I will briefly introduce each of these sections in turn below.

Local leadership analysis

The more I work abroad, the more I realise that it takes more than just a survey to examine and classify national cultures. More specifically, there is too much cultural heterogeneity and nuance, which substantially impacts upon how one effectively operates in a particular country, but yet simply does not fit within prevailing academic constructs on this topic. Notwithstanding the many good Western-centric books on a variety of countries, what is invariably obfuscated in these texts is the local perspective. The need to address this lacuna in the field by prioritising localised perspectives became pivotal to our approach to investigating country-specific leadership styles and practices. This approach comprises gathering data from indigenous sources, including: (i) survey-results and what local respondents say, (ii) a local leadership scholar, (iii) a local cross-cultural trainer, (iv) and an in-country best-selling book on leadership. While having to conduct research sometimes in other languages and even scripts has proven to be incredibly challenging for some of our students, it has undoubtedly produced rich local-based data that provides insight into how leadership styles and practices are enacted in these selected markets.

Understanding hierarchy in a country

Most of the trends in Western leadership across the twentieth century were centred on moving away from hierarchical command-and-control processes. To this end, both management literature and business school education began to introduce a more egalitarian and facilitative style of leadership. For example, we started to see open-plan office architecture and 360-degree feedback.

However, it is important to note that there are profound cross-cultural differences with respect to how authority is viewed. In India, for example, the teaching staff are addressed by Madam or Sir, while I also observed on occasion students standing up when their 'senior-lecturer' entered the classroom. Conversely, on my own Dutch course (CCBS - the authors of this book) local students address me by my first name, and at times feel free to contradict me in front of the class.

Relational hierarchy

Eight out of ten Swiss survey respondents (CCBS Survey, 2021) reported that employees greeted their leaders by their first name. This low-level of hierarchy results in equal and harmonious relationships between superiors and their employees, which are based on mutual trust. Being acutely aware of someone's relative level of authority is of critical importance in a country such as South Korea. This is because it determines how colleagues interact with each other, including choosing between the many different linguistic levels of politeness. For example, organisations tend to have far more levels of management compared to some other countries, each of which have their own corresponding forms of address. Hence, the informal way in which business is conducted in Australia, for example, would likely completely confuse the average Korean employee. This would especially be the case for those Korean workers who have attained senior positions within their organisations, and are wholly accustomed to VIP treatment.

Power Distance

The words Hierarchy and Power Distance are often used interchangeably. The latter can be defined as "the degree to which members of an organisation or society expect and agree that power should be stratified and concentrated at higher levels of an organisation or government" (House & Javidan, 2004, p. 12). Countries that have scored high Power Distance values in either Hofstede or Trompenaars' respective research, believe that power dispenses agreement, social order, and role stability, and, hence, should be concentrated within those in the upper echelon of organisations. In high power distance cultures, leader-subordinate relationships are characterised by paternalism, whereby a leader assumes a parental role and feels obligated to provide support and protection to subordinates under their care (Yan & Hunt, 2005). Many of the country profiles in this book reference their country's Power Distance Index score (PDI), as measured by Dutch cultural scientist Geert Hofstede. However, the value score in and of itself cannot fully explain how hierarchy operates within a particular

11

culture. For example, despite Greece and South Korea both having equally high PDI values (60), leadership is enacted in a fundamentally different way in both countries. Therefore, in this book we attempt to account for such cultural contingencies by conducting culture-specific qualitative research, including interviewing local cultural experts.

How to achieve leadership empathy

This section addresses a specific people-oriented leadership requirement: empathic soft skills. Here, empathy is defined as a leader's capacity to relate to the feelings and experiences of their employees. Empathy is an altogether broader category than sympathy, and, in fact, several researchers consider empathy to be both a key part of emotional intelligence and a critical element of being an effective leader (Bar-On & Parker, 2000). Of course, the ability to successfully build and maintain relationships has long been regarded as a fundamental managerial skill; however, in accordance with the Center for Creative Leadership, the point being made here is that, in some cultures, empathy is more important to job performance than other aspects of leadership (Gentry, Weber, & Sadri, 2016). In addition to this, the way empathic understanding is expressed varies dramatically from country-to-country. Above all, empathy touches upon a leader's understanding of role requirement. To understand its importance across different cultures, several questions in our online survey (CCBS Survey, 2020) pertained to the specific expectations that local leaders had towards empathy. Furthermore, each team attempted to interview local experts, scholars and cross-cultural trainers on the country-specific ways in which empathy is effectively utilised. To cite an example: whereas in Nordic countries empathy is partly established through low-key and modest behaviour, Latin countries prefer a warm, personal and 'simpatico' approach, while, conversely, South Koreans value a courteous leader who, above all, attempts to save face (Kibun). It is well-established that how we connect with people is dependent on our cultural background, and, as such, the ability to be empathetic is especially important for leaders working across cultural boundaries (Alon & Higgins, 2005). The results of our CCBS survey (2020) reflect this, insofar as a large majority of the respondents from the different cultures examined in this book agreed with the statement that a manager should actively spend time on the personal wellbeing of their team members. When one compares the actual country scores (Dell, Eriks, 2018), South Korea and Ukraine score significantly lower on empathy than countries such as Uruguay and Portugal, due, in part, to the fact that Ukrainian and South Korean leaders generally prefer to keep more personal distance from their employees.

However, it is important to stress that having empathy for others is not the same as demonstrating empathy; this is because staff expectations may vary considerably across culture in terms of: (i) the amount of verbal attention employees require; (ii) the praise and encouragement expected by staff; or (iii) the daily routine of managers. When managers increase their awareness of the cultural context in which empathy takes place, it often has a direct impact on employee performance, the organisational climate, and the quality of the productive working relations between leaders and employees.

Concluding Remarks

It was Darwin who first showed us the supreme value inherent to diversity. With this in mind, both the increased cultural heterogeneity of today's workforce and the increasingly global footprint of contemporary organisations transforms the styles and practices through which we lead teams. This calls for leaders with an ability to decode cultural differences and adjust their leadership-style to fit the cultural milieu in which they are operating. In summary, I hope that our findings contribute to increasing the richness of extant leadership literature, alongside aiding professional leaders to recalibrate their skills and mindsets in a manner advantageous to themselves, their employees, and, above all, the organisations they serve.

de Baas

ප්‍රධාන විධායක නිලධාරී
தலைமை நிர்வாக அதிகாரி

Big-man

प्रबन्धक

Chief Executive Officer

Gerente general

Manajer umum

Generálny Riaditeľ

المدير التنفيذي

総監督

Président Directeur Géneral

Consejero Delegado   генеральний директор

MAIN DUDE

Australia

Casper de Groot, Domenico Testa, Gabriela Castillo de Sales, Kıvılcım Kafkas, Lisa-Marie Cardoso, Warsha Tamang.

Situated in the Southern Hemisphere of Australia, the country also referred to as the "land down under" for its geographical location, is one of the most economically progressive nations in the world (IMF, 2023). Renowned for its diverse wildlife, picturesque coastlines, and distinct accents, the total population of the country amounts to 26.6 million people (Australian Bureau of Statistics, 2023), of which three-quarters live along these aforementioned coastlines. Despite being one of the smallest continents, Australia is actually the sixth largest country in the world and is home to a myriad of different cultures and ethnicities, which contributes the cultural tapestry of the country. Indeed, it is home to one of the oldest indigenous cultures, that is, the Aboriginals, who have inhabited the land for over sixty thousand years (Camilleri, 2007). Across its history, the country has experienced significant mass migration, with the most notable of these being the British migration in 1788, which explains why English is the primary language spoken by seventy-two percent of the population (Statista 2018). This mass migration, in turn, has resulted in the country's culture greatly resembling that of Western society (Yoa & Collins, 2019). Alongside its riches in natural beauty, the country also possesses sizeable natural resources; indeed, it is home to the second largest and fifth-largest reserves of iron ore and coal, respectively (Statista 2024). Due to its geographical positioning spanning between the Indian and Pacific Oceans, Australia unsurprisingly has strong economic ties with East Asian countries. As a result of its dynamic economic landscape, the Australian work culture is characterised by collaboration, egalitarianism and preserving the work-life balance of citizens. Deeply rooted in the egalitarian and people-oriented nature of Australian business leadership (Baird & Harisson, 2017), these values translate into a commitment to equal treatment of all employees, fostering a supportive, team-oriented environment that prioritises knowledge sharing and a people centric approach (Baird & Harisson, 2017). The upcoming chapter further explores the underlying process of Australian business leadership styles and practices through recourse to both primary and secondary data from Australian experts and professionals.

How Australians characterise leaders

Australia's distinct leadership style is characterised by a multicultural work environment. According to Brian and Lewis's study (2004), Australians have an affinity for a hybrid transactional-transformational approach to leadership. Their study highlights leaders' emphasis on setting clear expectations from their employees, which they achieve through setting specific, measurable, achievable, relevant, and time-bound (SMART) goals for projects. SMART goals give diverse teams clarity and direction, whilst, simultaneously, promoting Australia's "mateship" culture of collaboration through shared goals (Brian & Lewis, 2004). This defining feature of Australian leadership was evidenced in our interview with a leadership consultant, Noel Mifsud (30 April 2024), who noted that *"there is a sense of a friendship, and we call it mateship here…and there's a real thirst for this national collaboration, and I think that's really healthy"*. However, Australian leadership goes beyond merely setting expectations. Brian and Lewis (2004) also emphasise the importance of leaders focusing on the individual development of their team members, which primarily takes place via performance feedback. For example, Australian managers prioritise giving their employees immediate performance feedback coupled with a developmental coaching session. This method, on the one hand, satisfies the direct expectations of Australian employees, whilst, on the other hand, promoting personal development, an essential characteristic of a transformational leadership style (Brian & Lewis, 2004). By integrating transactional elements that offer guidance and transformational elements that foster growth, in the Australian context, this leadership style cultivates a harmonious multicultural workplace whilst also being pragmatic and inspiring. As aforementioned, Australian organisations are also known for their cultural heterogeneity, which, in turn, requires leaders to be flexible, adaptable, and culturally intelligent (CQ) in their approach (Deng & Gibson, 2008). Leaders who effectively harness their CQ are better able to understand the importance of adaptability and recognise the need to tailor their approach to the unique dynamics of their team. This aspect of Australian leadership is supported by the results of the CCBS Survey (2024) insofar as the C-Level leaders who took part reported that Australian leadership was characterised by a flat and open management style, informal relationships with co-workers, being good listeners and seeking consensus. These findings are corroborated by a study by Wipulanusat et al. (2017), who underscored that fostering innovation within Australian public sector organisations requires transformational and considerate leadership styles. Empowering employees through such considerate forms of leadership has been associated with enhanced levels of organisational innovation and effectiveness (Wipulanusat et al., 2017). This requires leaders who possess CQ and can adapt their approach to capitalise on the capabilities of their diverse workforce (Deng & Gibson, 2008). Further support for this characterisation of Australian leaders comes from the results of the CCBS Survey (2020- 2024), where Australian leaders are described as being visionary thinkers who are resourceful and collaborative in their approach, in conjunction with leading by example and focusing on developing trust and high performance. However, it is important to note that, according to De la Rey (2005), the landscape of leadership in Australia is constantly evolving, specifically in ways that challenge the traditional view of leadership as an individual trait. According to the findings of Sarros et al. (2002), Australian work environments prioritise social responsibility and performance orientation over competitiveness. This can be attributed to several aspects of Australian culture, such as the strong sense of "mateship", where collaborative workplaces ensure that all employees have a chance to succeed (Brian & Lewis, 2004). Moreover, Australian leaders have been shown to prioritise work-life balance and wellbeing (Sarros et al., 2002). In this vein, Odengo and Kiiru (2019) highlight initiatives such as flexible working arrangements, telecommuting, and compressed work weeks that are expressly designed to boost productivity, employee satisfaction and commitment. The need for this was corroborated by our interviewee, Mifsud, who noted that especially post-pandemic, the need for a better work-life balance is much greater,"...*people are expecting more work, home life balance*" (30 April 2024).

This is further evidenced by the CCBS Survey (2020), where Australian leaders were described as spending active time on the personal well-being of team members and achieving organisational aims whilst looking after one's team, thus indicating a focus on both task accomplishment and team well-being. This testifies to the significant impact that Australian leaders have on the cultures of their respective organisations. In summary, then, Australian leadership is characterised by a balance of transactional and transformational strategies, placing equal importance on inspiring individuals and setting clear expectations. CQ and effective communication are fundamental for success in Australian workplaces. Furthermore, cultivating a culture that fosters innovation and high performance as well as prioritising work-life balance are all essential components of leadership development in Australia.

Survey results and what local respondents say

The CCBS survey (2024) was administered as a means of gathering country-specific data on the leadership styles, attributes, and practices of Australian leaders. Various C-suite members and directors were surveyed and given the opportunity to share their knowledge, expertise, and personal experiences of Australian organisations to better paint a picture of what it means to be a leader in Australia. The most significant findings emerging from the survey are discussed in turn below. Firstly, the majority of the respondents strongly agreed with the statement that managers should actively spend time ensuring the personal well-being of their team members, whilst just over half of the respondents stated that they do not prefer to retain a personal distance from their employees. This is in line with the findings of Sarros et al. (2002), who stated that Australian leaders prioritise work-life balance and wellbeing and is suggestive of a people-oriented leadership approach that prioritises employee welfare (Brian & Lewis, 2004). When it comes to decision-making, just under half of the respondents expressed agreement with the statement "*Once a manager has made their decision, they are not likely to change it easily,*" which appears to point towards a degree of decisiveness and commitment to decision-making amongst Australian leaders (CCBS Survey, 2024). Furthermore, one-quarter of respondents stated that they do not consider missing a deadline to be synonymous with failure, thus suggesting a more flexible and outcome-oriented mindset (CCBS Survey, 2024). The survey also demonstrated that Australian leaders tend to have a collaborative leadership style. As one respondent noted, leadership styles and practices in Australia, "*tends to be less formal with a focus on outcomes/results and employees being encouraged to share ideas and feedback*". Similarly, another respondent opined that Australian leadership was characterised by more "*collaborative, casual and informal leadership styles*", which further supports this observation (CCBS Survey, 2024). With respect to employee-leader relationships, the vast majority of the respondents reported that they allow their employees to address them by their first name, which is indicative of the egalitarian and less formal dynamic highlighted by our interviewee, Mifsud, who also said that Australian leaders treat their employees like they would their own families (30 April, 2024). This characterisation of Australian leadership is corroborated by the finding that most of the respondents strongly disagreed that it is important for subordinates to address leaders by their titles or positions (CCBS Survey, 2024). When analysing the specific attributes that Australian leaders value, the survey results show a focus on organisational experience, technical competence, and market expertise. Moreover, the respondents also stressed that Australian leaders are expected to be good listeners and visionary thinkers (CCBS Survey, 2024). When asked about the level of gender (in)equality within the Australian business sector, the respondents provided relatively mixed responses, with over one-quarter of them strongly agreeing that men and women have equal opportunities to attain senior leadership positions, whilst almost half of the respondents responded somewhat disagree or strongly disagree (CCBS Survey, 2024). This suggests that whilst some progress has been made, there is still room for improvement in achieving gender parity in Australian leadership positions (CCBS Survey, 2024). Overall, the survey results depict an image of Australian leaders as approachable, collaborative, and people-oriented, with a focus on technical and organisational expertise.

Local leadership analysis

Noel Mifsud: an Australian leadership consultant

To gain a deeper understanding of Australian leadership skills and practices, we conducted an interview with Noel Mifsud, an educational leadership consultant with over forty years of experience in leadership and education (Mifsud, 30 April 2024). His perspective on Australian leadership offers a unique lens into the cultural nuances that shape business and organisational leadership down under. Central to his perspective is the concept of mateship, a cornerstone of Australian culture, which fosters a spirit of camaraderie and collaboration within leadership structures. This sense of mateship translates into a non-hierarchical approach, where leaders are more accessible and less inclined to impose rigid structures. Mifsud began the interview by outlining the typical traits of an Australian business leader. From his perspective, Australian leaders are generally non-hierarchical, socially conscious, fairly national in their outlook, and relatively tech-savvy. This non-hierarchical approach has shaped the nation's ethos. As Mifsud noted: "*when we meet our Prime Minister, we call them by their first name,*" which serves to emphasise the relaxed and egalitarian nature of Australian society. Mifsud proceeded to explain that treating employees like family is key to fostering mutual respect. In his words: "*the Australian perspective is if you treat employees like you would treat your family, they're more motivated to work with you.*" (Mifsud, 30 April 2024). This philosophy encourages leaders to take a genuine interest in their employees' well-being and to cultivate and maintain a work environment in which everyone feels valued and respected. Within this approach, leadership is not something that is imposed from the top down but rather emerges organically from within. By breaking down these traditional barriers, Australian leaders create a more engaged and innovative workforce. Later in the interview, Mifsud moved

19

onto discussing the evolving nature of leadership in Australia. More specifically, he explained that Australian business leadership must adapt to changing times and new challenges. Moreover, he emphasised the importance of trust, noting that trust is built through clear strategic intent and by respecting individuals. In light of the fact that the world is becoming increasingly interconnected, Australian leaders also are and need to embrace multiculturalism and to seeing people from diverse backgrounds as part of a larger family. Such open-mindedness in turn promotes national collaboration and the cross-fertilisation of ideas, which is a hallmark of contemporary Australian leadership. Mifsud's insights offer a compelling view of a leadership approach that is grounded in egalitarianism, adaptability, and a deep sense of community which makes Australian leadership unique and effective in a global context.

Australia Social media review

Other sections of this chapter have drawn upon academic research, survey and interview data and YouTube in order to explore how individuals or businesses in Australia discuss leadership skills and practices. This section extends this analysis further to encompass all social media platforms utilised specifically for discussing leadership styles and practices within the region. Firstly, David Cheng, Associate Professor in Leadership and Management at the Australian National University, uses his LinkedIn profile to promote recent topics that are of importance in the context of Australian leadership. In a recent post, he focused his analytical gaze upon the area of gender inequality in senior-level leadership positions within Australian organisations (LinkedIn, 2024). This assertion corresponds with the aforementioned argument that achieving success as a manager or leader in Australia necessitates the equitable treatment of all individuals within one's purview. On Spotify, Claire Delahunty hosts the Rural Leadership unearthed podcast, which discusses various issues related to Australian leadership and business practices, in conversation with a variety of guest speakers who share their knowledge and expertise with both her and her listeners. In every episode of the podcast, she delves into various topics that can be associated with the concept of leadership. The first episode, *Leading our regions through disaster; and how it does not have to be complicated,* explicitly refers to Steve Tinker's leadership approach, which, amongst other things, prioritises leaders being less complex than telecommunications itself (Tinker, 2024, 02:48). This perspective puts forward the argument that, above all, effective Australian business leaders should focus on being as simple as possible in their everyday practices, especially when communicating with their employees. Furthermore, Dr. Richard Chambers, a popular leadership consultant in Australia, speaks in a post on LinkedIn of the numerous benefits deriving from offering flexible workspaces (LinkedIn, 2024). More specifically, he showcases a modern approach to effective ways of leadership and sharing insights about effective ways of creating cultures of sustainable peak performance in Australian organisations, alongside psychosocial resilience, and high-impact leadership. Allan Keogh, from Keogh Consulting, shares his knowledge and expertise regarding how wonderful it is to see their CEO make a difference as a mentor for women in Australian businesses (LinkedIn, 2024). In particular, Keogh underscores the fact that Australian leaders, and society more broadly, are striving to make a difference in the area of gender inequality, which serves to add more weight to our aforementioned argument concerning the fact that achieving success as a leader in Australia necessitates the equitable treatment of all individuals within one's purview (LinkedIn, 2024).

In-country leadership best seller

In their insightful book "*Australian Leadership Paradox*," Geoff Aigner and Liz Skelton, who are esteemed figures within Social Leadership Australia at The Benevolent Society, delve deep into the complexities of business leadership in Australia. Renowned for their expertise in change management and leadership theory, Geoff, as Director of Social Leadership Australia and adjunct faculty at the Australian Graduate School of Management, and Liz, in her capacity as Principal Consultant, bring nearly two decades of invaluable experience in guiding social change organisations across the country. The book explores the unique challenges facing Australian business leadership, stressing the importance of adaptation in response to complex, evolving problems. Through insightful analyses, it encourages business leaders down under to address fundamental questions related to values, lifestyles, and the costs of change in order to navigate Australia's leadership landscape successfully. According to the authors, Australian business leadership stands at a crossroads, facing critical challenges in the spheres of ethics and responsibility. The prevalence of flawed leaders and organisations only serves to underscore the urgent need for a stronger emphasis on ethical behaviour and accountability within the business sector. Moreover, effective leadership in Australian businesses must extend beyond individual interests or short-term gains. Rather, it is imperative for Australian leaders and organisations to prioritise their impact upon society as a whole. "*Australian Leadership Paradox*" examines the intricate dynamics of leadership in Australia, shedding light on four pivotal paradoxes: blaming leaders for not demonstrating leadership yet turning on them when they tackle difficult issues; hesitance amongst passionate and talented individuals to take up leadership roles due to perceived challenges; the tension

21

between Australians' historical relationship with authority and the cultural values of mateship and egalitarianism; and the contrast between the perception of Australia as a nation leading during times of adversity versus the reality of living in *"the lucky country."* Utilising their extensive experience working with leaders across government, business, and community sectors, Geoff Aigner and Liz Skelton reveal how Australian leadership can be both inspiring and effective. Their insights offer new perspectives on the essential qualities needed for leadership in Australia, providing valuable guidance for readers seeking to make a positive impact in the world. Both Geoff Aigner and Liz Skelton delve into purposeful leadership, offering practical strategies for inspiring and encouraging effective leadership across a diverse range of sectors.

Local leadership book	
Title	*The Australian Leadership Paradox*
Subtitle	What it takes to lead in the lucky country
Author	Geoff Aigner and Liz Skelton
Publisher	Allen & Unwin
Year	2013
ISBN	978-1-74331-030-4

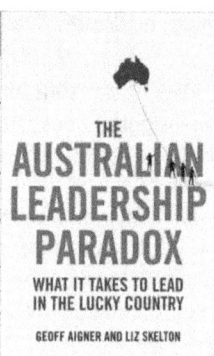

**THE
AUSTRALIAN
LEADERSHIP
PARADOX**
WHAT IT TAKES TO LEAD
IN THE LUCKY COUNTRY
GEOFF AIGNER AND LIZ SKELTON

Australian leadership YouTube review

In order to understand Australian leadership, it is instructive to consider diverse voices from various forms of data, each of which can contribute towards gaining a multifaceted viewpoint of leadership in the country. In an interview, Professor Peter Gahan, Director of the Centre for Workplace Leadership, discusses the findings of his groundbreaking study which represents the first-ever comprehensive review of Australian leadership. The study uncovered significant shortfalls in business performance and innovation, pinpointing a widespread lack of effective leadership and management capability (Gahan, 2016).

Many businesses are failing to meet performance targets, particularly in terms of return on investment and profitability, impeding innovation and overall success. Moreover, basic management practices, such as, for example, setting targets, measuring performance against KPIs, and continuous improvement are frequently overlooked. This failure in management is exacerbated by a dearth of leadership skills that are necessary to navigate the evolving business landscape, resulting in organisations struggling to adapt. Consequently, employee engagement and the ability of employees to utilise their talents are compromised. The solution proposed is to invest more in developing leadership and management capabilities to address these challenges comprehensively. Gahan emphasizes the urgency and ambition as follows: *"Forget 'The Lucky Country' if we want to become the innovation nation"* (Gahan, 2016, 1:40). With respect to Australian leaders specifically, Gahan asserts: *"Leadership matters in many different ways at different levels of the organization for performance, for innovation, and for the way the employees experience work"* (Gahan, 2016, 1:01). Alarmingly, approximately forty percent of Australian organisations are falling short of performance targets, which is indicative of a widespread deficiency in leadership and management skills. Gahan's research thus underscores the urgent need for organisations to invest in leadership development to navigate change and drive innovation. The next video to be summarised comes from the Creating Synergy Podcast, where the host explores the career of Martin Haese, the former Lord Mayor of Adelaide, and an entrepreneurial trailblazer. The discussion covers his journey from founding successful fashion ventures to leading significant civic and business initiatives in South Australia. Topics include building a 25 million USD fashion empire, strategic leadership in business and governance, contributions beyond business as Lord Mayor and CEO, commitment to sustainability, and his vision for South Australia's future (Hease, 2023). In response to a question about business leadership, Haese underscores the importance of strategic planning and nuanced communication. He advocates for leaders to carve out dedicated time for strategic thinking and adapt their communication styles to suit the diverse members of their teams. Haese's approach thus highlights the need for flexibility and empathy in leadership, ensuring that messages are effectively conveyed, whilst, simultaneously, remaining sensitive to individual differences. As he aptly puts it, *"Being nuanced is actually really important... You stay on message, but you deliver it differently."* (Haese, 2023, 1:20). The final video to be explored involves Michael Peroumal, Founding Director at Lion Private Equity Melbourne, Garry Pesochinsky, Director at Lion Private Equity Melbourne, and John Sader, Co-Founder & Director at Lion Private Equity & Lion Property Group, who engaged in an insightful discussion on Australia's *"tall poppy syndrome"* (Peroumal, 2019). The hosts explore how success can lead to criticism and its implications for personal growth and the business landscape. Peroumal shares, *"The person observing it going no no stay with me like. Don't drift away from me. Don't be better than me don't be this that or the other than me."* (Peroumal, 2019, 12:54). Peroumal's observation on the "*tall poppy syndrome*" underscores the cultural nuances that impact upon individual leadership journeys. Collectively, these perspectives paint a picture of Australian leadership as characterised by humility, moral integrity, and adaptability.

Understanding hierarchy in Australia

Australia, a country known for its laid-back attitude and egalitarian values, nevertheless exhibits distinct hierarchical structures within its business culture (Mackay, 2011). The Australian Public Service Commission (APSC) demonstrates this in their "Hierarchy and Classification Review" (2019), insofar as they report that whilst social settings might feel equal, hierarchies become more pronounced in specific situations, such as, for example, governmental jobs. This system, with its different levels and specific roles, ensures a clear chain of command and ensures that everyone is accountable within the organisation (APSC, 2019). Similarly, educational institutions and large corporations in Australia also often have well-defined hierarchies in order to ensure efficient operation (APSC, 2019). Hofstede's power distance index (PDI), which encapsulates the extent to which cultures accept differences in power (Hofstede Insights, 2024), adds an additional layer to the story. Australia scores low (38) on this index (Hofstede Insights, 2024), thus indicating a subtle interplay between informality and respect for authority in the country. Moreover, the fact that hierarchy is primarily established for convenience rather than the exercising of power, appears to suggest that there is also a preference for agility and innovation (Loh et al., 2019). Communication is open, and information is shared freely, allowing for informal participation in business settings, which translates to decentralised decision-making and greater employee autonomy (Loh et al., 2019). This depiction of Australian leadership was supported by out interview with a leadership consultant, Noel Mifsud, who opined that in Australia *"there's a lot more autonomy, you have the freedom to be creative, to make mistakes with integrity, and to think outside the square"* (30 April 2024). The results of the CCBS Survey (2024) lend further support to this characterisation of Australian leadership insofar as when the respondents were asked what distinguished Australian leadership from other countries, most of the respondents stated that leadership was *"Laid-back" "Informal" "Open"* and *"Collaborative"*. However, despite these assertions, the level of progress on gender equality in leadership is not quite in keeping with cultural shifts in the country more generally. Research by Yarram and Adapa (2021) highlighted this in their study with 214 Australian firms, which revealed that only 13% of Australian board of directors were women. Having said this, the percentage of female directors has increased from 10% in 2011, which indicates some degree of progress in terms of gender diversity in Australian boardrooms (Yarram & Adapa, 2021). Therefore, although there has been progress with respect to female representation in senior-leadership roles, women still occupy a disproportionately low percentage of executive positions compared to their male counterparts (Turnbull et al., 2020). The CCBS Survey further supports these insights insofar as the majority of the respondents disagreed with the statement that women and men had equal access to senior leadership positions. As one anonymous respondent noted: *"There is still a lot of male influence. In general, they give jobs to all the boys. Especially when they went to a private school. Also, men in their 50s and older are still very chauvinistic. A Dutch woman gets a lot more respect in the Netherlands than in Australia."* (CCBS Survey 2020; CCBS Survey, 2024). Furthermore, there is a complex dynamic in terms of how employees relate to their leaders in Australian organisations. On the one hand, the emphasis on open communication encourages employees to feel comfortable approaching their leaders with questions or ideas or to even challenge their leaders' decisions if they feel they have a valid point, and Australian leaders are expected to be receptive to these perspectives in return (Loh et al., 2019). On the other hand, the underlying hierarchical structures continue to hold a certain weight, with leaders typically being respected for their expertise and experience; this respect is often earned rather than automatically assumed. However, employees also expect a certain degree of respect from their leaders. Hence, leaders who can navigate this effectively, fostering open communication whilst maintaining clear roles and responsibilities, are likely to be the most successful in engaging their teams (Franken et al., 2019). Therefore, even though Australians are known for being relaxed and down-to-earth, there are still clear levels of management in place to keep things running smoothly. This in turn creates a unique work environment in which everyone can speak up and share ideas; however, leaders are still respected for their experience and knowledge. To be a successful leader in Australia, it is important to strike the requisite balance between encouraging open communication, maintaining clear roles, and treating employees with respect.

How Australians achieve Leadership empathy

In the Australian context, where cultural diversity and egalitarian values are prominent, empathy assumes especial significance. Recent research conducted in Australia has sought to delve into the intricacies of leadership empathy, exploring its antecedents, manifestations, and consequences within a variety of organisational contexts (Gahan et al., 2016). Research suggests that the

25

development of leadership empathy in Australia is influenced by various individual and contextual factors. One key determinant in this respect is emotional intelligence (EI), which encompasses the ability to perceive, understand, and manage emotions effectively. Australian leaders demonstrate empathy with their employees by actively listening to their concerns, showing understanding and compassion, and taking the appropriate actions to address their needs and concerns (Aimazrouei, 2023). Some key practices through which empathy is achieved involves holding frequent one-on-one meetings to discuss workload, concerns, and career goals, alongside fostering open communication, and building trust (Aimazrouei, 2023). Leaders also often offer flexibility in terms of working hours and location, in order to support employees' work-life balance (Sarros et al., 2002). Besides this, leaders often maintain open communication channels, encourage their employees to voice concerns without fear of repercussions, which, in turn, cultivates a transparent workplace culture. Empathetic leaders acknowledge employee achievements through formal and informal recognition, reinforcing a positive work environment. Leaders might also invest in training, mentorship, and career growth opportunities, demonstrating a vested interest in employees' professional advancement (Sarros et al., 2002). A study by Parrish (2015) also highlighted the positive association between EI and leadership empathy, suggesting that leaders with higher levels of EI are better equipped to empathise with their followers. Additionally, the organisational culture and leadership styles prevalent in Australia, which are characterised by openness, inclusivity, and a focus on relationship-building, contribute towards the cultivation of empathy amongst leaders (Davis et al., 2016). This was corroborated by one of the respondents of the CCBS Survey (2024), Leanne Williams, a Chief Executive Officer, who reported: *"You get the most out of your people when you as a leader empower them, support them and are kind. This must be matched with ensuring accountability is in place so everyone and the organisation succeeds. Psychologically safe and supportive workplaces are essential in the modern age of leadership."* Furthermore, Australian companies also prioritise diversity, which reflects the multicultural nature of the country. This inclusivity encourages leaders to be empathetic by valuing a wide range of perspectives and experiences. Practices like diverse hiring and anti-discrimination policies reinforce this ethos. This aspect of Australian leadership was also underscored by our interviewee, who noted that leaders in the country typically favour building relationships over rigid hierarchies (Mifsud, 30 April 2024). Other research has also pointed towards the emphasis on creating personal and meaningful connections with employees within Australian business leadership (Samad, 2015). Studies have consistently shown that leaders who demonstrate empathy foster higher levels of employee engagement, job satisfaction, and organisational commitment (Loh et al., 2019). Moreover, empathetic leadership is associated with reduced levels of workplace stress, burnout, and turnover amongst employees (Chlap et al., 2022). Finally, research by Loh et al. (2019) with 150 male and 151 female Australian employees, found that Australian workers exhibited higher job dissatisfaction and withdrawal from work when faced with workplace incivility. This underscores the importance of respectful interactions between leaders and their employees within Australian organisations. Ultimately, the ideal relationship between employees and leaders in Australia appears to walk a delicate line between informality and respect (Loh et al., 2019). These findings underscore the pivotal role of leadership empathy in terms of shaping both the organisational culture and organisational performance in Australia.

Brazil

Anastasia Otabil, Bianca Motta, Joe Gimpel, Paul van den Ende, Soraya Panoet
& Vanessa Vieira de Sousa

Brazil, renowned for its abundant sunshine, spectacular carnival, and famous soccer legacy, possesses various lesser-known realities beyond its iconic sights, such as Rio de Janeiro, the country's second largest city, and the Amazon, the world's largest rainforest (Eakin, 1997). Brazil, or *República Federativa do Brasil* (Federative Republic of Brazil) as it is otherwise known, is the largest country in South America. The name *"Brazil"* itself derives from the Portuguese word for *"brazilwood"*, *"pau-brasil,"* which is a tree that once grew plentifully along the Brazilian coast (Meade, 2002). The country is the most ethnically heterogeneous country in the world, whose ancestry can be traced to a wide variety of groups, including, amongst others, Africans, Asians, and Europeans (Costa, 2001). The country has a population of more than two hundred million people, with the prevailing language being Brazilian-Portuguese due to its status as a Portuguese colony for over three centuries (Scarato, 2019). Brazil's vivid and heterogeneous culture is celebrated through spectacular street parades, local festivals, and, of course, the world-renowned *Carnaval*. The musical genres of *Samba*, *Axé*, *Bossa Nova*, and *Pagode* fascinate travellers from all over the world, whilst its diverse cuisine, which includes staples such as rice, beans, and coxinha, serves as a cultural emblem for the country (Santos et al., 2023). The Brazilian export economy has grown markedly in recent years, with its principal export destinations being China, the US, and the Netherlands, driven by its key export products: soya beans, coffee, and corn (Canuto et al., 2013). This economic dynamism is complemented by a business leadership style that emphasises accessibility, visibility, charisma, and relationship-building in order to navigate the complexities of international trade (Casado, 2018). The importance of these leadership traits is encapsulated in the following expression: "*Quem não é visto não é lembrado,*" ("He who is not seen is not remembered") (Casado, 2018). The following chapters explores Brazilian leadership skills and practices by drawing on primary and secondary data from Brazilian experts and professionals.

How do Brazilians characterise leaders

According to Casado (2018), Brazil's distinct cultural values and traits significantly impact upon the preferred business leadership practices and skills in the country's organisations. Brazilian leaders frequently take on a protective and paternalistic role, which serves to position them as so-called "*hero-leaders*." This leadership style emphasises the value of social ties and influential figures within organisations, such as, for example, founders or senior-level leaders, who embody its values and beliefs, serve as role models, and shape the organisational culture through their actions and behaviours (Casado, 2018). The importance of role-models was confirmed by the results of the CCBS Suevey (2024) insofar as the respondents stressed the importance of Brazilian leaders possessing a strong charismatic personality (CCSB Survey 2024). The importance of having trust in leaders has been found to be higher in companies where leaders support and influence workers, encourage decisive behaviour, and employ planning and training (Pinto, 2005). This aligns with the democratic leadership profile found in the Brazilian banking sector, where collaborative decision-making and investment in training helps to build trust and confidence amongst employees (De Souza, 2021). This aspect of Brazilian leadership was emphasised by our interviewee, André Brandao, a cross-cultural trainer, who stated that Brazilian leaders best build trust with their employees through strong relationships. According to them, this necessitates not only being *"acquainted with people but becoming really close to people and it must be in a genuine way"* (Brandao, 12 April 2024). In line with this, unsurpirisingly paternalistic tendencies are prevalent in Brazil, not only in small companies with high-levels of paternalistic control, but also in larger, more complex companies, which results in a unique Brazilian version of oversight (Moreira, 2005). This paternalistic leadership approach is grounded in the broader societal inclination towards personalism and the creation of archetypes. Within this milieu, leaders are simply required to protect and guide their subordinates and provide guidance to them in order to build trust and reliance (Casado, 2018). This is supported by the results of the CCBS Survey (2024) insofar as the respondents reported that leaders actively spend time to ensure the wellbeing of their team members. Consequently, Brazilian leaders are more likely to adopt authoritarian approaches than transformational behaviours with their subordinates (Cavazotte et al., 2013). This has been observed in public organisations, which were found to be characterised by highly stable structures, resistance to change, bureaucratism, political interference external to the organisation, centralised authoritarianism and paternalism (De Souza Pires & Macêdo, 2006). However, the leadership dynamic has shifted over time towards a model that prioritises trust, fostering personal relationships with employees, and actively seeking their input on various matters, according to the interviewee who took part in our research (Brandao, 12 April 2024). This was supported by our Brazilian leadership scholar, Marcel Zorovich, (16 April 2024), who noted that in comparison to other South American countries, Brazil places importance on collaboration via team-based techniques, a paradigm shift which he refers to as *"corporate diplomacy"*. This approach encourages employees to *"delegate many projects to develop their skills in terms of leadership too"* (Zorovich, 14 April 2024). Investing in collaborative decision-making and training programs not only enhances employee trust and confidence but also plays a crucial role in developing new leaders, ultimately contributing to organisational success (De Souza, 2021). Brandao (12 April 2024) stated in our interviews that due to people's increased aversion to working under authoritative leaders, companies are investing in leadership training programs to gradually phase out this style. Nonetheless, Brandao (12 April 2024) expressed: *"every company still has the authority issue present"* and that *"[although] it's changing it still happens"*. Furthermore, Dias and Borges' (2015) research showed that, according to the perceptions of employees in the public sector in Brazil, the most prominent trait amongst leaders is *"management by exception"*, which is embelmatic of a transactional leadership style and entails leaders actively seeking out deviations from established rules and standards, intervening only when these standards are not upheld (Dias & Borges, 2015). An example of management by exception would be when leaders punish their employees for their failures, demonstrating a focus on irregularities in the process rather than routine operations (Da Silva, 2016). However, transactional leadership, driven by performance-based rewards, may lower employee engagement. Therefore, a shift towards transformational leadership is needed in public sector management to improve team performance and engagement, emphasising individual development and recognition beyond monetary incentives (Dias & Borges, 2015). Finally, professionals in *Brasília* have also been found to exhibit a strong preference for transformational leadership, driven by its perceived effectiveness in fostering organisational commitment, loyalty, satisfaction, and performance (De Oliveira Fonseca et al., 2012).

Survey results and what local respondents say

In order to gain additional insight into leadership skills and practices in Brazil, the CCBS Survey (2015-2024) was administered to C-Level managers in order to learn from their knowledge and expertise. The results of this year'survey were combined with results from previous iterations of the survey in order to enhance both the generalisability and validity of the findings. Overall, the data reveals several significant trends and beliefs that influence leadership behaviours across Brazil. The first noteworthy finding is that Brazilian leaders tend to stick to their decision once it has made been in Brazilian organisations (CCBS Survey, 2015-2024). This rigidity in organisational structures, coupled with the high value placed on deadline observance and responsibility, has significant implications for leadership practices in the country. The results also provide insights into leadership traits and behaviours. Specifically, around two-thirds of the respondents reported that leaders will confront team members in staff meetings in order to achieve the desired outcomes (CCBS Survey, 2015-2024). However, team members' well-being is also accorded significant weight it seems, insofar as more than half of the respondents agreed with the statement that managers should spend time on the wellbeing of team members. This is indicative of a more sophisticated leadership style that balances team member needs and task-oriented outcomes (CCBS Survey, 2015-2024). With respect to whether leaders should retain personal distance from their mployees in order to ensure the necessary respect, just under half of the respondents agreed with this statement, in comparison to the remaining respondents who stressed that it is important to develop a personal rapport with their subordinates (CCBS Survey, 20215-2024). The survey results also underscored how the subtleties of Brazilian culture influence business leadership, insofar as sixty percent of the respondents cited personal connections, informality, and a penchant for teamwork over strict hierarchical systems as being key characteristics that set Brazilian leaders apart from their foreign counterparts. Furthermore, the results of the CCBS Survey (2025-2024) also demonstrate that the significance occorded to academic titles and formality in leadership is waning in Brazil, as evidenced by the fact that over forty percent of the respondents disagreed with this practice. This finding is also in accordance with the belief expressed by almost half of the respondents that personal declarations, as opposed to meritocracy, define leadership in Brazil. Alongside this, the respondents acknowledged the significance of interpersonal skills and emotional intelligence in effective leadership, with almost seventy percent of thcm agrecing with statements highlighting the relevance of traits like being a good listener, consensus seeker, and visionary thinker (CCBS Survey, 2015-2024). Finally, in response to a question regarding the level of gender (in)equality in terms of access to senior-level leadership positions in Brazil, over forty percent of the respondents claimed that there was equal acccss to these positions for both men and women, whilst around thirty percent suggested this was not the case, thus signalling the persistence of gender-related challenges in business leadership in Brazil (CCBS Survey, 2015-2024).

Local leadership analysis

Marcelo Zorovich: a Brazilian leadership scholar

Marcelo Zorovich is a Professor of International Relations and Business at ESPM Brazil. Professor Zorovich has over twenty-seven years of commercial experience, spanning numerous countries including Brazil, Argentina, Uruguay, and others, as well as nearly 18 years in leadership positions, which makes her ideally suited to provide insights into the problems and dynamics of leading multicultural teams. According to Zorovich (16 April 2024), the ideal leader in Brazil is someone who is always looking for results from subordinates and is able to manage multicultural teams. From the interview, it became evident that managing multicultural teams is an exciting yet challenging task because, as Professor Zorovich opined, *"There is a lack of personal interactions and personal relationships when people work from different countries, and this has developed greatly in reaction to the global shift such as COVID-19."* (16 April 2024). Successfully adapting to this evolving paradigm necessitates striking a delicate balance between human-centred methods and technological improvements. Next, he proceeded to discuss how Brazilian leaders are flexible and their approach to leadership has evolved significantly in recent years (Zorovich, 16 April 2024). In response to a question about what distinguishes Brazilian leadership styles and practices from their foreign counterparts, Marcelo Zorovich stated that whilst hierarchical systems are strong across several Latin American countries, including, amongst others, Mexico and Colombia, Brazil emphasises collaboration through the utilisation of team-based techniques (Zorovich, 16 April 2024). He proceeded to explain that, whilst hierarchy is important, it is less pronounced in Brazil. Rather than merely adhering to the top-down approach, the focus is instead on working in teams and creating a collaborative environment: *"We are creating teams and squads to facilitate collaborative efforts, aiming to align individuals and promote interconnectedness, rather than relying solely on the top-down approach"* (16 April 2024). This shift, which he refers to as *"corporate diplomacy,"* denotes a strategic approach to navigating organisational dynamics. Another difference he highlighted between Brazilian and international practices concerned time management. Whilst North Americans and Europeans value punctuality and straightforwardness, Brazilians tend to be more flexible and less time-conscious (Zorovich, 16 April 2024). He recounted a story from his time managing key accounts for Nestle when he met a Swiss director of Nescafe. He explained that despite warning the director of a minor delay, he was chastised upon arrival for failing to adhere to the agreed-upon time. Whilst taken aback by the criticism, he promptly apologised and recognised the value of punctuality in other countries. Later, he discussed how Brazil's history as an immigrant nation has resulted in a diverse society marked by tolerance for opposing viewpoints. However, he also stressed the difficulties foreigners face concerning bureaucracy and the pervasive awareness of security issues in Brazil, stating *"Every day in our life we tend to be alert because we grew up in violence."* (16 April 2024). With respect to empathy in leadership, he underscored the significance of leaders understanding and assisting employees with their problems. He referred to his own practice of joining colleagues for coffee breaks to discuss both personal and professional issues, offering assistance regardless of the topic at hand (Zorovich, 16 April 2024). Furthermore, he explained that effective leadership in Brazil is dependent on trust, communication, and making subordinates feel appreciated. To foster this, leaders should practice transparency by openly discussing ongoing projects and challenges with their team (Zorovich, 16 April 2024). Finally, he empowers his own subordinates by giving them the freedom to choose their projects and allowing them to develop their skills. He concluded by noting: *"People want to be exposed, to lead, and to have their way so I give them the opportunity to do that"* (16 April 2024).

Andre Brandao: a Brazilian cross-cultural trainer

Andre Brandao is a CEO at LINUXtips, a cultural consultant at Barret Values Centre, and a Training and Human Development Specialist. With over eleven years of experience, he is ideally positioned to provide us with important insights into leadership and business practices in Brazil. At the beginning of the interview, Brandao (12 April 2024) stated that a Brazilian leader is young and more knowledgeable on the technical aspects than the leadership and management aspects. He proceeded to note that these leaders often develop their leadership abilities through on-the-job experience (Brandao, 12 April 2024). Next, he explained that there has been a shift in Brazilian leadership dynamics in recent decades. More specifically, whilst previously leadership was autocratic in nature with a strong emphasis upon hierarchy, where leaders gave out orders and subordinates complied without question, the landscape has changed to a model that emphasises trust, personal relationships with employees, and soliciting their input on matters (Brandao, 12 April 2024). Mr Brandao also argued that there are different types of leaders in different organisations. Interestingly, he noted that some leaders continue to show authority but do so cautiously because they are acutely aware of the potential impact of unfavourable publicity on their leadership skills. As a result, there is a reluctance to demonstrate excessive control, because public criticism can quickly destroy one's reputation (Brandao, 12 April 2024). He moved onto explain that increasingly people hate working with authoritative leaders, which has given companies the impetus to invest in leadership training programs (Brandao, 12 April 2024). In response to a question about what distinguishes Brazilian culture from others, Mr Brandao stated that Brazilian culture is relationship-oriented in that it is a warm culture that emphasises personal relationships which go beyond delegating and completing tasks. In this vein, later in the interview, Mr Brandao discussed the welcoming nature of Brazilians towards outsiders and their eagerness to assist them. He did note however that foreigners may have difficulties overcoming the language barrier, whilst those accustomed to a more direct culture may find it difficult to adjust to Brazil's *"beating around the bush"* communication style (Brandao, 12 April 2024). Towards the end of the interview, Mr Brandao expressed that in Brazilian culture, trust is built through personal connections with employees, which involves going beyond knowing their names to being acquainted with their families, pets, and even attending family events (Brandao, 12 April 2024). It is important for leaders to show interest in their employee's lives and occasionally show vulnerability. This approach fosters an environment of trust and openness within the workplace (Brandao, 12 April 2024). Finally, he recounted a time when one of his employee's mother fell ill and required blood. He organised groups within the company, who went to the blood centre to donate (Brandao, 12 April 2024). He recalled this as one of the most memorable days of his life. He reaffirmed this dedication, by stating; *"If someone needs help, I will do my best to meet their needs."* (12 April 2024).

In-country leadership bestseller

Brazilian global leaders for the 21st century: how you can follow in the footsteps of successful international Brazilian leaders, is authored by Brian Guest, a seasoned executive coach and leadership writer. In this book, he outlines strategies for emulating the achievements of accomplished Brazilian leaders on the world stage. Drawing from his extensive experience as a former CEO in various countries including Brazil, Guest primarily caters to senior-level executives and promising managers in large multinational corporations in Brazil.

Encouraging readers to envision their personal growth beyond perceived limitations, Guest employs his dynamic coaching approach to facilitate their development. His methodology, rooted in profound leadership experience within diverse international contexts, offers practical tools for navigating challenges and seizing opportunities. Characterised by its challenging yet inspiring nature, Guest's coaching style equips individuals to overcome obstacles and maximise their potential. There are several key takeaway messages from this book for aspiring leaders in Brazil. Firstly, adaptation and innovation are of critical importance for being a successful leader in Brazil, due to the importance of adapting to diverse markets and innovating to meet varied consumer demands and challenges. Secondly, cultural competence is vitally important, namely in terms of being sufficiently equipped to understand and navigate the different cultural landscapes in the country. The book is critically important in this regard insofar as it provides guidance into how these leaders can leverage their unique Brazilian cultural insights to influence and negotiate in the global business environment. Thirdly, sustainability and responsibility are vital. Many Brazilian companies are leaders in sustainability, due to Brazil's rich natural resources and the global emphasis upon environmental responsibility. In summary, targeted towards Brazilians aspiring to pursue or enhance their careers in international management and leadership, this book addresses the common hurdles encountered along this journey. From seizing initial opportunities to contemplating relocation decisions, it provides insights specifically tailored to the unique experiences and aspirations of Brazilian professionals venturing into the global arena. This perspective on the evolving landscape of work delves into the nuances of cross-cultural communication and international business, with an especial emphasis upon the virtual realm.

Local leadership book		
Title	Brazilian global leaders for the 21st century	BRAZILIAN GLOBAL LEADERS FOR THE 21ST CENTURY
Subtitle	How you can follow in the footsteps of successful international Brazilian leaders	
Author	Brian Guest	
Publisher	Independently published	
Year	2022	BRIAN GUEST
ISBN	979-8414363194	THRIVE CAREERS LTD

XYZ leadership YouTube review

Alongside academic research and survey and interview data, YouTube also constitutes an interesting source of data through which to learn about Brazilian leadership skills and practices. In the first video to be summarised, Simone Costa, a senior coach and specialist at TCO international, summarises the nuanced

35

complexity of leadership in Brazil. In her interview with the chief digital officer of TCO, she explains that whilst one can flourish as a leader elsewhere, navigating the Brazilian setting requires a distinct strategy in order to flourish (Costa, 2015, 2:51). She emphasises that acceptance comes before leadership effectiveness, which, in turn, necessitates an investment in cultivating and maintaining personal ties with subordinates in order to win their respect and build trust (Costa, 2015, 3:25). In Brazil, communication goes beyond words; *"it is based on relational depth and understanding."* (Costa, 2015, 4:14). Ms Simone also argues that flexibility is a key component of effective leadership in Brazilian teams, as rigidity undermines trust and reduces productivity. This highlights the importance for Brazilian leaders to tailor their methods by prioritising relational dynamics and adaptability to develop trust and achieve success (Costa, 2015, 2:36). She concludes that there is high informality in Brazilian organisations as they have seen this to be more productive and effective than formal approaches (Costa, 2015, 3:32). In the next video, Erika Linhares, CEO of Telecom and founder of B-have, discusses female leadership in Brazil. She emphasises that there is an imbalance of female representation in leadership roles, despite Brazil having such a high proportion of women. Linhares outlines four major variables that contribute to this imbalance. Firstly, she accepts that women still bear the burden of balancing professional responsibilities with caregiving roles (Linhares, 2020, 1:28). Secondly, there are persistent biases that impede women's professional development (Linhares, 2020, 6:00). Pregnancy, Linhares notes, is the final barrier, since women encounter difficulties in career advancement owing to maternity-related absences (Linhares, 2020, 7:35). In the final video to be summarised, in a TedTalk Felipe Barreiro recounts his journey of leadership from two decades of experience within Brazilian organisations. He shares that when he first started working as an internal controller, Brazilian organisations were more vertical and he aspired to instigate a shift towards a more horizontal approach (Barreiro, 2022, 5:40). Later in his career, he worked hard to create a culture of horizontal leadership by encouraging collaboration through team-building activities and the involvement of his employees (Barreiro, 2022, 7:15). Above all, he stressed the need for leaders to establish proximity with their employees, which represents not just access to information, but also close interpersonal connections that help people realise their goals. He also talked about purpose emphasising the alignment of activities with larger goals and perseverance corresponding to resilience in the face of adversity (Barreiro, 2022, 10:01). Finally, Barreiro noted that if leaders incorporate these principles into their practices, it will cultivate discipline and produce a harmonic and productive operating cycle within Brazilian firms.

Understanding hierarchy in Brazil

In Brazil, hierarchy and status play a notable part in terms of forming leadership preferences within the professional landscape (Schroevers, 2024). According to Hofstede Insights (2024), Brazil's society is charactered by the acceptance of inequality and respect for hierarchy. This is reflected in the relatively high score of 69 on the dimension "power distance" (Hofstede Insights, 2024). Based on data from a sample of Brazilian managers, the authors concluded that Brazilian culture is characterised by hierarchy, paternalism, and authoritarian management approaches. Brazil's workplace hierarchies reflect significant cultural norms and societal ideals shaped by historical legacies and economic realities. Organisational hierarchies often mirror societal divisions, with power concentrated at the top and subordinates expected to follow orders (Da Silva et al., 2017). However, effective Brazilian leaders recognise the limitations of this traditional model and understand the importance of engaging with employees at all levels. By actively involving employees in strategy formulation processes and fostering an environment in which their input is valued, leaders can break down hierarchical barriers and encourage collaboration. In doing so, they mobilise resources for evaluation and discussion, harnessing the collective intelligence of the organisation to drive innovation and adaptability (Bernardo et al., 2017). De Souza and Dourado (2016) explain that the hierarchical structure of Brazilian companies is well-defined, exhibiting a conventional top-down arrangement in which decision-making power and accountability are centralised at the top and distributed downwards. At the upper echelon of the organisation, senior-level management demonstrates traits associated with strategic leadership. They oversee establishing the organisation's broad goals and objectives, determining the strategic direction of the business, and speaking on behalf of the firm to external stakeholders, including the public, investors, and government officials (De Souza & Dourado, 2016). Their choices impact upon the entire company and direct the behaviour of intermediate and lower-level managers. Within organisational hierarchies, middle management operates as a liaison between senior-level management and lower-level staff members. Their actions are defined by how they carry out the plans and directives that upper management has established. In so doing, they ensure alignment with the organisation's broad objectives by converting high-level goals into workable plans for their departments or teams. Middle managers oversee staff members at the lower levels, giving them direction and advice, keeping an eye on performance, and assessing their results (De Souza & Dourado, 2016). The CCBS Survey (2015-2024) findings also testify to the persistence of these hierarchical dynamics within Brazilian organisations, insofar as the respondents reported that once leaders have made their decision, they are not easily altered, which is indicative of a top-down approach to decision-making. Similarly, the respondents indicated a strong preference for adherence to hierarchical timelines and expectations, alongside seeing missing deadlines as being synonymous with failure (CCBS Survey, 2015-2024). These insights illuminate the hierarchical dynamics within organizations and further underscore the importance of middle management in ensuring alignment with organisational objectives whilst overseeing lower-level staff, providing guidance, and evaluating outcomes. Somenzari et al. (2017) indicates that the preference for hierarchical structures is prevalent within public institutions in Brazil, such as federal government agencies insofar as these organisations are distinguished by a distinct separation of roles and duties in which managers and their deputies supervise teams of operational employees. Decision-making processes ordinarily follow a top-down methodology, where senior-level management issues directions that are then carried downstream to ensure adherence to institutional norms and principles (Somenzari et al., 2017). A distinct but nevertheless hierarchical dynamic similarly operates within private sector organisations in Brazil. Although the management structure of private companies is frequently more flexible and adaptive, hierarchy is nonetheless a distinguishing feature. Da Rocha (2018) explains that hierarchical structures are shaped in large part by gender, with women consistently having difficulty obtaining high-ranking jobs across a range of industries. Gender gaps persist despite progress because women still face obstacles to equal pay and job development. The results of the CCBS Survey (2024) lend credence to these assertions, inasmuch as only a minority of the respondents strongly agreed or somewhat agreed with the statement that men and women have equal opportunities to attain senior-leadership roles in Brazilian organisations, which underscores the persistent challenges faced by women.

How the Brazilians achieve leadership empathy

Flávia et al. (2014) state that Brazil is a country in which power, social and work relationships appear to be profoundly interwoven. This is because organisations in Brazil operate based on a "relational logic", which is to say that individuals continually strive to be included by prioritising and nurturing personal connections (Casado, 2018). The strong emphasis on personal connections and admiration for heroes within Brazilian society results in a tendency for people to rely heavily on their leaders, viewing them as both saviours and protectors (Casado, 2018). This aspect of Brazilian leadership was corroborated by our interviewee, Brandao, a specialist in human development, who stated in our interview that Brazilian leaders prioritise the cultivation and maintenance of warm relationships. This was also supported by the results of the CCBS Survey (2024) insofar as the respondents stated that it is important for leaders in Brazil to have a strong charismatic personality. Indeed, it is more important for leaders to maintain warm relationships than it is to engage in direct communication with their employees, which stands in marked contrast to the straightforward approach often observed in other cultures (12 April 2024). That is to say, Brazilians tend to communicate subtly, offering context and choosing their words carefully, unlike the more direct forms of communication observed in other cultures (Brandao, 12 April 2024). In light of these cultural nuances, it is essential to consider how leadership styles align with Brazilian cultural values. In relation to this, Senosiain (2012) argues that in Brazil, the prevailing leadership styles are Charismatic/Value-Based and Team-Oriented. According to our interviewee, these leadership styles are particularly effective in a cultural context in which warm relationships and subtle communication are highly valued (Brandao, 12 April 2024). To elaborate further on the importance of aligning leadership styles with cultural values, it is crucial to recognise the significance of team dynamics in Brazilian workplaces. Whilst individual interactions with team members are essential, dedicating time to collective engagement is equally vital (Javidan et al., 2016). Javidan et al. (2016) emphasise the necessity of both formal work settings and informal gatherings for fostering such cohesive teamwork. Moreover, given Brazil's low rules orientation, managers must clearly establish the rules and procedures to be followed, along with providing the rationale for their decisions. Javidan et al. (2016) state that considering these aspects within the strategy development process is essential in terms of allowing input from employees, and requires leaders to be patient and proactive in fostering and supporting their participation. The Brazilian leadership scholar we interviewed, Zorovich agrees that fostering trust involves leaders assigning tasks and seeking input from team members, thereby empowering them, and cultivating a sense of accountability within the team (16 April 2024). These strategies should avoid appearing too risky or ambitious and should instead be on generating short-term outcomes to strengthen employee understanding and support (Javidan et al., 2016). Alongside trust, Sobrinho and Porto (2012) argue that in order to be a successful leader in Brazil, leaders must also display sincere care for the individual welfare of their team members. Specifically, the authors argue, leaders can cultivate a healthy and empathic organisational environment by giving their employees autonomy and recognising their performance (Sobrinho & Porto, 2012).

Canada

Christopher Chin, Savino Every, Thea Hughes, Kemeal Khaddage,
Katherine Landry & Margaret MacLellan

Canada, or *"The Great White North"* as it is popularly known, is a diverse country both in terms of its people and its natural landscapes. Contained by the longest coastline in the world, this North American country boasts multicultural communities from the coasts of the Pacific to the Atlantic Ocean (Statistics Canada, 2016). Canada encompasses ten provinces and three territories, each with distinct provincial laws, capitals, and distinct identities (Government of Canada, 2017). Despite having only two official languages, English and French, there are over 200 languages spoken across the country (Government of Canada, 2019). Canada is a major global player, with strong trade relationships and a large economy (World Bank, 2023). In this respect, the country utilises its geographic positioning and infrastructure to its advantage with respect to exporting and importing goods and doing business with other countries. As a result of free trade agreements, Canada's top exports such as crude petroleum, cars, and gold can move freely across the world (OEC, 2023). For Canada to maintain its large economy in the modern business climate, a great deal of acceptance is required, especially given that Canada is renowned for its ethnocultural and religious diversity (Statistics Canada, 2022). Hence, an important trait of both Canada's business and political leaders is their ability to collaborate and include diverse perspectives within decision-making. Besides this, the Canadian business norms also place emphasis on adhering to a performance-driven corporate culture, whereby career advancement is only achievable through working long hours and remaining ahead of the "competition" (Duxbury & Higgins, 2003). The consequence of this is that work takes precedence in the lives of many Canadians, driven by the prevailing belief that, irrespective of one's background, everyone can access all the opportunities Canada has to offer as long as they are hardworking. Canadian leader Justin Trudeau sums this up in the following quote; *"leadership should be focused on extending the ladder of opportunity for everyone"* (Parker, 2016). This chapter explores Canadian leadership through recourse to primary and secondary data from Canadian leaders and experts.

How Canadians characterise leaders

The community-oriented culture of Canadian society generally and the workforce specifically influences the characterisation of leaders in the country. In Canada, leaders are defined by an effective, quiet style that relies more on charisma than flash or showiness (Henein & Morissette, 2007). Allied with this, Canadian leaders distinguish themselves from their international counterparts by adopting a more "lateral" leadership style that promotes democracy and inclusivity (Hartney et al., 2022). This characterisation of Canadian leadership is supported by Arber Zaplluzha, a Canadian manager in Settlement Services and Programs, who stated that *"Canadian leaders tend to adopt a consultative and consensus-building approach, valuing input and feedback from various stakeholders before making decisions"* (CCBS Survey, 2023). With the former in mind, Canadian organisations, and their leaders thus search for employees who are self-aware and engaged, committed to learning and able to develop new skills, appreciative of change and accepting of challenges, or accountable and committed to achieving the organisation's vision and values (Crawley-Low, 2013). Therefore, knowing one's workforce through inclusion and process expertise is critical for leadership success in Canada (Henein & Morissette, 2007). This emphasis on inclusion is supplemented by House (2004), who observes that countries like Canada, which typically accept a large volume of immigrants, are driven by the mindset that professional advancement is possible no matter what level of the organisational ladder you enter the workforce at. Consequently, it is common for Canadian leaders to implement policies related to employment equity and DEI training, which seek to eliminate bias and promote diversity in the workplace (CCBS Survey, 2023). This finding from the CCBS Survey (2023) is in line with Hartney et al. (2022), who underscore the importance of Canadian leaders being suitably equipped to integrate diverse perspectives within their decision-making process. The aforementioned focus on a more lateral leadership approach in Canada is also supported by the fact that leadership in Canada is determined by one's behaviour rather than one's position (Skelly, 2017), a philosophy which ensures that all employees have the opportunity to both provide and receive motivation from their colleagues. In an attempt to generate feelings of empowerment and trust amongst their workforce, Canada's participative leaders aim to motivate employees by granting them autonomy and decision-making responsibility (Huang et al., 2010). Participative leadership can also affect the volume of potential leaders present in an organisation, as mentorship is a key aspect of enabling future leaders. As noted by Henein and Morissette (2007), apprenticeship empowers self-discovery, positive reinforcement, and growth that is sustained through the community mindset. In the public sector, leaders themselves have acknowledged that vision, communication, teamwork, worldview, and an ability to learn are five leadership competencies that must continue to be developed going forward (Dantzer, 2000). Moving forward, possessing a worldview is set to become a standard for successful leadership in Canada given the ever-increasing diversity of its population. For example, as the workforce grows in terms of culture and experience, it is important for organisations to value the cultural and religious heterogeneity of their employees. This provides one clear explanation for why the ability to learn is ranked highest amongst the required competencies of Canadian leaders. In the same vein, the CCBS Survey (2024) clearly showcased the meritocratic principles that govern Canadian organisations, with respondents highly valuing leadership characteristics such as skillset, knowledge, and ability to adapt to varying circumstances. In contrast to the long prevailing view that the public and private sectors required notably different types of leaders, research by Dantzer (2000) indicates that there is consensus over the leadership competencies that will be required in the future, irrespective of the sector. Visionary leadership is commonly valued in Canadian business leaders, insofar as it helps them to provide a strong sense of direction and articulate realistic goals to those they lead (Javidan & Carl, 2005). As a result, Canadian managers are more concerned with advancement and therefore are commonly viewed as individualistic. Nevertheless, as the definition of a Canadian leader continues to grow, it is expected that senior-level leaders will continuously add new skills to their repertoire and expand their leadership capacity (Henein & Morissette, 2007).

Survey results and what local respondents say

To obtain further insights into Canadian leadership dynamics, C-Level Canadian executives with extensive leadership experience within Canadian organisations were asked to complete the CCBS Survey. Presented below are the key findings gathered from over 60 respondents, who provided valuable insights into the prevailing leadership styles and practices in Canada. The first notable finding in the survey is that in Canada, there exists an egalitarian attitude within the workplace, as evidenced by the fact that 74% of the respondents disagreed with the notion that subordinates must address leaders solely by their formal titles or positions (CCBS Survey, 2024). Similarly, 70% of the leaders affirmed that within their organisations, privileges are not exclusively reserved for leadership, thus signalling towards a more democratic environment (CCBS Survey, 2024). These survey findings are in line with Al-Alawi and Alkhodari (2016), who report that employees are considered almost as important as the people in management in Canadian organisations. Considering the aforementioned, it is also common for subordinates to address their leaders by their first names, highlighting that status and hierarchy are indeed not of significant importance in Canada (CCBS Survey, 2024). In addition, the survey respondents reported that leaders in Canada are also characterised by their informal and approachable management style (CCBS Survey, 2024). This was illustrated by one of the respondents, Cameron Cummins, a Canadian Content Marketing Manager, who noted that *"subordinates seldom feel pressured when approaching their managers with questions, concerns, or complaints"* (CCBS Survey, 2024). In fact, open communication lines and follower engagement in the co-creation of strategies are encouraged in Canada, a sentiment which is shared by both Hartney et al. (2022) and the CCBS Survey (2024). Moreover, the survey also underscored the importance of skills, knowledge, and versatility as key attributes of a Canadian leader. Skillset was found to be essential, with organisation, market, and technical proficiencies highly valued across the board, thus showcasing the meritocratic principles that govern Canadian organisations (CCBS Survey, 2024; Schroevers, 2024). Conversely, other factors such as age, family background and physical appearance, were found to collectively hold relatively minor significance according to the respondents (CCBS Survey, 2024), insofar as only 9% selected this attribute. Finally, there was a clear sentiment from the respondents regarding the importance of valuing their employees, with 91% of the respondents reporting that they actively devote time to ensuring the wellbeing of their team members (CCBS Survey, 2024). This result is in line with the strong emphasis that Canadian leaders place on a healthy work-life balance (CCBS Survey, 2024), as well as being in accordance with Henein and Morissette (2007), who state that leaders in Canada acknowledge that they cannot achieve their objectives without the support of their subordinates. This was further corroborated by one of the respondents, Arber Zaplluzha, who referred to the distinct leadership style of Canada as being a *"servant leadership"* approach, where leaders prioritise the needs of their team and seek to empower and develop their employees (CCBS Survey, 2024). In conclusion, the core essence of the Canadian leadership style was summed up by one of our respondents, an IT manager in Ottawa, who described it as *"a collaborative and consensus-based approach, emphasising inclusivity, equality, and fairness"* (CCBS Survey, 2024).

Local leadership analysis

Canadian social media review

This section showcases examples of how effective leadership skills and practices can be shared via social media and, in so doing, serve as an educational tool for current and aspiring Canadian business leaders. The Global Leadership Network Canada (GLN Canada) uses their X page to teach members about what it takes to cultivate and maintain positive and effective leadership within Canadian workplaces. GLN Canada places strong emphasis upon empathic leadership stating, *"leadership is not just about power – it is about empowering others. True leaders guide even when absent"* (Global Leadership Network Canada, 2024). Through this tweet, GLN Canada is once again underscoring the aforementioned point about leaders providing equal opportunities and placing value on all employees. GLN Canada also shared the qualities of good leaders with their followers, stating *"clarity, consistency, and accountability are the pillars of building a culture of trust"* (Global Leadership Network Canada, 2024). This reinforces the idea that Canada is focused on maintaining business relationships through empathetic leadership. George Couros, who operates under the Instagram handle 'Gcouros' has grown a following on multiple social media platforms, educating followers on innovative teaching, learning, and leadership consulting. Specifically, Couros (2022) reflects on the significance of lifting others up and making them better, which suggests that Canadian leaders prioritise fostering a culture of support and development within their organisations. Similarly, Couros (2024) stresses that inclusion and collaboration are vital, posting that *"innovative organisations are not about a top-down or bottom-up approach as much as it is about all hands-on deck"*. He suggests that using all resources and talents at one's disposal regardless of their hierarchical positioning epitomises a collaborative leadership style to addressing the challenges and opportunities that organisations face. Sterlin Martin is a Canadian leadership coach, who is active on LinkedIn, and shares insights on what leadership looks like in Canada. His perspective on what makes a good Canadian leader is shown in a 2021 LinkedIn post that notes that *"as a great leader it is imperative that you know that one style does not fit all"* (Martin, 2021). Rather, a leader's ability to adjust their leadership style to different team members and under different circumstances is at the core of what constitutes a great leader in Canada (Martin, 2021). Moreover, Martin (2021) points to the flat hierarchical approach in Canadian leadership, stating that *"the title is an obstacle for what the person really brings to the table"*. Instead, a good Canadian leader focuses on the unique competencies of a person, underlining the meritocratic principles that govern Canadian organisations. Finally, Martin (2021) argues in a different post that *"one of the biggest errors a leader can make is not taking the time to listen"*. He proceeds to state that *"the generation and communication style of those being listened to may be very different"* (Martin, 2021). Terrence Thomas Kevin O'Leary, better known as Mr. Wonderful or Maple Man, is one of the most successful Canadian businesspeople in history. He is highly active on his various social media platforms, generating content for his sizeable audience on different business leadership-related topics. On December 30, 2023, he shared on X his depiction of a great leader, stating, *"The definition of leadership is that you have to find great people and ask them to do extraordinary things"* (O'Leary, 2023). A great Canadian leader must thus be able to find eager individuals who are prepared to seek innovation, regardless of their current position, which is in line with the finding of Jill Crawley-Low (2013). Both highlight the importance of identifying top-tier talent and placing them in an enabling and encouraging environment. Moreover, traditional hierarchical standards become less apparent in these work cultures insofar as the shared effort of employees and management intertwine (O'Leary, 2023).

Dave Kernaghan: A Canadian leadership expert

To gain a deeper understanding of Canadian leadership in a cross-cultural context, we conducted an interview with Dave Kernaghan, a business professional with over thirty years of experience in leadership and teaching. Kernaghan, who held roles in project management and consulting prior to beginning his teaching career at the University of Manitoba, is passionate about international project management and exploring the leadership skills required to manage heterogeneous cultures in the workplace (Kernaghan, 15 April 2024).

At the beginning of our interview, Kernaghan described a typical business leader in Canada, drawing a clear distinction between English-speaking Canadians and French-speaking Canadian leaders. On the English-speaking Canadian side, leaders often exhibit a participatory, flexible style, in recognition of the importance of treating employees as people in order to build mutual respect (Kernaghan, 15 April 2024). Rather than adopting a more traditional approach, English-speaking Canadian leaders attempt to break down the hierarchy in order become closer to their employees. As Kernaghan himself put it: *"the Canadian perspective is if you treat people with respect, they are more motivated to work with you"* (15 April 2024). In contrast, from a French-speaking Canadian perspective, leadership is generally more formal and rigid in nature. On top of the respect that they earn through their work, French-speaking Canadian managers also expect to gain automatic respect based on their title and position in the organisational hierarchy (Kernaghan, 15 April 2024). When it comes to building trust as a leader in Canada, Kernaghan proceeded to explain that good leaders emphasise that everyone is important to the organisation's success (15 April 2024). In many instances, he noted, executives and managers will also exercise empathy and compassion as a means through which to increase trust. As he put it: *"if you really want to motivate your people to work hard for you, to like coming to work, you have to respect them as individuals"* (Kernaghan, 15 April 2024). Hence, rather than treating employees as numbers, resources, or assets, it is important that Canadian managers treat their employees as people in order to sufficiently motivate and inspire them (Kernaghan, 15 April 2024). For example, simply recognising when employees are working hard or holding open office hours to procure feedback are two ways in which leaders can connect with their employees on a human level. However, Kernaghan also stressed that leaders must be cautious not to take these ideas too far, as managers can sometimes become burdened with personal problems if their employees feel too comfortable sharing (15 April 2024). He is of the belief that in Canada, good leaders recognise how to walk the line between exercising empathy and focusing on the business. As Canada continues to grow in terms of both population and diversity, the leadership environment also continues to change. Given the diversity of cultures now present in the Canadian business world, Kernaghan explained that leadership styles have changed drastically in recent decades to be able to adapt to the potential variance in values, beliefs, and leadership expectations (Kernaghan, 15 April 2024). More specifically, Kernaghan posited that leaders must learn to be flexible in their management style, as a *"one style fits all"* approach will fail to meet the expectations of those coming to Canada from other business cultures (15 April 2024). Finaly, in order to have leadership success in Canada, one must adjust their style to be as effective as possible (Kernaghan, 15 April 2024). To conclude, Kernaghan noted *"the perspective of leadership is evolving very quickly in Canada, simply because there are so many different cultures trying to learn to work together"* (Kernaghan, 15 April 2024).

In-country leadership bestseller

'*Made In Canada Leadership*' by Amal Henein and Françoise Morisette (2009), is a Canadian top ten bestselling business book, which has received many accolades from CEOs. The first author, Amal Henein, CHRP, has worked for over twenty years in various sectors as an internal practitioner and external consultant, and is an expert in coaching and leadership development. The second author, Françoise Morisette, is a French-speaking and English-speaking HR consultant, who also specialises in leadership development and executive coaching. Together, these two HR professionals collaborated on an extensive research project focused on uncovering the collective wisdom of Canada on the art and practice of effective leadership. The book explores effective strategies for cultivating leaders, drawing upon the best practices of 295 outstanding leaders and 66 professionals in leadership development across various sectors of the Canadian economy. In their book, Henein and Morissette extensively describe the answers to their three main research questions, which are related to leadership development. Firstly, they establish that the best way to develop competent Canadian leaders requires a commitment to service, fostering a collaborative vision for the future and encouraging individual and collective growth. Secondly, to ensure Canada has a reliable supply of capable leaders in the future, a key takeaway from the book is the shift from individual heroism to a shared responsibility for leadership, emphasising the need to mentor and grow more capable leaders and a reliable talent pool. The book also highlights distinctive Canadian leadership qualities, characterised by effectiveness, collaboration, humility, and a commitment to fairness and good governance, which are imperative to the successful functioning of a leader in Canada. Finally, to enhance Canadian leadership, the book draws attention to the international appeal of the unique leadership style in Canada, which blends North American expertise with European social responsibility. It highlights the inclusive and process-oriented nature of Canadian leadership, fostering tolerance, consensus-building, and democratic decision-making. In short, Henein and Morisette's book 'Made in Canada Leadership' equips readers with insights into Canada's unique leadership traits and provides tools for nurturing a diverse pool of competent future leaders.

Local leadership book		
Title	*Made In Canada Leadership*	
Subtitle	Wisdom from the Nation's Best and Brightest on the Art and Practice of Leadership	
Author	Amal Henein, Francoise Morissette	
Publisher	John Wiley & Sons	
Year	2009	
ISBN	9780470739549	

Canadian leadership YouTube Review

Whilst analysing the various types of leadership within Canada, it is clear two distinct types of approaches are often brought to light, which are those of the public and private sectors. Although they often share the same goals and attributes, the difference in their practices is noteworthy. These are very well communicated through the expertise of Jocelyne Bourgon, President of Public Governance International, and Vince Molinaro, CEO of Leadership Contract Inc. Their views, which are presented in two different YouTube videos, yield valuable insight into two diverse methods of leadership. Jocelyne Bourgon, in her presentation for the CSPS Virtual Café Series, shares her experience of leadership in the Canadian public sector. She describes public sector leadership as inherently collaborative, necessitating the collective involvement of all members within an organisation. Significant emphasis is placed on the need for an integrative approach, which she illustrates when stating that, "*leadership is not an individual activity, it is a collective sport*" (Bourgon, 2024, 9:55) This implies that the success of the public sector is largely dependent on the ability to marshal the collective leadership capacities of all people in the entire business. Bourgon argues that the distribution of power and empowerment of all partners equips public sector organisations with a more subtle and flexible approach to tackling the multifaceted challenges of business governance. This sentiment sheds light on the transformative potential in every individual within the public sector when provided with the right conditions to develop and exercise leadership (Bourgon, 2024). In contrast, Vince Molinaro discusses the leadership landscape within the Canadian private sector in an interview with Canadian HR Reporter TV. He suggests that the private sector leadership in Canada demands resilience and a preparedness to face increasing difficulties, which is encapsulated in his assertion, "*Leadership is hard today and will continue to be harder and get harder, and so we all need to be tough*" (Molinaro, 2011, 2:16). Molinaro emphasises the weight of responsibility that leaders must shoulder in a competitive business environment. This is in line with the idea that work takes precedence for many Canadians, as career advancement is achievable only through remaining ahead of the "competition" and working long hours (Duxbury & Higgins, 2003). The final video to be discussed involves Don Wheaton, a Canadian CEO, who was awarded the Canadian Business Leader Award in 2021. In a video from the Alberta School of Business, he states that there is "*value in paying attention to the front end of the business*" (Alberta School of Business, 2021, 16:48). From his years of experience, he has gathered knowledge on effective leadership and what it takes to be successful in Canada. He labels a business's top priority as "*the front of the business,*" implying that employees are the most valuable assets and the main

48

reason for success in Canada. Overall, this implies that a business should aim to take care of their employees in any way possible if they want to be successful. Another key takeaway from Wheaton is the idea of teamwork in the Canadian workforce, and how it contributes towards a better business environment, insofar as it allows for fast responses and creates a better work environment. Overall, as Don Wheaton explains, effective leadership in Canada can be attributed to the value leaders place upon their employees, and the opportunities they provide them with to be able to succeed.

Understanding hierarchy in Canada

The Canadian business culture places strong emphasis upon interdependence and a high value on egalitarianism. As a result, employees are considered almost as important as the people in management positions (Al-Alawi & Alkhodari, 2016). According to Henein and Morissette (2007), leaders in Canada recognise that they cannot achieve their goals without the support of their followers. This conceptualisation of Canadian leadership is corroborated by the fact that Canada scores low (39) on Hofstede's Power Distance scale (Hofstede Insights, 2023). Consequently, there is no *"superiority wall"* separating the work of management and employees within Canadian organisations' power structures (Al-Alawi & Alkhodari, 2016). Rather, one sees a synergistic relationship between management levels, in ways that generally follow what one sees in a clan-based employee culture (Dastmalchian et al., 2000). Clan cultures are more likely to have innovative leadership styles and be characterised by participatory forms of leadership (Dastmalchian et al., 2000). Indeed, in Canadian organisations, the value of friendship and non-instrumental relationships often replaces hierarchy. According to Pooler, the mutuality of friendship that stems from early childhood later becomes the social norm for the hierarchical organisation of social and work contacts in Canada (2000 as cited in Pooler, 2017). Alongside this explanation, the increase in the diversification of Canadian firms from 1960 to 1975 also provides further reasons for the adoption of flatter hierarchical structures in the country, insofar as there arose a need to decentralise decision-making responsibilities amongst executives across various hierarchical levels (Martz & Semple, 1985). The results of all of this is that superiors tend to be always accessible in Canadian organisations, and, even more than this, managers rely on the expertise of individual employees and teams, which, in turn, makes Canadian workplaces social settings built upon teamwork, trust, and mutual respect. Regarding the latter, respect is not typically tied to age in the English-speaking Canadian workplace. Rather, respect is gained through one's ability, prior experience, and knowledge

(Kernaghan, 15 April 2024). To further understand the Canadian hierarchy, Henein and Morissette (2007) note that Canadian leadership focuses on empowering its followers by providing them with opportunities to develop and grow as individuals, which, in turn, promotes a sense of ownership and responsibility amongst employees. Similarly, Hartney et al. (2022) posit that a "shared leadership" approach is a common hierarchical principle of Canadian business structures, which is to say that teamwork in Canada adopts a democratic style where there is an open line of communication at all levels and team members are encouraged to participate in decision-making processes (CCBS Survey, 2023). Due to the team-oriented nature of Canadian businesses, it is customary for Canadian managers and their subordinates to consult one another and freely engage in a straightforward exchange of information, especially when faced with uncertainty (Hostede Insights, 2023). Naturally, it is leaders' responsibility to create a web of inclusion and mutual respect to support collaboration and flexibility (Helgesen, 2005). Although the aforementioned leadership approach is applicable across Canada, there are some subtle differences between English-speaking Canadian and French-speaking Canadian leadership styles that warrant mentioning here. Specifically, Hofstede Insights (2023) describes French-speaking Canadians as more formal and hierarchical in their organisational structures. Similarly, our interviewee noted that the French-speaking Canadian style is indeed less flexible, with titles and positions holding great importance (Kernaghan, 15 April 2024). Nevertheless, regarding Canadian leadership, the preferences observed through decision-making, teamwork, and leadership styles tend to be based on meritocracy over rigid hierarchical structures (Schroevers, 2024). Therefore, Canadians uphold a high standard of performance and have a strong preference for an organisational hierarchy that promotes empowerment, inclusivity, collaboration, straightforward communication, and mutual respect.

How Canadians achieve Leadership Empathy

Considering that the Canadian workforce comprises people from an increasingly diverse set of cultural backgrounds (Dujay, 2023), the first significant step for achieving leadership empathy in Canada is the prioritisation of inclusivity and multiculturalism (CCBS Survey, 2024). Besides this, Canadians also place high value on egalitarianism. As a result, Canadian leaders have "*a commitment to creating an inclusive workplace environment where all individuals feel valued and respected*" (CCBS Survey, 2023). This finding is in accordance with Hein et al. (2018), who purport that being cognisant of the evolving needs and beliefs of various cultures, generations, and other social groups, as well as utilising situational empathy, is highly valued by subordinates. Thus, it should come as no surprise that, as one of our survey respondents stated: "*Canadian leaders prioritise inclusion and embrace cultural differences, recognising that diversity can lead to greater creativity, innovation, and productivity*" (CCBS Survey, 2023). Further support for the empathic nature of Canadian leadership comes from the fact that over 90% of the respondents in the CCBS Survey (2019) reported that managers should actively spend time ensuring the personal well-being of their team members. As a matter of fact, Frédérique Dombrowski (2023), a manager in Corporate Communications in Ottawa, considers the well-being of staff to be "*a central aspect of the employee experience*" (CCBS Survey, 2023). He continued to state that Canadian leaders tend to place strong emphasis on "*ensuring staff feel valued, respected and provided with the right environments and tools to thrive in their role*" (CCBS Survey, 2023). As a result, leaders in Canada understand that a healthy work-life balance can lead to increased employee satisfaction, engagement, and productivity. The commitment of Canadian leaders to ensuring employee well-being is evident in specific policies like paid parental leave, flexible work arrangements, vacation time, and mental health programs (CCBS Survey, 2023). Hence, even though Canada is characterised as a highly meritocratic and performance-oriented society, Canadian leaders still prioritises the personal well-being of all their employees to achieve leadership empathy (Dujay, 2023). Thirdly, Pooler (2017) purports that friendships tend to replace hierarchy within Canadian organisations, thus encouraging open lines of communication between managers and subordinates. By utilising the knowledge gained via these personal relationships, Canadian leaders can exercise empathy to a degree that would otherwise not be possible. Indeed, Salari and Nastiezaie (2020) confirm that the level of familiarity between employees and employers in Canada results in an in-depth understanding of each other's sensitivity to work-related problems, which, in turn, allows for reduced occupational stress and lower costs stemming from a lack of coordination. Finally, the development of leaders is a constant priority in Canadian organisations, particularly in terms of involving employees from all levels in the workplace within participative leadership. Despite appearing contradictory at first glance, this relates to Canada's relatively high score of (72) for individualism (Hofstede Insights, 2023), because participative leaders in Canada aim to motivate employees by granting them autonomy and decision-making authority. Huang et al. (2010) argues that participative leaders frequently evoke a sense of empowerment and trust within the Canadian workforce. To develop this "*shared leadership*" approach, Canadian leaders promote task ownership and self-determination (Hartney et al., 2022). Allied with this is the fact that Canadians value charismatic leaders, which leads employees to feel greater reverence, trust, and satisfaction with them as well as heightened sense of collective identity (Conger et al., 2000). To conclude, a mindful leader who prioritises inclusivity and the well-being of staff, builds genuine relationships with subordinates, encourages open and straightforward communication, and empowers employees with autonomy and decision-making power, possesses all the necessary competencies to achieve leadership empathy in Canada.

Curaçao

Chislaine Andrade Costa & Sander Schroevers,

with: Mark van Heijningen, William Horsford, Abel Fego, Janou Dihal, & Jamiro Rozendaal

Curaçao is the largest ABC island in the western Leeward Antilles, nestled in the crystal-clear waters of the Caribbean Sea. 16th century Portuguese sailors referred to the island as *Ilha da Curação* (Island of Healing), after they recovered from scurvy resulting from eating oranges. When the Netherlands Antilles were dissolved in 2010, Curaçao became an autonomous constituent country of the Kingdom of the Netherlands. Curacaoans are deeply proud of their heritage and origins, as illustrated via the expression: *'Kaminda mi lombrishi ta derá'* (where my umbilical cord is buried). Indeed, there is a tradition of burying one's umbilical cord there, as also practiced by Jamaican, Surinamese, Māori, Navajo, and many African cultures as a symbolic act of ongoing life (Van Marrewijk, 2004, Koot & Ringeling, 1984). Curacao's capital Willemstad was home to the administrative seat of the West India Company in the Americas and was referred to as the Amsterdam of the Western Hemisphere, due to the 17th century settlers' penchant for gabled rooftops. Today, tourism is the island's primary source of income, attracting half a million visitors each year (Curaçao Chronicle, 2023). Curaçaoan culture is heterogeneous. Whilst the island experienced immigration from the enslaved West Africans, Dutch colonials, and Portuguese Jews, later, René Römer (1981) argued, Latin American, South Asian, East Asian, and Levantine migrants were attracted by the island's industrialisation. More recently, Haitian, Venezuelan, and Colombian immigrants have added to the country's multicultural fabric (Roe, 2016). This plurality of ethnicities has strengthened debate on cultural identity, through the *Yu di Kòrsou* ideology ('children of Curaçao' in Papiamentu) (Allen, 2016), which sought to evoke a sense of unity. An interesting subsegment of Curaçaoans are those that were educated or born in the Netherlands and returned to work professionally on the island, who are often referred to via the expression: *Makamba pretu,* which means they are Afro Curaçaoan acting as traditional Dutchmen.

The island's inhabitants are known for their multilingualism, using *Papiamentu*, Dutch, English and often Spanish, with equal aplomb (Maris, 2013). Papiamentu is a captivating creole blend of African, Portuguese, Venezuelan Spanish, Dutch, and

Arawak Indian influences. This is driven by *Créolité*, which is a movement stemming from the French Caribbean, which valorises the use of Papiamentu in literary and academic contexts (Badiane, 2012). Moreover, Papiamentu is also coming to be the language used by student teachers at the University of Curaçao, (Broek, 2017). Despite this, Dutch is the language of choice when it comes to career and social advancement within the business sector in Curaçao (Allen, 2010). In terms of the prevailing business leadership style, Mr. Verton, a researcher and advisor in governance and nation-building in Curaçao, posits that there is a preference for an authoritarian leadership approach within Curaçaoan organisations (27 April 2024). In the following chapter we will explore what leadership in the business sector in Curaçao entails precisely from the perspective of Curaçaoan experts and professionals.

How the Curaçaoan characterise leaders?

Both leadership and Curaçaoan society more broadly cannot be understood without acknowledgement of the 1969 Curaçao uprising, known as *'Trinta di mei'*, which can be understood alongside other social conflicts and political movements against racism, neo-imperialism, and the anti-establishment counterculture at that juncture. In the Caribbean region, the social unrest was also connected to the Black Power movement (Jamaican riots of October 1968, Trinidadian unrest of February 1970). The second reason for the uprising stemmed from unemployment owing to layoffs in the oil industry, as well as wider discontent with Curacao's subordinate relationship to the Netherlands (Dalhuisen, 2019). Curaçao's Fidel Castro-esque figure, Stanly Brown, together with Godett and Nita directed the 1969 protest rally, which turned violent after Papa Godett was shot, leading to widespread looting and destruction in the central business district of the capital Willemstad (Römer, 1979). *Trinta di mei* marked a clear sociopolitical breaking point in Curaçao's society (Goede, 2022). This history of Curaçao is significant insofar as it has had a detrimental impact upon the prevailing management styles that are adopted within organisations there. Generally speaking, managers often display authoritarian and punitive tendencies, which, in turn, impinges upon employee initiative and autonomous decision-making (Korpodeko, 2022b). During our interview with Peter Verton, a researcher and advisor in governance and nation-building on Curaçao (27 April 2024), he emphasised the necessity of authoritarian leaders within Curaçaoan culture. As he himself put it: *"Yes, it seems like people also prefer and value authority, and they tend to hold it in higher regard"*. Within the Curaçaoan government, power-sharing amongst managers is minimal, according to research by De Pablo (2002). This characterisation of

Curaçaoan leadership was also corroborated by our interviewee, Dr. Miguel Goede (2005). Other research has demonstrated that Curaçaoan leaders, however, lead by example, upholding ethical standards and fostering transparency, honesty, and mutual respect amongst their teams (Arnoud, 2008). One key explanation for this is that forms of unethical behaviour are swiftly noticed in small, tight-knit societies, and, hence, can significantly damage an individual or company's reputation (Smith, 2017). Similarly, in international relations, perceived trustworthiness and accountability have been shown to bolster diplomatic ties and levels of cooperation (García & Van Der Voort, 2020). Notwithstanding the importance of communal values that prioritise social harmony and collective well-being, in practice, Curaçaoan managers often lack the competence and knowledge required for successful implementation (Goede, 1999). This perspective is supported by a seasoned Willemstad-based consultant, who argues that there is presently something of a leadership crisis in Curaçao. As they put it: *"If I were to walk around now and ask who the leaders are and who people consider to be good leaders, it is a difficult question to answer on the island. It was not like this 10 to 15 years ago".* As aforementioned, Curaçao is a heterogeneous society (Roe, 2016). The existence of such cultural differences necessitate leaders striking the requisite balance between global strategies and local customs in order to ensure both competitiveness and relevance (De Bruin & Johnson, 2021). Hence, leaders in Curaçao are expected to embody participative leadership styles, which seek to integrate feedback and cultivate and maintain social harmony within their organisations (Martinez, 2018). However, it was noted by our interviewee that there remains a notable lack of knowledge amongst managers with respect to effective business management and leadership, which, in turn, hinders effective strategy implementation (Goede, 26 April 2024). Dr. Miguel Goede, a management consultant, proceeded to inform us in our interview with him that the biggest difficulty in Curaçao currently is the inconsistency in the national culture itself, where reduced performance due to organisational members' inability or unwillingness to adhere to implementation concepts can negatively impact upon their implementation. As Miguel Goede opined: *"The point is, even after explaining the story to them, I do not see any change in behaviour. But that is just how people are; many simply follow the herd without really seeing. There are only a few who truly grasp it. And now, that is where I think many people lack the ability"* (26 April 2024).

Survey results and what local respondents say

In order to gain a deeper understanding of the prevailing leadership styles, practices and dynamics in Curaçaoan business culture, C-level executives from various Curaçaoan organisations were invited to participate in the CCBS Survey (2024). This section explores the most significant findings emerging from the survey, shedding light on significant trends and noteworthy deviations from global leadership standards. The first notable finding emerging from the survey was that the majority of the respondents reported that they are prepared to confront subordinates during staff meetings in order to obtain the desired results (CCBS Survey, 2024). To strengthen both the generalisability and validity of our findings, it is instructive to also draw upon the results of extant academic research or insights from our interview data. In this respect, the first survey finding is in accordance with the perspective of Curacaoan leadership put forward by our interviewee, Peter Verton, who told us that Curaçaoan culture value authoritarian leaders and hold them in high regard (27 April 2024). Interestingly, however, a little more than half of the respondents stated that they do not encourage some degree of competition within their teams in order to achieve better results (CCBS Survey, 2024). This finding is in line with Miguel Goede's point that Curacaoan leaders place emphasis upon direct communication and prioritise collaboration over competition (26 April 2024). The second significant finding is that nearly half of the respondents disagreed with the notion of maintaining a personal distance from employees in order to uphold the appropriate level of respect (CCBS Survey, 2024). This preference for establishing a personal rapport with their subordinates was also supported by later responses in the survey. For example, the majority of the respondents indicated that subordinates are allowed to address them by their first name. Similarly, approximately half of the respondents expressed indifference towards being addressed by their titles or position within the organisation (CCBS Survey, 2024). Curacaoan culture is often characterised by an aversion to confronting issues in order to preserve relationships, a trait that is sometimes seem as hypocritical. This was evidenced by the survey insofar as half of the respondents strongly agreed with the statement that business leaders in Curaçao are more likely to discuss criticism in an indirect matter (CCBS Survey, 2024). One of the respondents shed light on the nature of the relationship between leaders and their employees, noting that; *"In Curaçao a group of subordinates can strike and have their leader removed from their position"* (CCBS Survey, 2024). This perspective from one respondent goes some way to explaining why many leaders cultivate a sense of mutual respect with their subordinates. Finally, with respect to what qualities, traits and behaviours are valued in Curacaoan leaders, one-third of the respondents stated that it is important for business leaders in Curaçao to be a respectable age, thus indicating that business leaders are respected on the basis of their age. Next, one-third of the respondents reported that technical competence is an important skill for Curaçaoan business leaders to possess (CCBS Survey, 2024). Further competences that employees expect from Curacaoan business leaders is to be eloquent speakers and to be able to make powerful decisions. The final quality upon which Curacaoan business leaders are judged is whether they have a charismatic personality, allied with having good political connections (CCBS Survey, 2024).

Local leadership analysis

Miguel Goede: a Curaçaoan leadership expert
In an effort to comprehend Curaçaoan leadership from within a cross-cultural framework, we engaged in an enlightening discussion with Dr. Miguel Goede, a business practitioner with over three decades of expertise in leadership and education. Goede's expertise extends far beyond the role of that of a mere scientist; rather, he is a visionary strategist, prolific author, captivating radio talk show host, and a seasoned management consultant. At the beginning of the interview, Goede delineated the complexities of leadership in Curaçao deriving from the small-scale of the country, drawing a pivotal comparison between leadership in the Netherlands. As Goede himself stated *"You could bump into each other. For instance, right now he might be the boss, but then at the football club, he is the chairman"* (26 April 2024). Moreover, the compact size of the island introduces other unique dynamics, besides proximity alone. Generally speaking, when it comes to business leadership, whereas countries such as the Netherlands operate across micro, meso, and macro levels, in Curaçao, Goede argued, due to the small size, everything operates predominantly at the micro level (26 April 2024). Next, in an effort to provide us with more in-depth insight into leadership in Curaçao, Goede proceeded to delve into the historical roots that underlie the distinctive leadership style prevalent in Curaçao. He underscored that although the culture of Curaçaoan organisations plays a role, the history exerts a more potent impact upon the prevailing leadership approaches. This understanding derives from his tenure in multinational corporations. As Goede opined: *"In our society, the dynamics mirror those of a plantation. Power is concentrated at the top, instilling fear among those below. Consequently, individuals strive to conform to this hierarchy, yet beneath the surface, there is a subtle resistance as the base attempts to undermine the authority at the summit"* (26 April 2024). However,

Goede told us that he believed that leadership has changed a lot in recent decades, in part because: *"we have a highly fragmented culture, and this fragmentation is reflected in organisations"* (26 April 2024). This rational approach to leadership is compounded by its introduction into a feudal society, especially at the beginning of Shell. In the early stages of industrialisation, the precursor to today's oil refinery emerged, which rapidly led to the country transition from a feudal system. Shell swiftly became the largest employer, introducing modern management practices and forms of rationalisation (Goede, 26 April 2024). Later in the interview, Goede explained that although Curaçaoans dislike the authoritarian leadership style, they often find it necessary for achieving better results. More specifically, he believes that operating in an authoritarian hierarchical manner and prioritising productivity tends to yield higher output, thus leading to enhanced organisational performance. However, as Goede himself stated: *"People may not love you for it, though"* (26 April 2024). As our interview came to a close, Goede stated that beyond the economic and political spheres, the scarcity of leadership in Curaçao is increasingly palpable. Within various domains of Curacaoan society, there is a general lack of vision, charisma, statesmanship or corporate leadership (Goede, 26 April 2024). Despite these problems, Dr. Goede expressed that he remains hopeful about the prospects for change in Curacao, buoyed by the growing number of well-educated young professionals as well as the gradual acceptance of modern leadership methodologies (26 April 2024).

Peter Verton: a Curaçaoan researcher

Peter Verton is a researcher and advisor in governance and nation-building in Curaçao, with decades of experience in a wide variety of roles, including, amongst others, a project coordinator, team leader, university lecturer, institutional development expert, public sector governance advisor, not to mention the fact that he is an author of governance publications. Moreover, he has been actively involved in and worked on management development projects in the (former) Netherlands Antilles and Aruba. At the beginning of our interview with him, Peter Verton provided an overview of several critical issues in Curaçao's political and management landscape (27 April 2024). Firstly, Verton told us that patronage serves to reproduce social disparities as opposed to addressing them in Curacao. Secondly, the prioritisation of power over effective governance has resulted in nepotism and favouritism within public appointments in the country. Thirdly, patronage within political parties serves to undermine fundamental democratic principles and the separation of powers (Verton, 27 April 2024). Later in the interview, Mr. Verton proceeded to explain the preference for an authoritarian leadership approach within Curaçaoan organisations. Specifically, Verton (27 April

2024) posited, the interaction between employees and leaders in Curaçao is often characterised by a power dynamic in which the leader's authority is simply unquestioned. This hierarchical framework is defined by distinct roles and centralised modes of decision-making, wherein senior-level leaders in Curaçaoan organisations wield significant authority, frequently to the detriment of engagement at lower echelons of the organisation. As Verton himself put it: *"Throughout Curaçaoan society, there is more of a "I am the boss, and you are the listener" dynamic" (27 April 2024).* Later, in response to a question about how leaders achieve empathic understanding in Curaçaoan organisations, Mr. Verton explained that the hierarchical nature of Curacaoan society, allied with the general lack of empathy, in turn makes it challenging for leaders to foster empathy with their employees. Moreover, Verton proceeded to inform us, some individuals may actually prefer and value a more authoritarian style, thus complicating any efforts to promote empathy in leadership in Curacaoan organisations (27 April 2024). In this respect, he stressed that changing deeply ingrained societal norms will take considerable time and effort. In his words: *"So pervasive is this characteristic throughout society that it cannot be easily brushed aside or eliminated" (27 April 2024).* To conclude the interview, Mr. Verton underscored the significance of embracing long-term strategic thinking over the prevalent short-term focus observed in numerous Curaçaoan leaders. More specifically, he advocated for strategic planning and leadership that prioritises future-oriented decision-making in order to guarantee both enduring success and sustainability for organisations (27 April 2024).

In-country leadership bestseller

One of the better books about leadership in Curacao was written by Peter Verton in 2017 and is called *Burgers & Broeders*. With an extensive background in governance, alongside being a notable figure in Curacao's intellectual circles, Verton has long been a respected voice on matters of leadership and governance in the country. In *"Burgers & Broeders,"* Verton delves into essential management principles that are crucial for success in Curacao's ever-changing business landscape. Through a lens of adaptability to volatility and complexity, Verton offers invaluable insights that are tailored to the specific needs of current and aspiring Curaçaoan professionals. His principal objective in this book is to elevate Curacao's work culture by integrating local practices with global standards of excellence. In our interview with him (27 April 2024), Peter Verton expounded further about this particular book, which explores leadership in the form of politicians and administrators. He told us that the first important point of the book pertains to the fact that political patronage in Curaçao renders voters dependent on elected leaders, thus further exacerbating existing social inequalities rather than remedying them. Secondly, politicians prioritise acquiring and maintaining political power, which overrides their responsibility for effective public administration. Thirdly, he argues, this focus on power serves to undermine the civil service in Curaçao by promoting nepotism and favouritism over merit-based appointments, thus compromising the checks and balances of democracy itself. Finally, and perhaps most concerningly, is the existence of patronage within political parties, where loyalty to the party leadership supersedes democratic principles, in turn, eroding the separation of legislative and executive powers (Verton, April 27 2024). In conclusion, the book systematically examines Curacao's distinct management practices and features, juxtaposing them with international best-practices, in an effort to bring Curaçao closer to global standards and lead to more success and greater recognition for the island.

Local leadership book		
Title	*Burgers & Broeders*	
Subtitle	Goed bestuur en natievorming in Curaçao	
Author	Peter Verton	
Publisher	LM Publishers	
Year	2017	
ISBN	9789460224553	

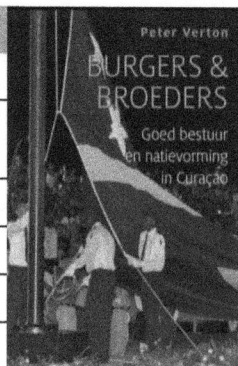

Curaçaoan leadership YouTube review

In addition to academic research and interview and survey data, YouTube also constitutes an invaluable resource with respect to deepening our comprehension of leadership dynamics in Curaçao. In the forthcoming summary of the video entitled *'Small Business, Big Leadership,'* Carla Hueck, a psychologist and proprietor of Experientia, outlines the qualities that define effective leadership. In the interview, the following question arose: Can anyone become a leader in Curaçao? In this respect, the answer appeared simple: *"Yes, anyone can, but not everyone excels in leadership. Some are born with the qualities of a good leader, much like the ability to teach"* (Korpodeko, 2022a, 2:08).

subordinates are simply expected to comply with directives without questioning (Verton, 27 April 2024). This perspective also resonates with the insight provided by one of our survey respondents who opined: *"The leader is always right, and one should respect that. Different opinions or criticism are not appreciated"* (CCBS Survey, 2024). Goede's (1999) research underscored both the preference for a top-down management style in Curaçao and the negative consequences of this approach for strategy implementation, including, amongst other things, low strategy commitment, failure to tap into specialised expertise of lower-level organisational members, or reduced self-confidence of organisational members. A study by Heijes (2010) also indicated that the Curaçaoan organisational context is marked by a significant power asymmetry between Curaçaoans and Dutch. This is illustrated by the fact that professionally active Dutch people on the island barely undergo a process of *'Curaçaoanizing,'* whereas Curaçaoans working in the Netherlands strongly invest in a process of *'Netherlandizing.'* As aforementioned, an especially interesting subsegment of Curaçaoans are those that were either educated or born in the Netherlands and returned to work professionally on the island, who are often referred to via the expression *Makamba pretu*, which means they are Afro Curaçaoans acting as traditional Dutchmen (Heijes, 2010).

It was writer Boeli van Leeuwen who stated in his book *Geniale Anarchie* (genius anarchy), that most Curaçaoans don't appreciate hierarchy nor predetermined structures, with as sole exceptions: baseball and carnival...

How the Curaçaoans achieve leadership empathy

In order to understand how business leaders in Curaçao both exhibit and receive empathy to and from their subordinates, it is critically important to understand the culture of the island. First and foremost, Curaçao is a relatively small island where *"iedereen kent iedereen"* (everyone knows each other) (CCBS Survey, 2015-2020). Secondly, Curaçaoans place tremendous value on personal honour, and preventing the loss of face. The consequence of this is that in some instances matters may be presented in specific ways so as to not lose face, both in everyday contexts as well as within the business setting. This aspect of Curaçaoans culture is illustrated further by the fact that White and Boucke (2024) note that Antilleans consider it polite to say 'yes' (which can lead them to make impossible promises) and rude to say 'no', which derives from the regional *mañana* mentality. Thirdly, the Curaçaoan writer and poet Boeli van Leeuwen highlighted that Curaçaoans are characterised by tolerance that consists of a remarkable combination of lenience, self-mockery, and tractability. This is important because it means that Curaçaoans do not take it too seriously if someone says one thing but does something wholly different. Consequently, exhibiting emotional intelligence within leadership in the Curaçaoan organisational context requires communicative subtleness. This is illustrated by one of the respondents of our survey, who noted that: *"Curaçaoans are not always waiting for know-it-all 'cheesed' Antilleans"* (CCBS Survey, 2024). Moreover, the majority of the respondents in the survey also reported that the key to exhibiting and receiving empathy in Curaçaoan organisations as a leader is finding the right balance between maintaining one's authority and connecting with one's subordinates (CCBS Survey, 2015-2020). The importance of the latter was explained by Van Marrewijk (2004), who purports that Curaçaoan leaders first invest in establishing and maintaining mutual trust and personal relations with their employees, prior to executing orders. This aspect of Curaçaoan leadership is also in accordance with the findings of the CCBS Survey (2024), which reveal that the majority of the Curaçaoan C-level managers are expected to actively spend time on the well-being of their subordinates. Notwithstanding this, the survey results also indicate that around half of the respondents prefer to retain a certain distance from their employees, in order to maintain the right level of respect (CCBS Survey, 2015-2020). This distance between leaders and their employees has been observed in many companies in the Caribbean, with the negative consequences of this approach being that information is often not shared and those higher up in the organisation do not trust those at the lower levels (Punnett & Greenidge, 2009). Perhaps unsurprisingly, then, Miguel Goede, informed us that the level of leadership empathy in companies can be quite low in Curaçaoan; *"you can simply observe it in how people interact with each other"* (26 April 2024). Similarly, Peter Verton, a researcher and advisor in governance, recommended that empathy should be integrated earlier into management education, because *"a characteristic that permeates the entire society cannot simply be brushed aside overnight, nor even within a decade; it requires much more time and effort"* (27 April 2024). Finally, in recent years management and leadership have become more communicative and even participatory in Curaçaoan due to the nascent presence of multinational companies. As a result, it is becoming increasingly important for leaders to empower their employees and help them achieve success, which, in turn, showcases their empathic skills (Goede, 26 April 2024, Gonzales, 2014).

Dominican Republic

*Carmen Martínez-Almeida, Hamza Momand, Scarly Mayi Santos,
Gianna van Ommeren, Dylan Peeters & Noa Serra de Kloet*

"La República Dominicana" (Dominican Republic) is a sovereign state located, together with Haiti, in the island of Hispaniola, in the Greater Antilles archipelago of the Caribbean (Market Overview, 2024). The country is the second largest Caribbean nation, with a population of 11.2 million people, three million of whom live in the metropolitan capital of Santo Domingo (Schrank, 2003). Its economy, initially reliant on agriculture, has diversified to now be driven by the construction, manufacturing, mining, and tourism sectors. This growth propelled its GDP to $113.5 billion in 2022, making it the largest economy in the Caribbean and Central America (World Bank Open Data, n.d.). The country attracts around six million visitors annually, due to its stunning beaches and cultural offerings, such its UNESCO Colonial Zone in Santo Domingo, which is the inaugural European settlement in the Americas and served as the principal seat of Spanish colonial authority in the New World (James, 2011). After more than three hundred years of Spanish rule, the Dominican people declared independence in November 1821 (Schrank, 2003). However, the country's history continues to be felt at the societal level. Indeed, the Taíno, African, and Spanish cultural influences of the past are today expressed in the Dominican music, dance, religious practices, and language, with Spanish serving as the official language of the nation, albeit with a distinctive cadence and warmth (James, 2011). This warmth is also expressed in the everyday conversational parlance which is replete with informal slang, such as *"qué lo qué?"* (what's going on?) and *"yala"* (okay), which is emblematic of the the informal and friendly demeanour of the people. Unsurprisingly, strong interpersonal skills, along with adaptability and resilience form the basis of the leadership skills and practices that are required to thrive in the diverse business environments in the country (Entrada, 2023). The following chapter delves deeper into examining the Dominican style of leadership, utilising a combination of primary and secondary data sources.

How the Dominicans characterise leaders?

Leadership in the Dominican Republic is deeply rooted in its cultural history and societal dynamics, exhibiting a distinctive blend of hierarchical respect and *"personalismo,"* which is a leadership style that values personal relationships over and above institutional affiliations (De La Sota & Zaino, 2018). Badia (2011) argues that this leadership style has been shaped historically by a strong influence of autocratic norms which are prevalent even to this day in business practices in the country. Consequently, leaders in the Dominican Republic are often perceived as paternalistic figures, which mirrors the family-centric structure seen in many Dominican businesses in which leadership roles often pass down through the generations, irrespective of the merits of the individual candidates (Badia, 2011). This aspect of the business culture was corroborated by one of the respondents from the CCBS Survey (2024), who explained that: *"most companies are family-owned and therefore passed down to children without taking their skills into account, which proves to be an obstacle for companies to achieve their full potential"*. This familial approach emphasises loyalty to the group over the formal qualifications of candidates, thus underlining a unique leadership ethos in which personal connections dictate professional interactions and business decisions (Badia, 2011). The CCBS Survey (2024) supports the persistence of this *"personalismo"* management style and familial approach, insofar as several of the respondents described the prevailing leadership style in the country as being people-oriented, warm, and empathetic. This was supported by our interviewee, a Dominican scholar, Mr. Ureña-Espaillat, who told us that Dominican leaders are assertive, clear, honest, and most importantly a source of motivation for their employees. In addition to these aforementioned attributes, Montesino (2002) purports that the Dominican leadership style is characterised by a distinct 'high context' communicative style, where non-verbal cues and implicit understanding are crucial. The preference for this high context communication style is grounded in deeper cultural values, where more indirect forms of communication may help to avoid direct confrontation, thus aligning with a societal preference for maintaining harmonious interpersonal relations (Montesino, 2002). The political culture, according to Montesino (2002) also profoundly business leadership paradigms, insofar as the values that prevail in the political sphere permeate workplace dynamics. For instance, there is an observed tendency towards centralised forms of decision-making within Dominican organisations, which mirrors the political governance style, which historically leans towards centralisation and control (Montesino, 2002). Leadership in the Dominican Republic is also characterised by a notable degree of adaptability to globalisation and external business influences. As Montesino (2002) notes, there is both an increasing acceptance of and adaptation to global business practices, such as enhanced corporate governance and advanced communication technologies, which are challenging due to a historical preference for centralised, top-down decision-making in the country culture. The shift towards practices that promote greater transparency and forms of participative management not only require a departure from the established norms but also pose a significant cultural shift for leaders accustomed to autocratic forms of control (Badia, 2011). In summary, then, leadership in the Dominican Republic is a complex interplay of historical, cultural, and interpersonal dynamics. It is characterised by a strong hierarchical orientation, a preference for indirect communication, and a deep respect for familial and personal relationships.

Survey results and what local respondents say

Dominican executives with multiple years of leadership experience within Dominican organisations participated in the CCBS Survey (2024) in order to enrich our understanding of leadership dynamics in the country. This section presents key findings emerging from the responses of over 70 respondents. In order to enhance the generalisability and validity of the findings, we have opted to draw upon data from a previous period of data collection (CCBS Survey, 2017) as well as this year's survey data (CCBS Survey, 2024). The most significant findings will be discussed in turn below. The first key finding from the survey is that the respondents confirmed the hierarchical nature of leadership within the Dominican Republic, whilst still maintaining a people-oriented focus (CCBS Survey, 2024). This is in line with the research of Montesino (2002), who also argued that a top-down leadership approach prevails in the Dominican Republic. One of the respondents elaborated on this statement, noting that: *"the Dominican Republic has a paternalistic management style, whilst still maintaining a high level of respect and hierarchy, as leaders maintain a very formal relationship with their subordinates, also outside of the work floor"*. This formal side to leadership in the Dominican Republic was also confirmed by the fact that the respondents were in broad agreement over the importance of subordinates addressing leaders by their titles or positions (CCBS Survey, 2024). Moreover, 25& of the respondents indicated that a strong charismatic personality is the most important trait to have as a leader. In addition, 56.25% of the respondents indicated they do not prefer to hear criticism in an indirect manner, outside of staff meetings. This sentiment was shared by one of the survey participants, who explained that: *"Criticism in general and specifically personal criticism is not tolerated; it is not appreciated and is seen as a personal attack and public humiliation"*. Secondly, in regard to the people-oriented focus, the vast majority of the respondents reported that it is very important for leaders to spend time actively on the well-being of their team members. This aspect of Dominican leadership was illustrated by Victor Mendez (CCBS Survey, 2017), a senior audit manager, who opined: *"leadership in the Dominican Republic is evolving, with trends differing from other cultures. The emphasis on fostering a close relationship between staff and their manager is seen as highly important"*. The third notable finding emerging from the survey results is the importance of decisiveness in leaders' decision-making process. This was evidenced by the fact that the majority of the respondents agreed that once a manager makes a decision, they are unlikely to easily alter it (CCBS Survey, 2024). This indicates a preference for firm leadership and a respect for authoritative decision-making processes, which is in accordance with Montesino's (2002) framing of leadership in the Dominican Republic. The fourth key finding is that there is a strong emphasis on meeting deadlines, with failing to do so perceived as tantamount to failure (CCBS Survey 2024). Finally, in terms of leadership attributes, the respondents noted that employees in the country look up to their leaders based on various factors. Organisational experience and technical competency were the most significant, reflecting the importance placed on expertise and knowledge. Family background holds only a moderate level of significance, whilst an elegant appearance ranks the lowest in terms of influencing employees' admiration. In conclusion, the data from the CCBS Survey (2017-2024) indicates a clear vertical hierarchy in Dominican organisations, coupled with a strong emphasis on maintaining formal relationships in which mutual respect is highly important. Moreover, the active prioritisation of the well-being of team members makes the organisational culture people-oriented.

Local leadership analysis

Hayrold José Ureña Espaillat: a Dominican leadership scholar

To gain a more profound understanding of leadership in Dominican leadership, we conducted an interview with Hayrold José Ureña-Espaillat. He is a Dominican scholar, who wrote the research paper entitled *"Knowledge and innovation management in agribusiness: A study in the Dominican Republic"* (Ureña-Espaillat et al., 2022), where he discusses the impact of knowledge management as an integrating element for sustainable development. Mr. Ureña-Espaillat is also the director of fuels at the Dominican *"Ministerio de Industria, Comercio y Mipymes"* (Ministry of Industry, Commerce and MSMEs). He specialises in project and social management, and completed his PhD in Management Sciences at the *Universidad*

Politécnica in Cartagena (Ureña Espaillat, 24 April 2024).
At the start of our interview, Mr. Ureña-Espaillat stated that the Dominican Republic, even though it is a small country, is the third most popular tourist destination in Latin America, and is a very smart and dynamic country with its own particular rhythm. This, in addition to the level of migration occurring in the Dominican Republic at this juncture has a had a profound impact upon business leadership in the country. In response to a question about what distinguishes leaders in the Dominican Republic from their international counterparts, he responded that they have extensive cultural knowledge (Ureña Espaillat, 24 April 2024). He proceeded to explain that because of these cultural differences, leaders have to deal a lot with different communication styles. For that reason, they have developed excellent communication skills, and, most importantly, they are empathic in their approach; they respect everyone for who they are (Ureña-Espaillat, 24 April 2024). Next, he moved onto discuss that when it comes to hierarchy in the Dominican Republic, Mr. Ureña-Espaillat stated: *"Unfortunately, and from the perspective of organisations in the past, the leader was a hierarchical figure"* (Ureña-Espaillat, 24 April 2024). However, today, the hierarchy is more horizontal than it was in previous years, insofar as everyone collaborates with one another, employees trust each other, albeit there are still clear rules. Later in the interview, in response to a question about what specific characteristics Dominican leaders possess, Mr. Ureña-Espaillat responded that a Dominican leader is assertive, clear, honest, and most importantly a source of motivation for their employees. As he himself put it: *"To be able to create an environment that is not a work environment. But when people sit down to do tasks that are not so routine, that they can promote creativity, there is that internal [and] external motivation that has to be operationalised"* (Ureña-Espaillat, 24 April 2024). He continued to say that Dominican leadership is transformational in nature in that they are clear, grounded, and result oriented. However, knowledge, creativity, training, and motivation are also essential attributes that also must be present in any Dominican company. Having said this, he also said that the truth is that just like all people, every leader is different: *"If I told you that there is a thumb rule for this, I would be lying to you"* (Ureña Espaillat, 24 April 2024).

Social media review

In the Dominican Republic, the social media discourse around business leadership showcases a vibrant amalgamation of traditional insights and modern perspectives. *"Impulsa Tu Liderazgo RD"* on Instagram champions transformational leadership, emphasising the importance of nurturing future leaders in the Dominican Republic to create sustainable impact. They stress, *"Ser*

69

un buen líder implica guiar a otros, pero ser extraordinario va más allá; implica inspirar, empoderar y cultivar la próxima generación de líderes" (Being a good leader involves guiding others, but being extraordinary goes beyond that; it involves inspiring, empowering and nurturing the next generation of leaders) (Impulsa Tu Liderazgo RD, 2023). Francisco Javier García illustrates on their YouTube channel how strategic leadership in tourism in the Dominican Republic has driven substantial economic growth, blending economic savvy with strategic execution. More specifically, he points out that leadership has propelled the Dominican Republic to lead in regional economic growth (TurismoRD, 2023). Roberto Mourey, in a TED Talk, promotes *'metaleadership,'* advocating for a leadership model in the Dominican Republic where roles are dispersed across all organisational levels, thus encouraging a culture of inclusivity and collective responsibility. He argues that *"leadership is for everyone* [in the Dominican Republic], *not just the top ranks"* (TED, 2023). The UNDP (United Nations Development Programme) on Twitter advocates for the inclusion of more women in leadership roles in the Dominican Republic, underscoring the necessity for gender inclusivity in effective leadership practices. They highlight that *"the participation of women in leadership roles demonstrates that power is not just a man's domain"* (PNUD Rep. Dominicana, 2023). Additionally, Antonio de los Santos on LinkedIn reflects on historical leadership, drawing lessons from the leadership of Artigas during the Banda Oriental Revolution in 1811. He emphasises, *"El liderazgo de Artigas fue fundamental para la Revolución en la Banda Oriental en 1811"* (Artigas' leadership was fundamental to the Revolution in the Banda Oriental in 1811) (De los Santos, 2023). These narratives from different social media platforms highlight the heterogeneity of the dialogue around leadership in the Dominican Republic, which is at once progressive and reflective, valuing strategic growth, inclusivity, and the empowerment of future generations of leaders in the country.

In-country leadership bestseller

One of the best-selling books about leadership in the Dominican Republic was written by Ney Díaz in 2022 and is called *"Las 12 Preguntas"* (The 12 Questions). The author is the president and founder of INTRAS, a leading company specialising in training and consultancy in the country (Fernando, 2024). *"Las 12 preguntas"* is divided into twelve different questions asked to the reader, which are meant to encourage reflection and self-questioning (Ramírez, 2021). Díaz mentioned that he wrote the book from the point of view of Dominican leadership regarding the view of interpersonal relationships. Most of the chapters are influenced by his own life experience of going to organisations, and having to work with different leaders and speakers, from whom he had the opportunity to learn from and talk to (Hamid Yaryura, 2023). When the reader answers the twelve questions, personal learning will emerge (Fernando, 2024). It is supposed to motivate the reader to strive to be a better person and make the necessary adjustments in their life (*Las 12 Preguntas*, n.d.). The leadership style presented in this book is of a someone who is mystical, motivational, imposing, and charismatic, to whom we compare both ourselves and others to. However, the non-negotiable characteristics of a leader are recognising and making use of the potential of others and being a pressure filter for them. Ney Diaz also states that Dominican leaders are the ones who make things happen and who have allowed humanity to move forward (Ramírez, 2021). In addition, the host of the podcast, where Díaz was interviewed about his book, Hamid Yaryura (2023), said that one of the things he took away from the book was: "*Si tu eres una autoridad, lo menos que tu tienes que ser es coherente con tu mensaje*" (If you are an authority, the least you have to be is consistent with your message), to which Mr. Diaz responded: "*Una que yo amarraría y que va muy asociada es la integridad, que es básicamente hacerlo correcto aunque no nos resulte conveniente*" (One that I would tie in and that goes very much with it is integrity, which is basically doing the right thing even if it is not convenient). Ney Díaz's book "*Las 12 preguntas*" offers profound insights into Dominican leadership, emphasising the importance of reflection, personal growth, and integrity, serving as a valuable resource for aspiring leaders.

Local leadership book	
Title	*Las 12 Preguntas*
Subtitle	-
Author	Ney Díaz
Publisher	Biblioteca Nacional Pedro Henríquez Ureña
Year	2022
ISBN	978-9945807905

Leadership YouTube review

Raúl Burgos is the founder of the initiative *"Dominicana se Transforma"* (The Dominican Transforms), which is part of the well-known John C. Maxwell Leadership Foundation. He joined the Dominican talk show *Esta Noche Mariasela* (2023), where he and the host Mariasela talked about what makes a good leader and what specific traits and attributes are required in the Dominican Republic. In this video, he shares that good leaders in the Dominican Republic not only work with their teams, but also influence and inspire them. The characteristics of a good Dominican leader are being knowledgeable, which, in turn, helps influence their teams, in addition to always staying positive: they should never make excuses or complain. As he put it: *"Nadie quiere seguir a alguien que se esté quejando [y] que esté haciendo excusas"* (No one wants to follow someone who complains and who makes excuses). Dominican leaders should also have and be able to share a clear vision and show a contagious passion for this vision, never settling but rather always striving for ways to improve further. Notwithstanding the importance of these aforementioned attributes and behaviours, Burgos also stated that leaders also need good teams behind them. Mr. Burgos proceeded to say that before becoming a leader, they should first be a follower, in order to watch and learn (Esta Noche Marisela, 2023). The second interview to be summarised is another interview with Raúl Burgos, this time on the Super7fm (2023). In this interview, he stated that if leaders in the Dominican Republic do not show their vulnerability, and who they really are, then they are not empathic and they will never inspire people: *"Eres un líder porque te dieron la posición y ejerces esa actividad, pero no eres un líder en el sentido real de la palabra"* (You are a leader because you were given the position and you exercise that activity, but you are not a leader in the real meaning of the word). He then carried on to say that a true Dominican leader is someone who wants to develop you as a person and is followed by people voluntarily. It is someone who has a vision and a sense of direction, and lets their subordinates help them create the path to achieving their vision. However, leadership has changed throughout the years in the Dominican Republic. Mr. Burgos reported in another interview (2023): *"Si quieres ir rápido, ve solo. Si quieres llegar lejos, ve acompañado"* (If you want to go fast, go alone. If you want to go far, go accompanied by others). What he means by this is that in contemporary organisations in the Dominican Republic, the preferred leadership approach is that of someone who collaborates with their team, that is, leaders who readily acknowledge that they do not have all the answers to all the questions. These leaders feel secure enough to surround themselves with better people, with people that share their opinions without acting defensive (2023).

Understanding hierarchy in the Dominican Republic

In the Dominican Republic, hierarchical values in the workplace are deeply ingrained and can be understood through drawing upon some of the cultural dimensions identified in the GLOBE research. One such dimension, power distance, as conceptualised by Hofstede, reflects the degree to which authority and hierarchical order are accepted in society. With a relatively high-power distance Index (PDI) score, the Dominican Republic thus demonstrates a strong acceptance of hierarchical structures and authority figures (Lebrón Rolón, 2008). This cultural inclination towards deference to authority figures shapes leadership dynamics in the workplace. Leaders often adopt directive or paternalistic leadership styles, providing clear guidance and direction to their subordinates. Lebrón Rolón (2008) supports this framing of Dominican leadership, reporting that a paternalistic Dominican leader supports and mentors their subordinates as they feel like it is their duty to help and watch over them. Moreover, subordinates see their leaders as akin to father figures. For instance, historical figures like Juan Bosch exemplified paternalistic leadership during their presidency, reflecting the cultural expectation of strong, guiding leadership (Sánchez & Lozano, 2012). Moreover, the high-power distance influences organisational structures, which are typically characterised by vertical hierarchies with clear chains of command (Montesino, 2002). Because of the lingering effect of colonialism, an uneducated workforce, as well as the abundance of family businesses in the country, there is an observed unequal distribution of power in the country. This cultural inclination affects both how leaders are viewed and how authority is exercised within companies, resulting in a top-down approach to management in which senior-level leaders are expected to direct, and employees are expected to follow (Montesino, 2002). The fact that decision-making processes tend to be top-down, with little input from lower-level employees, was corroborated by the results of the CCBS Survey (2024), insofar as several of the respondents described the prevailing leadership style as being authoritarian in nature. Indeed, one respondent even went so far as to say that criticism is not really appreciated by Dominican leaders and rather is seen as a 'personal attack' or form of 'public humiliation' (CCBS Survey, 2024). Although this hierarchical structure aligns with the cultural values in the country, researchers have argued that it can serve to inhibit employees' empowerment and innovation within companies (Diaz, 2011). Therefore, effective leadership in the Dominican Republic requires a more nuanced approach that balances cultural norms with organisational effectiveness. Whilst hierarchical values may favour certain leadership styles, successful leaders also recognise the importance of empowering employees and fostering open communication (Diaz, 2011). By striking a balance between respecting cultural norms and promoting collaboration, leaders can thus better navigate the complexities of the Dominican workplace more effectively (LATAM Republic, 2024). In conclusion, the Dominican Republic is characterised by high power distance, which results in subordinates being afraid to disagree with their leaders, and decision-making being autocratic in nature (Lebrón Rolón, 2008). Whilst these values shape leadership dynamics and organisational structures in the country, effective leadership requires an understanding of cultural nuances and a willingness to adapt leadership approaches to foster collaboration and innovation (Diaz, 2011).

How the Dominicans achieve leadership empathy

In the Dominican Republic, organisations have gradually come to recognise the importance of emotional intelligence, with human resources departments now placing much greater emphasis on hiring individuals with both high performance and emotional intelligence (Feliz & Contreras, 2021). Building on this trend, Suriel and Escalante (2023) explored the competencies of emotional intelligence (EI) that are crucial for effective leadership in the Dominican context. Specifically, the authors identified adaptability, commitment, initiative, optimism, self-confidence, reliability, motivation for achievement, political awareness, ability to work in teams, innovation, and integrity as key competencies in the Dominican Republic (Suriel & Escalante, 2023). Support for this comes from the CCBS Survey (2023), insofar as one of the respondents noted that: "*an effective leader* [in the Dominican Republic] *is characterised by competitiveness, ambition, and challenge*". Leaders, or "*líderes*", who demonstrate competencies such as adaptability and effective teamwork, are more proficient at adopting empathy-driven approaches to conflict resolution, thereby fostering a culture of understanding and cooperation amongst their team members (Lawani et al., 2022). In the realm of meeting commitments, three-quarters of the participants from both the CCBS Survey (2017) and CCBS Survey (2024) equated missing deadlines with failure, thus underscoring the value placed on fulfilling one's commitments. This emphasis on commitment aligns with the Dominican cultural legacy, which places a strong emphasis on interpersonal interactions and communal values (Rodriguez, 2021). Indeed, the importance of relationships for Dominicans lays the foundation of the Dominican concept of "*solidaridad*", or solidarity, as highlighted by Arbino (2022). Further support for the importance of empathy within Dominican leadership comes from the fact that half of the respondents affirmed the importance of managers dedicating time to ensure the personal well-being of their team members (CCBS Survey, 2024). However, despite the value placed on interpersonal relationships in the country, the majority of the respondents also expressed a preference for maintaining a certain level of professional distance to maintain the necessary level of respect from their employees (CCBS Survey, 2024). Similarly, half of the respondents of the CCBS Survey (2024) agreed with the importance of addressing their leaders by their title or position, which testifies to the significance of maintaining a professional demeanour. Elaborating on this finding, Mr. Ureña-Espaillat (24 April 2024) emphasised in our interview that effective leadership in the Dominican Republic requires striking the requisite balance between a linear focus on results and empathy as a human skill. He suggested that systems that promote empathy and collaboration are crucial for motivation. However, he warned that without respect and discipline, a leader may struggle to maintain their effectiveness. Mr. Ureña-Espaillat thus advised that whilst empathy is important, leaders must ensure that respect and discipline are not compromised in the process (24 April 2024).

Egypt

Charlotte Dijkman, Anita Elzinga, Ramy Girgis, Mike Smith, Shanna Strube & Caroline Sweep

The Republic of Egypt, or as it is known in Arabic: جمهورية مصر العربية, lies at the crossroads of the continents of the ancient world of Africa and Asia-Europe. Egypt is one of the world's oldest civilisations and owes its prosperity to the Nile River. Often referred to as 'the Gift of the Nile,' this waterway facilitated the rise of Egyptian culture. The name *Egypt* itself has Greek origins, referring to 'The House of essence of *Ptah*,' an important god in early Egyptian beliefs, but locally Egyptians commonly refer to their country as *'Misr'* (Akroyd, 2014). Egypt's strategic location derives from the fact that it borders both the Red Sea and the Mediterranean Sea. It overlooks the Gulf of Suez and the Gulf of Akaba, with the Suez Canal serving as the primary transportation route connecting Asia and Europe. Despite facing challenges in recent few decades, the Egyptian economy has seen significant growth (World Bank, 2023). This growth has served to improve Egypt's competitive position on the international stage (Aliboni, 2017). Egypt's economy is incredibly diverse, encompassing agriculture, tourism, industry, and services (Raihana et al., 2023), with its most successful sectors being tourism and agriculture. This diversity is also seen amongst its population, insofar as Egypt also boasts a variety of dialects, including Nubian, Sa'idi and Bedawi, although Egyptian Arabic is spoken by the majority of the population and is the predominant dialect in the country. Moreover, Egyptian Arabic is also widely understood amongst other Arabic speakers due to the popularity of Egyptian movies, music, and other media platforms (Vollers, 2011). Today, most of Egypt's inhabitants follow the Islamic faith, alongside a Coptic Christian minority, which serves to cultivate a societal culture characterised by strong familial bonds. As will be explained in due course, these fundamental values also influence the behaviour of Egyptian leaders in a variety of key respects (Shanin & Wright, 2004). This chapter explores Egyptian business leadership skills and best practices, and sheds light on the prevailing organisational culture in the country.

How the Egyptians characterise leaders?

In Egypt, the leadership style tends to be a blend of cultural influences and organisational contexts. Transformational leadership is commonly regarded as an ideal approach through which to address the complexities of the business environment in the country (El-Zayaty, 2018). Egyptian leaders are family-oriented, relationship-driven and place value upon respect for authority, ancestors, and religion. This aspect of Egyptian leadership was confirmed by our interviewee, Ms. El Sokary, who argued that *"orders are expected to be followed without question"* (25 April 2024), which, she argued, can often suppress feedback and innovation within Egyptian organisations. Alongside this, other common characteristics of Egyptian leadership are expressiveness and formality, such as, for example, addressing leaders by Mr or Mrs (Lituchy et al., 2017). Furthermore charisma, courage, and the ability to lead organisations down a path to progress typically form the basis for assessing someone's leadership qualities (Atty et al., 2014). More specifically, Egyptian leaders with a strong personality and the ability to inspire, by sharing their vision, passion, and their ability to unite people, are often seen as charismatic figures who possess the power to influence and guide others (Altun, 2022). The results of the CCBS Survey (2018-2024) confirmed this aspect of Egyptian leadership as the respondents stated that charisma is greatly valued in leaders and is seen as a sign of their effectiveness, insofar as it helps them inspire and bring everyone together. This finding is in accordance with the work of Altun (2022) who also argued that charismatic leaders can really influence and lead others. Regarding the importance of leaders being able to move organisations forward, Egyptian leaders who can steer the organisation towards prosperity and triumph are considered competent leaders insofar as they have a clear vision of the future and possess the ability to make strategic choices (Kamel, 2017). Another style of leadership that is valued in Egypt is effective leadership, which in the Egyptian context is defined by values, namely showing honesty, fairness, and support towards one's subordinates. Moreover, both educational and work experience are highly valued, and leaders strive to ensure that there is *Asabiyyah,* which refers to the concept of social cohesion (Lituchy et al., 2017). In this respect, Egyptian leaders work hard to balance cultural awareness, tradition, vision, and practicality together with honesty in order to inspire their teams (El-Zayaty, 2018). Further Insights on Egyptian leadership can be drawn from our interview with Dr. Bekhit, who informed us that a typical Egyptian business leader must possess resilience, an understanding of cultural nuances and adaptability, which are all important traits for navigating the complexities of a global business environment (22 April 2024). This is reflected in further research, which states that in an Egyptian business setting, the majority of subordinates expect their leaders to be macro managers, encouraging, visionaries, coaching and result driven. This can also be observed during business meetings in which Egyptian leaders emphasise respect and authority for others, by addressing each other with their titles to maintain a sense of hierarchy (Asmaa, 2019). The results of the CCBS Survey (2018-2024) underscore that this pattern also holds true for employees, insofar as they highly value leaders who show courage in the face of challenges, both political and operational, and who make decisions without hesitation. These courageous leaders deserve the respect and admiration of their employees. In this respect, to become an effective leader in Egypt is to have a mindset that fosters leading by example, charisma, experience and supporting.

Survey results and what local respondents say

In order to gain valuable insights into the business skills and leadership styles of Egyptian executives, the CCBS Survey was administered to a select group of experienced C-level executives in Egyptian organisations. The CCBS Survey results were combined with data from previous years of the survey, in order to enhance the generalisability and validity of the findings (CCBS Survey, 2018-2024). This resulted in data from more than 50 C-level executives who shared their experiences and knowledge with us. The most significant findings are presented in turn below. The first notable finding is that, in line with Hofstede's research on Egypt and power distance, the majority of the respondents agreed with the notion that subordinates must address leaders solely by their formal titles or positions (CCBS Survey, 2018-2024). Similarly, 60% of the leaders agreed that privileges within their organisation were (somewhat) exclusively reserved for leaders, which is also suggestive of a more hierarchical environment (CCBS Survey, 2018-2024). In addition, participants placed considerable emphasis on the values of personal connections and relationships in effective leadership, recognising loyalty and trust as indispensable qualities. As one of the respondents opined: "*Leaders often wield significant power and are expected to command respect from their subordinates; also personal relationships and connections play a crucial role in leadership dynamics with loyalty and trust being highly valued*" (CCBS Survey, 2018-2024). This statement is in accordance with other results from the survey, namely the fact that the respondents agreed that managers should actively spend time ensuring the personal well-being of their team members. Consequently, it is apparent from the survey data that cultivating emotional connections with team members is a key element in boosting a leader's efficacy, which was again illustrated by the fact that the majority of the respondents reported that they do not retain personal distance from their employees, in order to maintain the right level of respect (CCBS Survey, 2018-2024). The next notable finding from the CCBS Survey (2018-2024) is that Egyptian leaders highly value maintaining connections with their teams and fostering a positive work environment. This demonstrates how Egyptian heavily influences the hierarchical structures within organisations, thus emphasising the importance of leaders staying connected with their teams instead of isolating themselves. Whilst some of the respondents noted the absence of formal leadership processes, others highlighted the necessity for leaders to adopt a more performance-oriented mindset. Further, the respondents placed significant emphasis upon the value of personal connections and relationships in effective leadership, recognising loyalty and trust as indispensable qualities (CCBS Survey, 2018-2024). Several noteworthy results were observed, indicating a shift towards more inclusive leadership styles in the country. This finding is consistent with the notion that effective leadership in Egypt is increasingly characterised by more democratic and inclusive approaches. The implications of this survey research are manifold. First, we can surmise that effective leadership in Egypt necessitates a blend of traditional hierarchical structures with more democratic and inclusive approaches. Secondly, consistent with Hofstede's findings, emotional intelligence is positively related to leadership effectiveness in the Egyptian context (CCBS Survey, 2018-2024). In summary, the results of the survey provide invaluable perspectives on the complex and diverse aspects of leadership in Egypt. It emphasises the significance of adaptability, emotional intelligence, and a nuanced comprehension of hierarchical systems for effective leadership within the Egyptian context.

Local leadership analysis

Dr. Khaled Bekhit: an Egyptian leadership scholar

Dr. Khaled Bekhit is an experienced professor at ESLSCA University in Egypt, a European institution of French origins, where he specialises in strategy and management. With an extensive background of more than twenty-five years in business, mainly in the industrial and manufacturing sectors, he brings a rich array of practical experience to his academic role. Prior to joining ESLSCA, Dr. Bekhit taught for ten years at the American University In Cairo as well as at Antalya International University in Turkey. His academic career is enriched by his considerable experience in various management positions, which deeply influence both this teaching approach and professional philosophy. It is for this reason that Dr. Bekhit describes himself as *"half businessman, half professor"* (22 April 2024), a dual identity that allows him to effectively integrate real-world business insights with theoretical academic concepts. At the beginning of our interview, Dr. Bekhit described the typical Egyptian business leader as a figure who is influenced by Egypt's rich historical and cultural heritage. According to Dr. Bekhit, such leaders are often characterised by a blend of traditional values with an acute awareness of market dynamics and international trends. Furthermore, a typical Egyptian leader is one who possesses resilience, an understanding of cultural nuances and adaptability, all of which are crucial for navigating the complexities of a global business environment. He proceeded to discuss how Egyptian leadership has evolved significantly in recent decades, moving away from traditional, hierarchical models towards a more dynamic and flexible approach. This shift was driven by numerous factors, including economic reforms, globalization, and the entrance of a well-educated, younger generation into leadership roles. As he himself put, this shift is " *primarily due to Egypt's efforts at economic liberalisation and the need to adapt to a "VUCA world"* (Bekhit, 22 April 2024) which stands for volatile, uncertain, complex, and ambiguous (Bennett & Lemoine, 2014). These changes have fostered an adaptability and resilience amongst leaders, preparing them for the international stage. This evolution reflects a deeper change within the Egyptian business community. Dr. Bekhit proceeded to explain the hierarchical structure of Egyptian businesses, which he described as *"bureaucratic and mechanistic"* (22 April 2024), with a strong emphasis on top-down management. However, he also emphasised the evolving role of empathy in leadership. He explained that true leadership goes beyond organisational power, suggesting rather that *"trust is earned"* (22 April 2024) and that effective leaders must *"walk the talk"* (22 April 2024). This approach to leadership involves leading by example and striving for clear and empathetic communication, which Dr. Bekhit sees as essential for fostering trust and respect within organisations. Dr. Bekhit defined empathy as *"putting yourself in the shoes of others"* (22 April 2024). Furthermore, he described the unique challenges and opportunities of Egyptian leadership. He underscored the cultural nuances that can be challenging for foreign leaders due to Egypt's high level of power distance and traditional reverence for authority. However, overall, Dr. Bekhit expressed optimism about the potential for change, driven by both the influx of well-educated young professionals and the gradual embrace of modern leadership practices, including digital transformation and the integration of modern technologies into business strategies. Dr. Bekhit ended our interview by defining Egyptian leadership in three words *"Respect, authority and influence"* (22 April 2024).

Ms. Rham El Sokary: An Egyptian cross-cultural trainer

Ms. Rham El Sokary is a certified international consultant and trainer with more than twenty-four years of professional experience in quality management. She began her career at El Sewedey Electric and has risen to the position of Global Director for Quality Assurance and Process Excellence at SI Paradigm in New Jersey, USA. She has been recognised by "PEX" as one of the top 50 thought leaders on operational excellence for 2023. Her expertise includes quality management, performance management and lean manufacturing. With an MBA, degree in Total Quality Management and certifications as an International Manager of Quality and Organisational Excellence, Ms. El Sokary is at the forefront of shaping leadership and quality management in Egypt. At the beginning of the interview, Ms. El Sokary described the typical Egyptian business leader as someone who combines a deep-rooted Egyptian cultural heritage with personal traits and experiences that shape their leadership style. Ms. El Sokary stressed that trust and personal relationships are particularly important in Egyptian culture. This is illustrated in the following extract in which she stated: *"the majority [of leaders] I have met consider trust more important than qualifications"* (25 April 2024), which emphasises the importance Egyptian leaders place on personal trust over professional qualifications. She then proceeded to explain that whilst Egyptian culture plays a role, organisational culture has a stronger influence upon leadership styles. She gained this insight from her experiences in multinational organisations, where she observed that *"corporate policies and practices often overshadow local cultural influences"* (25 April 2024). She elaborated on this, noting that: *"The organisation enforces all its policies and procedures on all employees, regardless of their country"* (25 April 2024). When asked about how hierarchy functions within Egyptian organisations, Ms. El Sokary argued that they often have a strict hierarchical structure, especially in Egyptian companies with a solely Egyptian native workforce. This structure is characterised by clear roles and centralised decision-making, with senior Egyptian leaders having sizeable authority, often at the expense of involvement from those working at the lower levels. She drew attention to a common problem in which *"roles and responsibilities are assigned without corresponding authority"* (25 April 2024), which impacts negatively on achieving goals and leads to inefficiency. With respect to adaptability, Ms. El Sokary noted that *"lower-level managers generally have greater adaptability than their senior-level colleagues, who feel confident enough to resist change"* (25 April 2024). On the whole, she was critical of the traditional exercise of authority in Egyptian leadership in which *"orders are expected to be followed without question"* (25 April 2024), as this often suppresses feedback and innovation. Her leadership philosophy stands in contrast to this norm and favours authority *"granted by team members based on respect and expertise, rather than imposed from above"* (25 April 2024). Furthermore, Ms. El Sokary addressed the sensitive issue of gender inequality in leadership, speaking out against differentiating leadership styles strictly based on gender. She argued that leadership effectiveness has more to do with personal traits and experiences than being male or female, opining that *"leadership is highly subjective and relative to personality itself and personal experiences, regardless of any other criteria"* (25 April 2024). Whilst she acknowledged that Egypt is still struggling with gender equality in leadership roles, she did highlight the government's efforts to improve the situation, albeit remarking that *"much work remains"* (25 April 2024). Finally, Ms. El Sokary underscored the importance of long-term strategic thinking rather than a short-term approach, which, form her experience, tends to be the case with many Egyptian leaders. Instead, she recommended strategic planning and leadership that looks beyond immediate gains to ensure the long-term success and sustainability of organisations.

In-country leadership bestseller

Dr. Ibrahim El-Feki, an Egyptian author and former expert within the field of personal development, is known for his many Egyptian best-selling books that have been translated into several languages. Dr. El-Feki has an impressive academic background, with twenty-three diplomas and the highest certifications in psychology, marketing & sales management, and human development. In addition, he has trained thousands of people around the world in his certification programs, workshops, and seminars. One of his best-selling books is *"The Magic of Leadership,"* which describes how to develop effective leadership, which can be applied within the Egyptian business culture. Dr. El-Feki disputes the idea that personal characteristics cannot be changed and presents seven secrets of effective leadership. Each of the chapters cover a specific aspect of personal development, which varies from decision-making to managing stress and relationships. The book also offers practical insights and strategies through which to unlock Egyptian leadership potential and achieve success. Alongside this, the book addresses the difference between a manager and a leader, and identifies nine common qualities of successful leaders, which are applicable within the context of Egyptian business culture. One inspirational quote from the author, " كل إنجاز كبير هو قصة روح ملأها التحفيز و هيجتها الحماسة" (Every great achievement is the story of a soul filled with motivation and fuelled by enthusiasm) (El-Feki, 2011, p. 28), highlights the impact of motivation and passion as key attributes of leadership success.

إن النجاح في الحياة لا يكون فقط نجاحاً مادياً بحتاً، و لا نحصل عليه فقط بالصحة الجيدة، كما أنه ليس بعدد الأصدقاء، او بنيل الشهادات العلمية".

82

(Success in life is not only a purely material success, and it is not achieved only by good health, nor is it achieved by the number of friends, or by obtaining academic degrees) (El-Feki, 2011, p. 84). This quote highlights the importance of adopting a broader perspective on success, which can be correlated with leadership. It suggests that true success is not just limited to external achievements, material wealth, good health, social connections, or academic achievement. It also has to do with inner growth, emotional well-being, and the pursuit of goals that resonate with one's values and passions.

Local leadership book	
Title	*The Magic of Leadership*
Subtitle	How to become an effective leader?
Author	Dr. Ibrahim El-Feki
Publisher	Sama For Publishing & Distribution
Year	2011
ISBN	9789776451155

Egypt leadership YouTube review

Authentic Coaching Academy is an Egyptian YouTube channel that was founded in 2019. The channel focuses on various aspects of Egyptian business culture and leadership. On November 16th, 2021, the channel hosted an online seminar with Dr. Ahmed Ibrahim Khalil from Analog Devices in Egypt. During this online seminar, Dr. Kalil talked about the success and the model of leadership and culture at Analog Devices. He stated that within the Egyptian management culture the prevailing point of view is that *"We don't trust you until you prove otherwise"* (Authentic Coaching Academy 2021, 11:20). He proceeds to explain that trust is a key element within the Egyptian business culture, and that it must be earned. One of the ways in which this trust can be earned is by being transparent and exhibiting an open mind towards questions. The second video to be summarised here comes from the Egyptian Banking Institute (EBI). The EBI hosted a conference entitled *"The Future of Work, Humanizing the Digital Age."* In this video, there is a panel discussion between various business professionals in Egypt. The focus of the conference was on Human Centred leadership in HR and L&D, The Future of

Business. The discussion centres on what traits the panellists believe are essential to Egyptian leadership and what challenges leaders are facing in the country. One key argument focuses on the necessity of driving traits that are more people related, whether it this be empathy, building authentic connections or applying emotional intelligence. Ms. Gen argues that *"Egyptian leaders need to now find a balance between financial acumen and the people factor and essentially empathy is the baseline"* (Egyptian Banking Institute 2024, 14:40). She proceeds to claim that it is imperative for Egyptian leaders to understand their organisation and people, that is, to understand what drives them. In her estimation, it is imperative that leaders adapt to the constantly changing priorities of their people, which, in turn, plays a critical role in terms of adaptability. The final video to be summarised here explores Egyptian business leadership from an educational perspective. The American University in Cairo hosted a business leadership online seminar on March 31st, 2022, and invited Dr. Sherif Kamel, Dean of the School of Business at the American University of Cairo. Dr. Kamel states in the video that *"in order to supply the market with the change agents, movers and shakers of tomorrow, business schools will be playing a key role in shaping Egyptian societies, but they need to act fast"* (AUC School of Business 2022, 54:56). He elaborates on this by noting that business schools need to think about innovative offerings, as change is continually needed if future Egyptian leaders are to keep up with the fast-evolving demands of global business.

Understanding hierarchy in Egypt

As Lituchy et al. (2017) explain, Egyptian culture has been influenced by its history, colonialism, wars, government power and the Islamic religion. The consequence of this, according to the authors, is that Egyptians value respect for authority, ancestors, and religion. Our interviewee, Dr. Bekhit, told us that hierarchy within Egyptian businesses is ordinarily bureaucratic and top-down in nature, with decision-making being concentrated at the upper echelons of companies, which he described as *"bureaucratic and mechanistic"* (Bekhit, 22 April 2024). Ms. El Sokary corroborated this framing of Egyptian organisational culture, asserting that in environments with solely Egyptian natives there often is a strict hierarchical structure. The result of this, she argued, is that senior Egyptian leaders have a great deal of authority and there are clear roles and centralised decision-making processes. She also highlighted a common problem of this approach, which is that *"roles and responsibilities are assigned without corresponding authority"* (El Sokary, 25 April 2024). To avoid such uncertainty, regulations and controls are put in place, which, in turn, means that Egyptian leaders, who are predominantly male, hold ultimate levels of power and authority (Lituchy et al., 2017). In relation to this aforementioned point about the gender composition of leaders in Egypt, Ms. El Sokary informed us that effective leadership has more to do with personal traits and experiences than gender (25 April 2024). However, there are social inequalities in Egypt in terms of power and wealth. This high- level of hierarchy is supported by the Power Distance Dimension of Hofstede's country comparison tool (Hofstede n.d.). Egypt scores 80 out of 100 on the dimension power distance. This is a high score, and according to Hawass (2015), in societies with high power distance, there is a greater acceptance of unequal power relations and decisions by management can be made without much objection from employees. Simply put, people accept that everyone has a place in the hierarchical order. Research conducted by El-Zayaty (2018) supports the high-power distance orientation in Egyptian society, indicating that it is characterised by rigid hierarchical power structures that tend to persist. Furthermore, El-Zayaty (2018) observes that more than three-quarters of the participants in their research describe their leaders as being inaccessible due to the high-power distance between them and management. This aspect of leader-employee relations is corroborated by the results of the CCBS Survey (2018-2024), insofar as the majority of the respondents reported that it is important for subordinates to refer to leaders by their title or position within the organisation when communicating with them, whether verbally or in writing. Similarly, when asked if employees are allowed to address their managers by their first name, the majority of the respondents responded no. This is in line with other research, which also demonstrated that job titles and job experience are clearly important in the Egyptian hierarchy; for example, the higher a leader's job title, the more respect and prestige they will receive in a company (Dajani, 2015). This was also confirmed by the results of the CCBS Survey (2018-2024) in that the majority of the participants reported that having organisational experience is highly appreciated by one's subordinates.

How the Egyptians achieve leadership empathy

The hierarchical and collective nature of Egyptian leadership as well as the high-power distance orientation in the country are recurring themes throughout this chapter. The high-power distance orientation results in a situation in which Egyptian employees tolerate power differences and obediently follow their leaders' orders (Hawass, 2017). On the other hand, the collectivist values of Egyptian society make it important for leaders to cultivate and maintain interpersonal relationships with their subordinates (Hawass, 2017). The Egyptian culture is a blend of Arab and Middle Eastern influences. Through a combination of cultural, social, and religious practices, the Egyptians have historically been able to cultivate leadership empathy (Tatomir, 2020). At the heart of this was their belief in *ma'at*, which encompassed the idea of cosmic harmony and justice. Leaders were encouraged to govern in accordance with *ma'at* by demonstrating empathy towards the needs and concerns of their people (Tatomir, 2020). This aspect of Egyptian culture is also reflected within the business context, insofar as it is important for employees to have good relationships at work with their superiors (Yousef, 2001, as cited in El-Kot & Leat, 2008). Egyptian leaders who are open, fair towards their employees, sincere and honest also enhance their employees' level of job satisfaction. In so doing, leaders also positively influence their own empathetic leadership in the sense that if employees are satisfied at work, then they will in turn exhibit greater empathy towards their leaders (El-Nahas et al., 2013). This point was corroborated by Dr. Bekhit, who informed us doing our interview that it is important for Egyptian leaders to display empathy by putting themselves in the shoes of their employees and exhibiting emotional intelligence. As Dr. Bekhit put it, empathy and understanding are thus important pillars for building trust and respect (22 April 2024). The fact that Egyptian leadership has a strong relational component was also apparent in the findings of the CCBS Survey (2018-2024). Specifically, some of the C-level executives emphasised the importance of emotional and personal connections with employees (CCBS Survey, 2018-2024). This is supported by Ms. El Sokary, who stated that having these type of connections Egyptian leaders enables them to earn their trust and, in turn, their empathy (25 April 2024).

United Arab Emirates

Omayma Amallou Garnat, Ghizlane Azzaoui, Dounia Belkas, Rafi al Gareb, Alaa Jabaly & Hajar el Yakoubi

Renowned for its thriving petroleum industry and impressively large human-made structures, the United Arab Emirates (الإمارات العربية المتحدة,) or simply UAE or the Emirates, is an Arab country in the Middle East. The Emirates consists of seven autonomous emirates, namely Dubai, Abu Dhabi, Sharjah, Ajman, Ras Al Khaimah, Fujairah and Umm Al Quwain. As of 2023, the population of the Emirates encompasses around just under ten million inhabitants (Ashour & Kleimann, 2024). Prior to the country gaining its independence from Britain in 1971, the Emirates' economy relied heavily on pearl diving and fishing (Aqil, 2018). As of 2022, it has one of the highest GDPs in the world at 507 billion USD (Shadab & Alam, 2024), which is why the Emirates is heralded as a great example of rapid economic development and diversification in the Middle East. In the space of fifty years, the Emirates went from having a predominantly Bedouin population, who lived in desert tents, to being one of the wealthiest countries in the world and noted for its innovative and modern architecture. The country is amongst the tenth largest oil producers in the world. Despite these notable oil reserves, it is actively pursuing economic diversification initiatives, focused on tourism, finance and technology (Arafat et al., 2017). As a result, the Emirates is now one of the fastest growing markets for goods and technology from Europe, North America and Japan. The Emirates is also characterised by its business-friendly environment that has attracted international investors. Beyond its economic impact, international investments have also ushered in a more diverse landscape within the country, exemplified by its large immigrant population who are known as 'incomers' (Ahmad et al., 2021). Committed to becoming a global hub for commerce and innovation, there is a growing emphasis on diversity and inclusion in leadership, with efforts to empower women and promote cross-cultural understanding in the workplace. Although organisations are often hierarchical, with an emphasis on respect for authority and traditional values (Ahmad et al., 2021), the country's rapid development is leading to a growing demand for innovative and adaptive leadership styles that can navigate complex business environments and foster creativity and entrepreneurship.

How the Emirati characterise leaders?

In the United Arab Emirates, culture, religion, and business are tightly intertwined (Metcalfe & Mimouni, 2011). Consequently, Emirati leaders are expected to uphold strict ethical standards and high levels of integrity, which are deemed essential in the Emirati business world, insofar as they foster credibility and trust amongst employees (Mohammed et al., 2023). Islamic principles play a significant role in guiding this ethical behaviour, emphasising integrity, accountability, and fairness, not only in the business sector but also within one's daily life (Metcalfe & Mimouni, 2011). Such Islamic values are emblematic of Middle Eastern culture generally, where tolerance and respect for others are prioritised, along with ethical principles like the "Golden Rule" and the "Ethics of Reciprocity" (Shurden et al., 2008). Alongside these aforementioned values, Emirati society also places significance upon community and collective well-being, which, in turn, influences decision-making processes within organisations (Shurden et al., 2008). Given that Emirati business leaders are often deeply connected with their communities, they naturally become influencers within their organisations, who inspire and motivate their employees (Taher Alav et al., 2021). This motivation is integral to increasing employee engagement, work satisfaction, and overall performance (Matira & Awolusi, 2020), as evidenced by research indicating the direct positive link between the motivations of business leaders and the achievements of their employees in the Emirates (Mohammed et al., 2023). These aspects of Emirati leadership were corroborated by the findings of the CCBS Survey (2024), insofar as the majority of the respondents reported that UAE employees admire leaders for their market expertise and organisational experience. Additionally, the respondents noted that they expect their leaders to demonstrate qualities such as strong decision-making abilities, visionary thinking, and access to valuable professional networks (CCBS survey, 2024). Alongside Islamic values and the aforementioned qualities and behaviours, at the heart of Emirati culture is the notion of polychronicity, which is one of the four key determinants identified by Al-Omari (2003) as extending beyond Arab nations to diverse regions like China, Africa, and Latin America. Polychronicity emphasises the importance of multitasking and embraces interruptions as simply part of life's natural flow, which is stark contrast to so-called monochronic cultures where time is strictly followed, and tasks are completed in a sequential fashion (Straub et al., 2002). Conversely, in the Emirates, individuals approach time with a degree of flexibility, using schedules merely as loose guidelines rather than rigid constraints. This cultural fluidity cultivates an environment in which adaptability and flexibility thrive, empowering business leaders to seamlessly manage multiple tasks and swiftly pivot in response to evolving circumstances (Straub et al., 2002). Finally, the study of Alnuami (2018) underscores the importance of fostering good relationships for leaders in the Emirati culture. More specifically, it is important for leaders to appreciate and recognise their team members, provide mentorship and offer emotional support (Ali et al., 2021).

Survey results and what local respondents say

In order to gain extensive knowledge of leadership styles and procedures in the Emirates, the CCBS Survey (2024) was administered to managers and C-level executives working in a wide range of UAE businesses and industries. Through their extensive knowledge and expertise, the survey provides useful insights into the UAE's different leadership styles and practices. Specifically, it provides an in-depth look at how leadership in the UAE is evolving, in light of both local cultural values and global business trends. The most significant findings emerging from the survey will be discussed in turn below. The first key finding is that most of the respondents reported that once a manager has made a decision, they are unlikely to modify it easily (CCBS Survey, 2024). This somewhat autocratic approach was also discernible in the fact that around 60% of the respondents stated that missing a deadline is basically considered a failure (CCBS Survey, 2024). The next significant finding sheds light on the hierarchical nature of organisations in the UAE. Specifically, nearly half of the respondents noted that as leaders, they are provided with office space and transportation, which is indicative of their position in the upper echelons of the organisation (CCBS Survey, 2024). Similarly, over 55 percent of the respondents also reported that in order to improve team members' performance and achieve better results, managers in the UAE should actively encourage competition within teams. This was illustrated by one of the respondents, Syed Noorulla Khadri, a Managing Director, who explained: *"Always look for scope for improvement and requirement of training for employees to increase their performance"* (CCBS Survey, 2024). In addition, a sales team manager, Shadab Shaikh, noted: *"Respect for the designation also, here leaders are always leaders who guide their team and make sure to deliver numbers. In the end, no one tries to be a boss and give orders, in fact, they are leaders and work with teammates to achieve successful results"* (CCBS Survey, 2024). Finally, when asked about the desired leadership attributes in UAE, the leaders of the UAE expressed a wide range of opinions. Organisational experience and market expertise were the most valued qualities according to the respondents, whilst having an elegant appearance and good family background were barely selected in the survey (CCBS survey,2024).

Local leadership analysis

United Arab Emirates Social media review

This section broadens our analysis to include all social media platforms that are used to discuss leadership styles and practices in the Emirates. Firstly, three creative leaders from the Emirates—Lucy, Dida, and Natalie—share their insights on leadership in Gerety Talks on YouTube. Gerety Talks offers a fresh perspective on leadership skills in UAE. Lucy Harvey is a Chief Growth Officer, Dida serves as a Design Director at Accenture Interactive, whilst Natalie Shardan is a Managing Partner at Serviceplan Group (Gerety Awards, 2024). When Dida was asked to share her tips on leadership in the Emirates, she emphasised the importance of community. She suggested fostering smaller communities of practice in which individuals can engage in discussions are helpful in terms of maintaining the motivation and skill development of employees. Moreover, she highlighted the significance of prioritising the well-being of employees within companies in the Emirates. As she herself put it: *"That is when you will start to see the best work quality"* (Gerety Awards, 2024). Nathalie expanded upon this by emphasising the importance of organisational culture. She proceeded to assert that the culture within an organisation can either make or break it, with Emirati leaders playing a pivotal role in shaping this culture. Nathalie stressed the importance of creating a culture that embraces individuals with diverse backgrounds, knowledge, and passions, insofar as this fosters a conducive environment for innovation (Gerety Awards, 2024). Complementing these individual perspectives, Ramy Jallad, CEO of RAKEZ, underscores the necessity of visionary leadership in navigating the dynamic economic landscape of the UAE (Jallad, 2024). Jallad highlights the need for visionary leadership in the UAE's dynamic economy (Jallad, 2024). He stresses the importance of adaptability, especially with respect to addressing talent attraction and retention challenges. To address this issue, Jallad advocates for a people-first approach, which prioritises employee well-being and developing flexible work policies. Further, he stressed the necessity for organisations in the Emirates to embrace global trends like sustainability and digital transformation in order to ensure continued success in the future (Jallad, 2024). Jallad's insights, published in Logistics Middle East, serve as a roadmap for business leaders navigating the evolving economic landscape of the UAE (Jallad, 2024). The accumulated insights from Lucy, Dida, Natalie, and Jallad offer valuable guidance for navigating today's professional landscape in the UAE, showcasing multifaceted approaches to effective leadership practices.

Abdallah Haidar: a cross-cultural trainer

In order to gain a comprehensive overview of business leadership skills and practices in the Emirates, as well as the nuances of intercultural communication, we conducted an interview with Abdallah Haidar, who is a cross-cultural trainer with over twenty-one years of experience in various industries across the Middle East. He co-founded the Cross Culture Consultancy in 2022 in Dubai, with the express aim of supporting growth and development within the creative and cultural sectors through research, strategy, and innovation. He also carried out several projects for clients such as the Dubai Culture & Arts Authority, working on strategies for different designs. In our interview, Abdallah Haidar provided nuanced insights into the intricacies of leadership within the UAE's diverse cultural landscape. At the beginning, he emphasised the necessity for leaders to cultivate a deep understanding of cultural nuances, particularly within the context of the UAE's multicultural environment. To achieve this, he stressed the importance of cultural sensitivity training, stating, *"It's crucial for leaders to undergo comprehensive cultural sensitivity training to gain insight and effectively navigate the diverse cultural fabric of the UAE."* (Haidar, 29 April 2024). Haidar then proceeded to underscore the importance of leaders in the UAE shedding any sense of cultural superiority and instead approaching each culture with respect and openness. As he himself put it, *"Leaders must recognise the uniqueness of each culture, particularly in a melting pot like the UAE, and abandon any preconceived notions of cultural superiority. Embracing diversity and fostering inclusivity are fundamental to effective leadership in the UAE"* (Haidar, 29 April 2024). In response to questions about the interplay between power dynamics and leadership within the UAE, Haidar offered valuable perspectives. Specifically, he informed us that hierarchical structures should not undermine the importance of emotional support within the workplace. He proceeded to explain this further, noting that: *"Even within hierarchical frameworks prevalent in the UAE, leaders must prioritise emotional support and empathy".* He continued as follows: *"Understanding and empathising with individuals across all levels of the hierarchy is essential for cultivating a cohesive and supportive work environment."* (Haidar, 29 April 2024). Towards the end of our interview with him, Haidar also underscored the need for leaders in the Emirates to adapt their leadership styles to accommodate for the aforementioned cultural diversity of their teams. As he himself put it: *"Leaders in the UAE must possess the agility to navigate between formal and informal interactions, depending on cultural expectations"* (Haidar, 29 April 2024). He concluded by explaining that such versatility is of critical importance for fostering collaboration and cohesion amongst team members from diverse cultural backgrounds.

In-country leadership bestseller

Tommy Weir's 2015 book, *Leadership Dubai Style* القيادة بأسلوب دبي (*The habits to achieve remarkable success*), is a bestselling book on leadership in the UAE. The author has lived and worked in Dubai for the past decade. He is a leadership maximiser and CEO counsellor who specialises in helping good leaders become outstanding. He earned a doctorate in Strategic Leadership from Regent University and teaches at Hult International Business School. In addition to releasing multiple books, he also writes leadership columns for major publications. The book, which is available in both English and Arabic, discusses the habits that have contributed to Dubai's leadership success - what he refers to as their 'secret sauce'. The author spent three years researching and interviewing over 200 leaders, in order to ascertain the city's leadership secrets before then narrowing these down to twelve habits. The goal of this book is to teach leaders in business, government, and other sectors how to become successful leaders. Through a storytelling style, he takes you on a journey through Dubai's history and helps you understand their culture of striving to always be better. According to Weir's book (2015), in Dubai دبي leadership is about the future. In technical terms, "*Hello, Tomorrow*" refers to seeing the future, a future that others do not yet see. The next thing leaders should ask themselves is what do they want to achieve? Next, be hungry and ambitious because leaders' level of ambition is ultimately their choice and will set the yardstick for what they can accomplish. As noted by Weir, (2015) even if you have a position of authority, followership is not taken for granted in Dubai. Rather, leaders must be loyal to those working under them. This loyalty can be cultivated by holding your own "*majlis*" مجلس (i.e., a conference chamber to consult and listen), giving people the opportunity to deliver once you have committed to your strategy, and creating an environment where others can thrive. The key word here is "*micro-monitor but do not micromanage*". If someone goes off track, speak out and help them get back on track and become better. Finally, he states (2015) that whilst leaders in UAE must be open to others' ideas and enable them to pursue goals that may be unfamiliar to them, they must also maintain their own identity and culture.

Local leadership book	
Title	*Leadership Dubai style*
Subtitle	The Habits to Achieve Remarkable Success
Author	Dr Tommy Weir
Publisher	EMLC Press
Year	2015
ISBN	9780996637503

Emirati leadership YouTube review

Alongside academic research and empirical data, YouTube also constitutes a resource for finding out information on leadership skills and practices, including in the Emirates. First, in an episode of Trade Around the World Talks, they discussed business etiquette and leadership with Salwa Alhammadi, Director of Quality & Excellence in the Abu Dhabi Government, UAE. In the video, Salwa emphasised the importance of adaptive leadership, collaborative Leadership, encouraging teamwork and inclusivity to drive innovation (Salwa Alhammadi, 2022). Throughout the conversation, Salwa emphasised the importance of authenticity, ethical leadership, and prioritising the well-being and growth of one's team members. (Salwa Alhammadi, 2022). Specifically, she noted that leadership in the UAE is about influencing, impacting, inspiring, and empowering others to achieve their full potential. Reflecting on her own experience and expertise, Salwa also talked about Emirati female leaders (Salwa Alhammadi, 2022). She shared that most of them are visionary thinkers because they need to think ahead of their time. She gave a message for female leaders working in the Emirates, which is to *"Be assertive when working in a tough environment because life is not easy* "(Salwa Alhammadi 2022, 28:32). The second video to be summarised here comes from Forbes Middle East and Visa United who organised an event that sought to illuminate the path for female entrepreneurs in the Middle East (Forbes Middle East, 2022). The event not only showcased their inventive pitches but also shared inspiring tales from accomplished female leaders in the region. Mona Ataya, the founder, and CEO of Mumzworld, serves as the perfect example of visionary leadership in pioneering e-commerce in the Middle East. In relation to the leadership skills that were required to achieve her success, she talked about how she exhibited resilience and innovation. Juggling entrepreneurship with motherhood, Ataya's dedication and adaptability can serve as an inspiration to others to overcome obstacles and achieve success in the dynamic world of online retail in the Middle East (Forbes Middle East, 2022). Ambareen Musa, CEO of souqalmal.com, exemplifies a leadership style rooted in authenticity and resilience. She empowers individuals to define their own success and fosters a culture of trust and collaboration within her organisation. As she put it in the video, "*love yourself, be passionate about what you do, ask for help and embrace failure*"(Forbes Middle East, 10:52). Finally, Hafsa Qadeer, CEO of ImInclusive, talks about the importance of compassionate leadership in the Middle East, emphasising inclusion and empathy in business (Forbes Middle East, 2022). Her focus on empowering marginalised groups reflects a visionary approach. *Qadeer's message to "open the door and open your own heart"* underscores her commitment to diversity and equity, inspiring transformative change through empathy and purpose (Forbes Middle East, 2022, 14:45).

Understanding hierarchy in the Emirates

In the bustling corporate landscape of the UAE, the business leadership culture is profoundly influenced by tradition and the rich history of Arab and Islamic values and societal norms. One of the ways in which this tradition continues to impact upon contemporary life in the Emirates is the high level of hierarchy, which is also reflected within their business organisational culture (McAdam et al., 2013). Arab cultures have consistently been found to have high levels of power distance, which Hofstede et al. (2010) define in terms of both the way people in society relate to each other on a hierarchical level and the amount of deference accorded to people in positions of authority. In Emirati business culture subordinates often submit to authority figures with reverence, expecting clear directives and guidance from their superiors in return. This reverence for hierarchy is emblematic of the deeply entrenched social classes within Arab culture in which respect for leadership and deference to authority are deeply ingrained from a young age (Alfaqeeh et al., 2019). At a societal level, lower classes in the Emirates have less political power than those higher than them (Hill et al., 1998). Similarly, in the business sector, senior-level positions in most companies are filled with older, more experienced employees. Resultantly, they are also the figures tasked with making the vast of majority of the important decisions (McAdam et al., 2013). In terms of the role of employees in this process, McAdam et al. (2013) argue that lower-level employees within the organisational hierarchy in UAE companies generally have very little influence in the decision-making process.

Rather, they are subordinate and are focused on doing merely what they have been told to do from the people above them (McAdam et al., 2013). However, besides being a country that places great importance on clear structures and hierarchy, the Emirati are also a highly collectivistic culture, which is to say that family, friends and community are accorded notable significance (ElKelish & Hassan, 2014). Indeed, at points one's family connections and economic class has more to do with where one is positioned in the organisational hierarchy than merit alone. Quite simply, the more money, status and connections someone possesses, the higher their position (Hill et al., 1998). However, this is not the entire picture. According to Hofstede (1985), collectivism involves placing the importance of the goals and well-being of the group above individual goals. In this respect, Arab workers also value the concept of collective unity, and solidarity extends throughout organisational structures, emphasising the importance of loyalty, harmony, and mutual support within tight-knit networks (Alfaqeeh et al., 2019). However, this collectivism can simultaneously lead to bureaucracies, which are firmly rooted in Arab culture, with privileges extended to those higher on the social ladder (Al-Omari, 2003). Gender also plays a significant role in this regard. Within the business culture there is a preference for male leaders in senior positions rather than women (Kemp et al., 2013). According to Alfaqeeh et al. (2019), this persistence of gender inequality in the Emirates derives from the continued bias that favours men leading corporations. Interestingly, however, the findings of the CCBS Survey (2024) show that the majority of the respondents reported that women and men have equal opportunity to attain senior-level leadership positions in Emirati organisations.

How the Emirati achieve leadership empathy

According to Iqbal et al. (2015), leaders must first understand themselves before implementing the best leadership style. They also need to demonstrate empathy for others in order to make decisions that are in line with societal demands. In this vein, a recent study conducted by Ali et al. (2021) demonstrated that Emirati business leaders have a highly empathetic leadership style. Specifically, they place significant value upon forming close relationships, engaging in active listening, providing assistance, being sensitive to cultural differences, and settling disputes in a constructive manner (Ali et al., 2021). This framing of leadership in UAE is also supported by the fact that HR departments are focused on diversity management and providing cultural sensitivity training, promoting understanding and appreciation for diverse backgrounds and beliefs within the workplace (Bealer et al., 2019). The importance of this approach within the UAE was shared by Abdallah

95

Haidar, who during our interview stated: *"By learning about and accepting other cultures, leaders can integrate traits like compassion and support into their leadership."* (29 April, 2024). In addition to being considerate of different cultures, Emirati leaders have also been shown to prioritise employee well-being (Bealer et al., 2019). They do so through the implementation of different programs, such as wellness workshops, mental health support services and promoting a healthy work-life balance to ensure the holistic health and happiness of their team members (Bealer et al., 2019). This healthy work-life balance is encouraged by providing employees with flexible work arrangements, understanding, and accommodating the diverse needs and responsibilities of employees (Valenta et al., 2019). This focus on wellbeing is corroborated by the findings of the CCBS Survey (2024) insofar as the majority of the respondents agreed that Emirati leaders spend time ensuring the personal well-being of their employees. One explanation for this is that like many other Gulf countries, the UAE values strong interpersonal connections, with leaders prioritising the cultivation of positive bonds with their employees, as this increases employees' job satisfaction (Alnuami, 2018). This argument is in accordance with the general observation that Emirati leaders often demonstrate compassion and empathy towards their employees (Agarwal & Gupta, 2021). Emirati business leaders exhibit their compassion and empathy by building personal connections, offering support to employees, being culturally sensitive and resolving conflicts constructively (Ali et al., 2021). Moreover, given that most employees in the Emirates are expatriates, and want to fly back home throughout the year to visit their home countries, it is standard practice that employers pay for return flights for their employees (Valenta et al., 2019). Finally, businesses that employ foreign workers and Emirati employers also largely fund accommodation and healthcare costs for their employees. In summary, these compassionate leadership techniques help to cultivate a productive workplace, encourage loyalty and trust, and advance both individual and corporate success within the Emirates.

Germany

Max Bijenveld, Pelle Brinkhof, Casper Dokter, Clara Weißenhorn
Amir Kila & Alide-Marie Hovenkamp

Germany, the country of *"Dichter und Denker"* (Poets and Thinkers) (Heussinger et al., 2020), is more than simplistic stereotypes, revealing instead a distinct blend of culture, history, and innovation. Whilst often associated with clichés such as beer, sausages, and lederhosen, such characterisations offer merely a partial perspective of Germany (Boonen et al., 2022). Beyond these traits one finds a nation defined by a unique combination of tradition and progress, where creativity and innovation coexist side-by-side (Radtke, 2003). Germany has become a key figure on the international stage, as a consequence of its economic strength, technological prowess, and political stability (Herzog-Stein et al., 2010). Worl-famous brands such as Mercedes-Benz and Siemens testify to Germany's excellence in engineering, which has also helped to position the nation at the forefront of global industry (Greer, 2008). The country's strategic positioning at the heart of Europe has profoundly shaped its historical and current relevance. Indeed, the intricacies of Germany's history is associated both with its fair share of triumphs and tragedies (Beattie, 2007). This history has contributed towards the formation of a resilient society that places significant value on democracy, human rights, and cultural diversity (Roseman, 1988). Across its history Germany has also had its share of powerful business and political leaders. In recent years, Angela Merkel, Germany's first female chancellor, left an indelible mark on global politics during her sixteen years in office. She was revered by many for her leadership style, which was characterised by ethical conviction and strong decision-making (Helms et al., 2018). In certain respects, her approach differed from traditional German leadership, which is often associated with low levels of compassion and empathy (Brodbeck et al., 2002), Although these stereotypes do not represent the entirety of the country, of course, they nevertheless form the basis of the country's leadership styles and practices. In this chapter the complexities of German business leadership and the prevailing organisational culture in the country will be explored in-depth through recourse to primary and secondary research with experts and professionals.

How the German characterise leaders?

Daniel Pinnows observes in his Book *"Führung - Worauf es wirklich ankommt"* that: *"Führung meint: Eine Welt so zu gestalten, dass andere ihr gern angehören möchten"* (Leadership means: designing a world in such a way that others want to be a part of it) (2015, p.303). In the specific context of German leadership this is translated into a strong focus on performance and efficiency. According to Brodbeck and Frese (2007), German business leaders prioritise attaining goals and increasing efficiency within their organisations, often at the expense of compassion or empathy. This preference for performance-driven leadership is well ingrained in German societal standards, where competence, discipline, and precision are highly valued (Brodbeck & Frese, 2007). Furthermore, Brodbeck et al. (2002) argue that the German leadership paradigm is distinguished by a pragmatic approach that places outcomes over relationship characteristics. In this respect, their findings support the widely held belief that German leadership approaches promote task-oriented behaviour and focus on achieving tangible results rather than cultivating interpersonal ties within the organisational setting. This characterisation of German leadership was supported by one of our respondents in the CCBS Survey (2024), Rainer Trometer, a COO, who opined that accuracy and precision are more pronounced in German leaders compared to their international counterparts. In contrast to these aforementioned characteristics, Lutz Von Rosenstiel et al. (2020) stress the importance of learning motivational, emotional, and interpersonal skills to succeed as a leader in Germany, showing a clear emphasis on empathy. Besides the efficiency and performance indicators (Brodbeck et al., 2002), it was evident from our interview with Aksana Kavalchuck (April 12, 2024) that there is also strong significance accorded to excellence with respect to German leaders. More specifically, she explained that a German leader has to be at least as good or better than their employees in specific subjects, along with possessing the ability to solve conflicts and problems whilst making decisions responsibly (Kavalchuck, April 12 2024). This was also underscored in the CCBS Survey (2015-2020), insofar as one of the respondents, Thomas Schindler, noted: *"Leadership is not appointed to an individual but earned through competency and knowledge."* (CCBS Survey, 2015-2020). During our interview with them, Kavalchuck also indicated that being cooperative as a leader is becoming increasingly important in the country. *"(...)you must be able to involve people in certain decision-making processes or in the process of finding solutions. That means, having the quality to encourage someone to contribute, to see who can contribute what, and where you can use someone"* (April 12, 2024). Nevertheless, the responsibility of the decision as an outcome of the collaborative process still rests with the leader themselves in Germany. In summary, shaped by cultural factors, German leaders must possess excellence which includes the ability to solve problems efficiently, be collaborative, whilst also showing a keen eye for precision and positive outcomes.

Survey results and what local respondents say

In order to gain further insight into leadership skills and practices in Germany, we administered the CCBS Survey (2024) to C-level executives who shared their vast first-hand knowledge and experience of leading German organisations. The most significant of the findings emerging from the responses of the 30 respondents are presented here in turn. The first notable finding is that the vast majority of the respondents reported that leaders in Germany are not likely to change their decision once it has been (CCBS Survey, 2024). This makes sense in many ways, especially given that every single one of the executives who took part in the survey also stated that German employees expect their leaders to be powerful decision makers (CCBS Survey, 2024). These findings are in accordance with the work of Brodbeck et al. (2002), who purport that German leaders have a dominant attitude, which is based on efficiency and performance. The second notable finding emerging from the survey is that although German executives tend to be dominant and stand behind their decisions, there does not appear to be an overly hierarchical relationship between leaders and their employees. This was evidenced by the fact that the majority of the executives stated that employees address their leaders by their first names in German organisations (CCBS Survey, 2024). Similarly, the majority of the respondents disagreed with the statement that subordinates need to address their leaders by their title or position (CCBS Survey, 2024). Kavalchuck (12 April 2024) helps us understand this further, insofar as they stated in our interview that people are comfortable addressing their colleagues and superiors with the casual *"Du"* or their first name. Interestingly though, over half of the leaders reported finding it important that they have their academic title on their business card or stated in their e-mail signature (CCBS Survey, 2024). The third significant finding is that one of the respondents stated that *"Work-life balance and employee well-being are very important* [in German leadership]" (CCBS Survey, 2024). This statement is supported by the finding that an overwhelming majority of the respondents noted finding it necessary that leaders should care about the well-being of their team members (CCBS Survey, 2024). The last key finding is that in Germany leadership is above all about competence, rather than being about someone's background or who they know (CCBS Survey, 2024). When queried about the attributes employees value most in their executives, most of the respondents underscored the significance of organisational experience. Alongside this, market expertise, high intellect, and technical competence also emerged as highly esteemed qualities (CCBS Survey, 2024). This is once again supported by Kavalchuk (12 April 2024), who stated that a leader has to prove they are competent enough with the skills that they have learned throughout their career.

Local leadership analysis

Dr. Anja Ebert-Steinhübel: a German leadership scholar

In order to gain a more comprehensive understanding of the leadership landscape in Germany, we conducted an Interview with Dr. Anja Ebert-Steinhübel. Besides owning a consultant firm with her husband and being the leader of the learning leadership institute, she has been appointed as professor of business administration with a focus on business psychology at Victoria International University. She has also published multiple articles focused on leadership and improving personal professional performance. Her book *"Learning Leadership: Führung lebenslang neu lernen"* was published in 2021. Currently, she is focusing on dealing with leadership in practice, working with executives, hiring them as well as assisting them with strategic issues. The interview began with discussing what characteristics are preferred in German leaders (26 April 2024). Before answering this question, she first pointed out that it is typical in Germany that *"(...) we still cling to the idea that a person's traits ultimately determine their leadership success"* (Ebert-Steinhübel, 26 April 2024). She proceeded to explain that leaders are usually selected, who are career-oriented, ambitious, transparent, but also respectful in their approach (26 April 2024). Nevertheless, she noted that she believes the current selection process is outdated and advocated for a shift from transactional to transformative leadership styles in Germany. She elaborated on this further by citing the following example: *"(...) meaning every leader automatically deals with communication, team development, dealing with conflicts (...) to stand behind or beneath the changes, to let others grow larger, to distribute leadership to different roles, to recognise people who may still be very low in the hierarchy, but who can already give significant impulses or are capable of innovation."* (Ebert-Steinhübel, 26 April 2024). She pointed out that this is still missing in the German leadership landscape. In response to a question regarding hierarchy, Dr. Ebert-Steinhübel began by saying that the term itself has started to become frowned upon in the German business landscape. She noted that many companies are becoming more flexible and are transitioning to flatter structures, in recognition of the fact that hierarchy hinders innovation and development (26 April 2024). On the other hand, she also emphasised that "(...) *the bigger, the older, the more traditional a company is, the stronger the hierarchy is* (...) (Ebert-Steinhübel, 26 April 2024). When it comes to building a trusting and respectful culture in German companies, Dr. Ebert-Steinhübel opined that it is only possible if the person in a leadership position deems this to be of importance. If leaders do not demonstrate trustworthiness, then it is simply impossible to foster such a culture. It is her belief that "(...) *there are simply people who, due to their personality structure, are more social, open, empathetic, communicative than others, who are more logically structured and only name things when it is extremely important.*" (Ebert-Steinhübel, 26 April 2024). However, to truly understand what each person needs and to be fair in different ways is what constitutes the art of being a good leader (26 April 2024). In response to a question regarding empathic leadership characteristics, she pointed out that listening and showing that you are listening are the most important factors. And whilst she believes you can stimulate your skill to emphasise through training, she stated that "(...)*someone who does not like people should definitely not be in a leadership position.*" (Ebert-Steinhübel, 26 April 2024).

Dr. Phil. Aksana L. Kavalchuk: a German cross-cultural trainer

Dr. Phil. Aksana L. Kavalchuk is the author of the Guide: "*Cross-Cultural Management: How to Do Business with Germans*" and the CEO of her own consultation firm called *Culture Leadership Communication Consult GmbH*. She has over twenty years of experience in training and coaching in the context of leadership and her lengthy career has enabled her to witness many changes in the German leadership landscape from the early 2000s onwards. She has worked in assessment centres for the selection of leaders and especially managers in large German companies. The interview began by discussing what characteristics make up German leaders (12 April 2024). According to Kavalchuck, a leader has to prove themselves as being competent enough with the skills that they have learned throughout their career. The journey to becoming a leader in Germany is often a long process with many different stages. She explained that due to these time-consuming steps it is rare to see someone in a leadership position before the age of forty (12 April 2024). Kavalchuck next proceeded to discuss that whilst corruption is not often visible in German business, nepotism is still an unspoken occurrence in Germany. More specifically, Kavalchuck (12 April 2024) pointed out that although it is unusual for someone to skip a step in the process of becoming a leader, having the right family, connections or mentor figures can definitely influence how fast you move through the process. Despite this, excellence and expertise from a leader is still demanded. After characterising German leaders Kavalchuck (12 April 2024) proceeded to describe the hierarchical structures within German organisations. She made it abundantly clear that the hierarchical structures are becoming ever-flatter in the country. However, this still depends on what type of management style the owner of the company adopts. Continuing our discussion of hierarchy, she told us that whilst the common polite form of address "*Sie*" in a business setting is fading away and people are becoming more comfortable with addressing their colleagues and superiors with the casual "*Du*" or their first name, some companies still have very clear hierarchical structures. She cited the example of hospitals where doctors are often referred to as "*Götter in weiß*" (Gods in white) (Kavalchuck, 12 April 2024) and where the polite address form is still enforced. However, she also opined that leaders are quite open to hearing suggestions when it comes to the decision-making process. One explanation for this is that Germans have the need to make the right decision, which is why they are open to hearing as many perspectives as possible to make the best decision (12 April 2024). In response to a question about how leaders achieve empathy in Germany, Kavalchuck acknowledged that whilst respect and appreciation are the norm in the workplace, the leadership approach is not always an empathetic one. More specifically, she argued, German leaders struggle to create an environment that fosters psychological trust in which employees feel able to show weakness and failure. She also expressed that you can either have empathy on a cognitive level and be born with it or develop it at a later stage in life. However, this development can only happen during certain time windows of a person's life, usually during puberty (12 April 2024). At the end of the Interview, Aksana Kavalchuk (12 April 2024) offered an additional unique insight into German leadership, emphasising that the development process of leaders in Germany is unique. Specifically, she talked about a certain seriousness and conviction that is not seen in other countries. This translates into a professionalised, systematic, and thorough development that provides leaders with the necessary toolsets and competencies (12 April 2024).

In-country leadership bestseller

"*Das Neue Führen*" by Bodo Janssen (2023) presents a paradigm shift in German leadership philosophy focused on the contemporary era, prioritising empathy, and interconnectedness. Janssen is a notable figure in the realms of entrepreneurship, leadership, and organisational development. As CEO of Upstalsboom Hotel + Freizeit GmbH & Co. KG, a prominent German hospitality company, Janssen has garnered acclaim for his innovative approaches to leadership and business management. In this particular book, Janssen argues that conventional hierarchical frameworks no longer align with the rapid pace of change and instead advocates for a more inclusive and participatory approach to leadership in Germany. Through a blend of anecdotes, insights, and actionable advice, he explains how German leaders can effectively navigate their way through the complexities of the modern landscape with authenticity and empathy. Central to Janssen's argument are the notions of cultivating robust interpersonal connections with one's employees, focusing on individual growth, and creating a supportive organisational culture. His work serves as a rallying call to German leaders across a diverse range of sectors and backgrounds, urging them to reassess their leadership and embrace a more human-centric method. By demonstrating understanding, respect, and active engagement, Janssen contends that German leaders can inspire meaningful change within their teams and organisations. *"Das Neue Führen"* thus stands as a beacon of guidance for those seeking to lead with purpose and compassion in an increasingly interconnected world. Through its blend of theoretical insights and practical wisdom, the book offers a roadmap for aspiring and seasoned leaders who wish to navigate the complexities of contemporary leadership with grace and effectiveness.

Local leadership book	
Title	*Das Neue Führen*
Subtitle	Führen und sich führen lassen in Zeiten der Unvorhersehbarkeit
Author	Bodo Janssen
Publisher	Ariston
Year	2023
ISBN	9783424202854

German leadership YouTube review

Alongside academic research and survey and interview data, YouTube also constitutes a vital resource for understanding German business leadership. The first video to be summarised involves Bernd Geropp, a German entrepreneur, speaker, and coach in the field of leadership and management (Führung auf den Punkt gebracht mit Bernd Geropp, 2024). He is known for his podcast *"Leadership in a Nutshell"* where he shares valuable insights on leadership, management, and entrepreneurship. Geropp primarily focuses on supporting *kmuunternehmer* (small and medium-sized businesses) through mentoring, coaching, and training. He also has a background as a self-employed entrepreneur, which means he has practical experience in running a business. The video provides valuable insights into recent developments at Gerob Leadership GmbH, a firm specialising in leadership and entrepreneurship. Bern Gerob, the company's founder, engages with his team to discuss their recent progress and plans for the year ahead. Bern underscores the significance of selecting employees capable of working autonomously and demonstrating initiative, noting: "*I chose my employees based on the motto: I'm not looking for employees but for colleagues*" (Führung auf den Punkt gebracht mit Bernd Geropp, 2024, 3:04). Furthermore, Bern elucidates his approach to fostering entrepreneurship within his team, enabling them to cultivate their own ventures alongside their commitments at Leadership GmbH, with Bern serving as their mentor. As he himself noted: "*And the best way to achieve that is, well, by supporting them in being entrepreneurial themselves*" (Führung auf den Punkt gebracht mit Bernd Geropp, 2024, 4:21). The second video to be summarised here (Business School 101, 2022) offers a comprehensive perspective on German culture and business practices, providing valuable insights into global business dynamics. The platform hosting this video, named *"Business School 101"*, comprises a consortium of US-based business professors, each of whom possess a Ph.D. in their respective fields. Their collective mission is to impart practical business knowledge and offer valuable insights into the real-world business landscape to those who seek it. The backbone of Germany's robust economy lies in its large export sector, which contributes around 40% of its national output. Key exports include vehicles, machinery, chemical goods, electronic products, and electrical equipment. Germany's status as Europe's largest manufacturing economy affords it resilience against financial downturns, bolstering its stability in the face of economic challenges. Furthermore, its commendable position on the Corruption Perception Index 2021, ranking 10th out of 180 countries with a score of 80, underscores its commitment to transparency and integrity in business practices (Business School 101, 2022). Delving into German societal norms through Hofstede's cultural framework reveals interesting insights. Germany exhibits low power distance and challenges leadership to demonstrate expertise. The society leans towards individualism, prioritising self-actualisation and personal preferences over collectivism. Given that it exhibits traits of a masculine society, Germany values performance, punctuality, and status symbols. Uncertainty avoidance is another notable aspect, with Germany emphasising deductive approaches, detail-orientation, and discipline. A high score on long-term orientation signifies a pragmatic outlook, emphasizing adaptability, perseverance, and a propensity for saving and investment. However, the culture also tends towards restraint, with less emphasis on leisure and gratification. According to the speakers in the video, the German organisational culture mirrors these social norms, and is characterised by a focus on tasks, attachment to rules and regulations, the strict separation of private and public spheres, and direct communication styles. When engaging with German counterparts, observing proper business etiquette is therefore crucial. Punctuality is important, meetings follow strict agendas, communication is direct and goal-oriented, and decisions are explained and documented. In conclusion, Germany's business culture is defined by efficiency, professionalism, and an adherence to established protocols (Business School 101, 2022).

Understanding hierarchy in Germany

According to Sorge (2017), the hierarchy in German business culture is characterised by a unique combination of standardised management and situation-specific problem-solving. This is reflected in the preference for a balanced management system, with the structured interaction between bottom-up and top-down activities (Heiß et al., 2004). During the interview with the cross-cultural trainer, Aksana Kavalchuk (12 April 2024), she pointed out that the typical polite form of address *"Sie"* in a business setting is slowly fading away and that people are now becoming more comfortable with addressing their colleagues and superiors with the casual *"Du"* or their first name. Moreover, she argued that the hierarchical structures within German organisations is becoming more horizontal and moving away from the strict vertical system seen before (Kavalchuk, 12 April 2024). This is supported by other research, which argues that in terms of corporate culture, German companies tend to favour a 'clan culture', focusing on employee needs and development (Kampf et al., 2018). This focus on employees' needs is also reflected in decision-making processes in German organisations. According to Kavalchuk, German leaders are quite open to hearing suggestions when it comes to the decision-making process. One explanation for this is that Germans have the need to make the right decision, which is why they are open to hearing as many perspectives as possible to make the best decision (12 April 2024). However, for this to function effectively, senior-level management must ensure that their staff are highly motivated staff (Dan & Elena, 2014). Another effective lens through which to study the level of hierarchy within organisations is, of course, Hofstede's power distance dimension; in terms of this dimension, Germany scores relatively low (Moll & Kretzschmar, 2017). The concept of authority in German business leadership is deeply intertwined with the country's culture and historical context. Both Richardson et al. (2014) and Larsen (2003) both underscore the influence of culture on leadership styles, with the former specifically noting the authoritative nature of German leadership. This is further supported by Brodbeck et al. (2002), who emphasise the high-performance orientation and low compassion in German cultural practices. In order to align with the performance orientation, it is important to have the right people in the right positions. Despite some progress, Holst and Kirsch (2014) observe that women remain significantly underrepresented in senior-level leadership positions within German businesses. Indeed, the overall progress towards gender equality in senior-level leadership positions in German businesses remains slow (Holst & Kirsch, 2014). Similarly, Heinrichs and Sonnabend (2022) found that women are less likely to hold postdoctoral positions, a key step in the academic career ladder, despite having similar qualifications to men. This suggests a potential leaky pipeline for women in academia, which, in turn, impacts upon the business world. A suitable German proverb that resonates with the changing landscape in which more women are ascending to leadership positions is *"Die Zeiten ändern sich"* translating to *"Times are changing."* This adage underscores the evolving nature of societal dynamics, wherein traditional norms and structures transform in response to emerging perspectives.

How the Germans achieve leadership empathy

According to the results of the CCBS survey (2024), the majority of the C-level managers who took part agreed with the statement that actively spending time to ensure the personal well-being of their team members is part of leaders' responsibility. However, the survey results also indicate that the majority of the respondents would rather retain a certain distance from their employees, in order to maintain the right level of respect (CCBS Survey, 2024). This underscores that managers in Germany acknowledge the need for empathy towards their employees but are nevertheless reluctant to cultivate and maintain close relationships with their subordinates. This tension between hierarchy, respect and empathy was also touched upon in a study conducted by Aulinger and Schmid (2009). In their study, the authors observe that the breaking down of hierarchical structures in Germany and the shift towards a more empathic style can be viewed as a disadvantage in certain respect. Their study, which drew upon the insights of thirty-three leaders in Germany, also stressed that having empathy as a leadership skill is not dependent on age but rather on the willingness to respect and acknowledge employees (Aulinger & Schmid, 2009). This was also highlighted in our interview with a German scholar, who stated that if leaders do not demonstrate trustworthiness, then it is simply impossible to foster an empathic culture. It is her belief that "(...) *there are simply people who, due to their personality structure, are more social, open, empathetic, communicative than others, who are more logically structured and only name things when it is extremely important.*" (Ebert-Steinhübel, 26 April 2024). Aulinger and Schmid's (2009) study argues that if German leaders are to cultivate this type of empathy in the workplace, then they must first self-reflect and understand their own attitude. This is in line with other research, which states: "*Emphatische Führung bedeutet auch, sich als Führungskraft seiner Haltung gegenüber den Mitarbeitern bewusst zu sein.*" (Empathic leadership also means being aware of your attitude towards your employees as a manager) (Ruhl & Ennker, 2012, p. 124). After this reflection, German leaders can achieve empathy by creating a space for trustworthy communication and motivation (Aulinger & Schmid, 2009). This communication entails active listening and fulfils the human need for emotional resonance, connection, and contact (Wiedel, 2019). Whilst displaying empathy as a leader in Germany has gathered attention in recent years, our interviewee, Aksana Kavalchuk (April 12, 2024), informed us that the German business landscape still has a long way to go to achieve empathy. Although she firmly believes there is already a lot of trust in German companies regarding structure and processes, a lot of employees still do not feel a certain psychological safety from their leaders. She expressed it as follows: "*this feeling of safety, that you can allow yourself to be ignorant, that you know, you can fantasize there, you won't be looked at sideways for seeking ideas*" (Aksana Kavalchuk, April 12, 2024). To show more trust in employees, she stated that German leaders have to create a space to allow their employees to show creativity but also weakness. Whilst she also believes that appreciation and respect have become the standard in the workplace already, she also pointed out to us that due to the absence of psychological safety, empathy is not the norm in German companies yet. Consequently, empathy has become a vital part of leadership training in German companies in recent years. Importantly, Aulinger and Schmid (2009) stress that only the affective abilities of empathy can be learned in such training, whereas true empathy can only be realised as an authentic experience and not through simulated acts (Aulinger & Schmid, 2009).

Gibraltar

Dóra Plébán, Beaudine Overtoom, Pariya Asfintabar, Sergio Mendez Vilas, Georgina Addai, Martijn Carels

Gibraltar is a small peninsula at the southern end of the Iberian Peninsula, towards the eastern end of the Bay of Gibraltar (Finlayson et al., 2014). English is the official language and, as such, is widely spoken across the territory. However, due to both the heterogeneity of its population and other historical influences, various languages, including, amongst others, Spanish are also commonly spoken in the country. Whilst Gibraltar measures a mere 6.7 square kilometres, this territory has nevertheless been of great interest to the international community throughout history due to its strategic location and historical significance (Bosque & Perera, 2021). Specifically, in light of the fact that it is nestled between Europe and Africa, Gibraltar has played an important role in shaping the course of history, insofar as it has served as a gateway between the Mediterranean Sea and the Atlantic Ocean. The consequence of this is that Gibraltar has had to face and overcome numerous geopolitical challenges and conflicts (Bosque & Perera, 2021). Considering both the small population and the multi-tiered nature of their governmental system, Gibraltarians have been described as the most governed people in the world (Dana, 2002). Leadership in Gibraltar is certainly complex and multifaceted, shaped by its unique history and geopolitical positioning. With respect to business leadership in particular, the most commonly adopted approach in businesses in Campo de Gibraltar is the democratic leadership style (Collante & Flores, 2018). This leadership style emphasises collaboration, participation, and decision-making through consensus amongst team members (Collante & Flores 2018). As will be discussed further in the chapter, upholding ethical standards, and promoting corporate social responsibility are also defining features of business leadership in Gibraltar (Feetham, 2015). These leadership styles and practices will be explored in this chapter using desk-based academic research and empirical survey data with Gibraltarian professionals and leaders.

How do the Gibraltarians characterise leaders?

Generally speaking, the prevailing leadership style in Gibraltar is characterised by a strong emphasis on relationship-building, open communication, and collaboration (Collante & Flores 2018). One of the ways in which managers cultivate good relationships with their employees, as identified by the results of the CCBS Survey (2024), is that they spend time ensuring the wellbeing of their team members. This was further corroborated by the fact that one of the respondents reported that Gibraltarian leaders have a high level of respect in terms of the local culture, which is important for collaboration and relationship-building (CCBS Survey, 2024). With respect to the predominant leadership styles that are adopted in the territory, Flores (2022) argues that the democratic and transformational leadership styles are the most suitable and commonly adopted approaches in the business sector in Gibraltar. These approaches are deemed to be the most suitable insofar as they have been found to positively influence the organisational culture, work stress, commitment, motivation, and conflict resolution (Flores, 2022). More specifically, leaders who adopt a democratic approach involve employees in the decision-making process, foster a positive attitude, skill development, and stronger results amongst their subordinates. This picture of leadership in the territory is evidenced by the findings of the CCBS Survey (2024), where the respondents informed us that leaders do not confront their employees during staff meetings in order to obtain the desired results. Given the aforementioned discussion, one plausible explanation for this would be that to do so would potentially negatively impact upon relationship-building and worsen employer-employee relations (Collante & Flores, 2018). Instead, Flores (2022) purports, leaders in Gibraltar cultivate an atmosphere of proactive, energetic teams who are listened to (Flores, 2022). Transformational leadership is distinguished by achieving improved organisational results through one's charisma, inspiring one's subordinates, and focusing on the organisation's interests. In this respect, this approach encourages and inspires teams to achieve the planned objectives and views them as significant individuals in the company (Givens, 2008). The importance of this in leadership in Gibraltar was stressed by Bering (24 October 2022), the CEO of AADS, who noted in a podcast that: *"You have to give away much trust and much responsibility to the people around you – that makes you and your team grow and develop."* Employees in Gibraltar are thus encouraged and supported to take responsibility for making decisions. Corporate leaders should be adaptable and focus on achieving growth (Feetham et al., 2023). Moreover, Feetham et al. (2023) proceeds to explain, leaders in Gibraltar emphasise building a strong and a diverse economy, which, in turn, contributes towards business development within the territory. Overall, the prevailing leadership skills and practices in Gibraltar emphasise collaboration, integrity, adaptability, and a solid commitment to achieving common goals. The employer-employee relationship is built on mutual respect, trust, and a shared vision for organisational success, thus contributing to a positive and productive work environment.

Survey results and what local respondents say

In order to gain additional in-depth insight into leadership skills and practices in Gibraltar, we administered the CCBS Survey to C-level professionals from across Gibraltar, who kindly shared their first-hand knowledge and experience with us. In order to strengthen the validity of the findings on leadership in Gibraltar, we combined data from this year with data gathered from a prior period of data collection (CCBS Survey, 2023-2024). The most significant results emerging from the survey are summarised in turn in this section. The first significant finding concerns the fact that the respondents had widely varying ideas about leadership skills and practices in Gibraltar (CCBS Survey, 2023-2024). One potential explanation for these differing perspectives may stem from the fact that although the respondents all held similar positions within their respective companies, they worked within very different sectors. Secondly, and interestingly, the majority of the respondents reported that employees in Gibraltar look up to their leaders on the basis of their organisational experience (CCBS Survey, 2023-2024). The third significant finding concerns the fact that most of the respondents stated that they prefer to avoid engaging in confrontation with their employees (CCBS Survey, 2023-2024). This is in accordance with previous research that showed that the prevailing leadership style in the territory is characterised by a strong emphasis on relationship-building, open communication, and collaboration amongst team members (Collante & Flores 2018). The importance of leaders being democratic in their approach and encouraging decision-making through consensus amongst team members (Collante & Flores 2018) was also supported by the fact that the majority of the respondents reported that employees are allowed to address their leaders by their first name (CCBS Survey, 2023-2024). Finally, with respect to what qualities, traits and behaviours are most valued in business leaders in Gibraltar, there was broad agreement over what qualities are essential in leaders, namely: 'strong charismatic personality,' 'resourcefulness,' 'eloquence,' and 'decisiveness.' (CCBS Survey, 2023-2024). This is in line with the views expressed by a Chief

Strategy Officer in Gibraltar, Nyreen Llamas, who in a panel discussion on gender inequality in organisations in Gibraltar noted that it is important for leaders in Gibraltar to be concise communicators, exhibit humility, and be good active listeners (Startup Grind Gibraltar, 2018). The last significant finding was that the respondents were evenly split over whether it is important for leaders to include an academic title in their business cards or email signatures.

Local leadership analysis

Gibraltarian leadership social media review

In order to again further insights into leadership in Gibraltar, we opted to go beyond academic research, survey data and YouTube to also include alternative digital platforms that provide information about leadership in the territory. In the digital era, where people primary consume information online, either in written or auditory form, outlets, and podcasts like, "Keeping it Civil," "Gibraltar Business Podcast," and Business Matters" provide invaluable insights on leadership in Gibraltar, both for current and aspiring leaders in the country and also for researchers. Firstly, as a guest on Spotify's Gibraltar Business podcast, Shimon Akad, COO of Playtech, a company in the territory, emphasises the importance of specific qualities, traits, and behaviours for leaders to embody and engage in in Gibraltar. As Akad (2022) himself put it: *"To be a really good leader* [in Gibraltar], *you need a few things: first, you need to have passion and love what you do; second, you need to always aim for excellence and make sure you work hard; and third, to build a really good business, you need a very strong team with you."* He proceeded to discuss how his leadership style prioritises flexibility and strategic vision, which he demonstrates by conducting yearly trend analyses to keep his team updated about market changes (Akad, 2022). The dynamic leadership environment of Gibraltar is strengthened by its heterogeneous corporate culture, which includes both local citizens and expats. Katherine Grant's experiences studying and working overseas provide crucial insights into how cultural factors affect leadership in Gibraltar. She proceeded to explain that: *'"The main difference in America was I always had a strong work ethic and not necessarily in a good way... You know, you are beholden to your company. So, coming back to Gibraltar and seeing the cultural difference here, I did not want to bring that"* (Your Gibraltar TV, 2020,3:38)'. Moreover, she worked in multicultural teams in Switzerland and learned how they manage conflicts and confrontation which was quite different from what she experienced in Gibraltar (Your Gibraltar TV, 2020).

111

From her experience, organisations in Gibraltar are characterised by a more dynamic and flexible approach to leadership, as evidenced, she noted, by the varied range of beliefs and experiences present in Gibraltar's leadership environment. Grant ends by stating that effective leaders in Gibraltar successfully manage problems and achieve success in an evolving business environment by drawing on a mix of individual experiences, cultural influences, and initiative-taking strategies. Thus, Gibraltar's leadership styles form a diverse range of experiences, cultures, and ideas, leading to a multiplicity of methods impacted by internal and external influences (Your Gibraltar TV, 2020).

In-country leadership bestseller

One of the best-selling books about leadership in Gibraltar was written by Kenneth Castiel and is called '*The Hero and the Villain Within.*' Kenneth, who is a high-performance Gibraltarian business coach, faced a fair number of setbacks during his youth. In this book, he sets out to tell his readers that everyone has the capacity to overcome the obstacles that we all encounter in life, whether these challenges occur in our social lives or as part of our business life (*Kenneth Castiel*, n.d.). The book provides a comprehensive strategy through which to help current and aspiring leaders in the territory to engage in a process of personal transformation. More specifically, the book does so by providing tools and exercises to the reader that can help to change their restrictive beliefs and thinking patterns, break unproductive habits, conquer their fears, and embark on a life filled with joy, wisdom, and self-understanding. In his book, Kenneth uses different real-life scenarios which he himself experienced, in order to show his readers how they too can make progress in their daily leadership practice within Gibraltarian organisations.

Local leadership book	
Title	*The Hero and the Villain Within*
Subtitle	Your Key to an Extraordinary Life Through the Power of Purpose, Freedom, and Abundance
Author	Kenneth Castiel
Publisher	Lioncrest Publishing
Year	2018
ISBN	9781544510040

Gibraltarian leadership YouTube review

Alongside academic and survey-based research, YouTube also constitutes an invaluable resource for gaining insight into leadership styles and practices in Gibraltar. The first video to be discussed in this section comes from 2018. Specifically, the video is a SGG and Girls in Tech Gibraltar event that sought to bring attention to the need for greater gender diversity in business leadership in the territory, as gender inequality remains an issue in Gibraltar despite the growing number of female leaders in the territory. As part of a panel discussion, Gemma Vasquez, Isabel Guggisberg, Naomi Quigley, and Nyreen Llamas all shared their respective stories and perspectives of female leadership and entrepreneurship in Gibraltar's corporate sector. The first speaker, Ms. Vasquez, addressed the persistent problem of silent discrimination against women in senior-level leadership roles within Gibraltarian organisations (Startup Grind Gibraltar, 2018). She proceeded to discuss how women in Gibraltar face persistent pressure to prove themselves, which, in turn, inhibits their ability to pursue leadership positions and exacerbates the issue of the lack of women in decision-making roles. According to Ms Vasquez, women have the ability to manage a multitude of responsibilities and bring unique skills to the table (Startup Grind Gibraltar, 2018). Next, Isabel Guggisberg's experience underscores the challenges that women encounter in male-oriented industries in Gibraltar. She explained how at first, she felt too inadequate to participate in conversations, even though the subjects being discussed were part of her occupation. Over time, she learned the value of resilience, observation and adjusting her communication style to become an effective leader in the territory, as she progressed in her career (Startup Grind Gibraltar, 2018). Furthermore, Chief Strategy Officer, Nyreen Llamas, addressed the need for concise communication, humility, and active listening for leaders in Gibraltar. When it comes to the business culture in Gibraltar, these qualities are essential for creating a cooperative and supportive workplace, says Llamas (Startup Grind Gibraltar, 2018). Finally, Naomi Quigley's observation in the panel discussion offers a valuable understanding of how departure encounters might influence future connections. In her words: *"How you leave people and how they feel when you leave their company will open or close doors for the rest of your lives."* (Startup Grind Gibraltar, 2018, 1:12:53). By highlighting the value of paying attention to nonverbal clues, the significance of building connections will endure in Gibraltar's corporate culture. Therefore, the experiences of the panellists underscore that diversity and inclusion in leadership roles require deliberate effort. By prioritising these principles and fostering a more ethical and useful business culture, Gibraltar may adopt more effective leadership styles to ensure future success (Startup Grind Gibraltar, 2018).

113

Understanding hierarchy in Gibraltar

The profoundly ingrained cultural characteristics of hierarchical norms in the workplace shape organisational dynamics and leadership styles in Gibraltar. We can identify the subtleties of Gibraltar's workplace hierarchy by drawing on the GLOBE research, which analyses cultural variables affecting leadership (House et al., 2004), as well as Hofstede's Power Distance dimension, which investigates the acceptance of hierarchical order (Hofstede, 2001). Based on Hofstede's cultural dimensions (Hofstede, 2001), we can see that Gibraltar has a moderate to low Power Distance Index (PDI), thus suggesting a preference for flatter organisational structures and a leaning towards egalitarianism. In these cultures, leaders are expected to cultivate and maintain a personal connection with their subordinates to promote a more participative and collaborative leadership style (Robbins & Judge, 2019). According to Yammarino and Bass (1990), transformational leadership is often more successful in situations with less power distance. Transformational leaders align with Gibraltar's egalitarian cultural leanings and inspire and motivate via the cultivation of personal connections and putting forward and subsequently pursuing a shared goal. According to a study on leadership styles in Gibraltar by Garcia-Morales (2012), subordinates view leaders who demonstrate transformational traits, such as, for example, individual concern and inspirational motivation, more favourably. This, in turn, lends credence to the idea that transformational leaders are typically more successful in societies with smaller power distances. It is important to understand, however, that organisational hierarchies may persist despite these cultural trends, albeit in less strict forms. Garcia-Morales et al. (2012) posit that leaders in Gibraltarian companies are given transportation and office space that corresponds to their rank, thus signifying the recognition of hierarchical positions within the company. To further understand these hierarchical positions within Gibraltarian companies, it is useful to refer to the results of the CCBS Survey (2024), which revealed different opinions with regards to whether leaders should interact with their employees. One-third of the respondents reported that they preferred maintaining personal distance from their employees. Moreover, a minority of the respondents indicated a desire for a personal relationship with employees but emphasised the importance of retaining enough distance to uphold the requisite respect (CCBS Survey, 2023-2024). Similarly, when asked whether it is important for employees to address their leaders by their position or title in Gibraltar, a little less than half of the respondents found this to be very important (CCBS Survey, 2023-2024). Furthermore, the survey indicated that in Gibraltar, leveraging personal connections to advance within a company is not uncommon.

Indeed, it is a routine occurrence within companies that someone further up the organisational hierarchy is either family or friends with someone who holds significant power within the organisation. This was confirmed by one of the respondents, who opined: *"In Gibraltar, people escalate all matters to the highest level of the hierarchy. They do not hesitate generally to use personal connections to achieve professional goals"* (CCBS Survey, 2024). In conclusion, understanding hierarchy in Gibraltar necessitates an appreciation of its cultural context, historical influences, and the interplay between personal connections and professional dynamics. Whilst the preference for flatter organisational structures and transformational leadership styles aligns with Gibraltar's cultural inclination towards egalitarianism, the persistence of organisational hierarchies underscores the complexity of navigating workplace dynamics.

How do Gibraltarians achieve leadership empathy?

In Gibraltar's business landscape, empathetic leadership shapes workplace dynamics and employee satisfaction. The results of the CCBS Survey (2023-2024) provide a clear indication that empathy goes beyond merely being a beneficial trait for leaders to possess; rather, it is an indispensable component of effective leadership in Gibraltar. This survey, which reflects the experiences of local employees, also captures the emerging shift in management focus towards empathy. The importance of empathy in leadership in Gibraltar has also been evidenced in previous academic research. For instance, according to a study on leadership styles in Gibraltar by Garcia-Morales (2012), subordinates view leaders who demonstrate transformational traits, such as, for example, individual concern and inspirational motivation, more favourably. Similarly, as aforementioned, Gibraltar has a moderate to low Power Distance Index (PDI), which suggests a preference for flatter organisational structures and a leaning towards egalitarianism. In these cultures, leaders are expected to cultivate and maintain a personal connection with their subordinates to promote a more participative and collaborative leadership style (Robbins & Judge, 2019). This was also corroborated by the work of Flores (2023), who noted in their research that a democratic leadership approach prevails in Gibraltar, an approach which is characterised by involving employees in the decision-making process, cultivating good relations with one's subordinates and fostering a positive attitude amongst one's teams, all of which requires empathic forms of leadership. The importance of empathy was also supported by various findings emerging from the CCBS Survey (2024-2024). Firstly, the majority of the respondents reported that leaders are not willing to confront subordinates during staff meetings to achieve desired results. This

115

signifies a strong call for leaders who approach conflict resolution with understanding and a commitment to collective problem-solving, rather than direct confrontation (Collante & Flores 2018). Similarly, the majority of the respondents noted that it is important for *managers to* actively spend time ensuring the personal well-being of their team members (CCBS Survey, 2024-2024). This approach by Gibraltarian leaders resonates with the inclusive and emotionally intelligent approach advocated by Jones (2020), who emphasises the significance of understanding and incorporating diverse perspectives within the decision-making process. These sentiments are not merely theoretical in nature, but rather are supported by empirical evidence. A study by Castro et al. (2012) demonstrates that leaders who are skilled in emotional intelligence can significantly enhance their teams' creativity, which is precisely the case in Gibraltar, insofar as scholars like Garcia-Morales (2012) have argued that subordinates in Gibraltar view leaders who demonstrate transformational traits, such as, for example, individual concern and inspirational motivation, more favourably. In conclusion, Gibraltar's inclination towards leadership empathy clearly indicates the evolving business landscape in the territory, where emotional intelligence is increasingly being recognised for its ability to unify teams and spur creative thought (Jones, 2020). It is evident that Gibraltar's businesses are championing a leadership style that prizes empathy, understanding, and the welfare of employees, which, in tun, enhances organisational effectiveness.

Great Britain

Daphne Jansen, Ekaterina Radeva (Екатерина Радева), Heejun Kim,
Mette Kabo, Vlad Milosteanu & Douwe Schmitt

Great Britain is located in the Northwest of Europe and stretches approximately 1,000 kilometres from its southern tip to the northernmost point, which is interesting when one considers that the Great Wall of China meanders its way across landscapes for more than 21,000 kilometres (Pang, 2024). Great Britain comprises four nations: England, Wales, Scotland, and Northern Ireland. England is significantly the largest of the home nations, housing over 80 percent of the entire population (Moore & Ramsay, 2021). The United Kingdom (UK) operates under a unitary government system wherein supreme authority resides with the central Westminster-based government. However, Scotland, Wales and Northern Ireland all have decentralised powers in specific sectors, such as in education and healthcare (Baldini et al., 2020). After the Second World War, Britain experienced a significant increase in immigration, leading to a fundamental transformation in its demographics. Formerly characterised by a predominantly white, ethnically British and Christian population, the country now encompasses diverse beliefs, cultures and communities from around the globe (Ashcroft & Bever, 2017). Panayi (2010) states that as a result of this mass immigration, locating a dish that is entirely native is almost impossible, so much so that Indian curry is widely regarded as the national dish. Whilst English is the primary language, the UK is also home to other languages such as Welsh, Gaelic, Scots, Irish, Ulster Scots and Cornish. These languages are often learned as a second language and are spoken in rural areas (British Council, n.d.). Economically speaking, the UK has the fifth-largest economy in the world. The most thriving of these sectors is the service industry, with business and finance sitting firmly at the top (Kingston University London, 2022). From the bustling business hubs of London to the serene landscapes of Scotland, Wales, and Northern Ireland, leadership in Britain is as varied as its rich tapestry of languages, customs, and traditions (Torrance, 2023). This chapter unravels the essence of British leadership, a blend of steadfast tradition and bold innovation that continues to inspire and shape the world.

How Great Britain characterises leaders

According to Brooks et al. (2022), the top five business leadership values in the UK are collaboration, integrity, excellence, customer service, and creativity. Indeed, these values are commonly listed in the value statements of UK companies, with collaboration and integrity being the most frequently cited values for any British leader to exhibit (Brooks et al., 2022). This is in line with the research of House et al. (2014) who state that there is a strong emphasis on integrity and ethical behaviour amongst leaders in the UK, which is in accordance with the global trend towards "charismatic and value-based leadership". Employees desire leaders they can trust, which, in turn, requires those leaders to be honest, transparent, and committed to moral ideals, both in terms of their actions and their decision-making. In addition to this, human-oriented leadership is also appreciated amongst British leaders, which is when leaders show empathy and compassion towards their team members (Beddoes-Jones, 2011). This characterisation of British leadership was underscored by Fiona Denney, a Professor in Leadership and Business education at Brunel University London, who expressed during our interview with her: "*So, I think leaders have got to know what motivates their staff, what issues and concerns their staff have, and they need to be seen as somebody who genuinely cares about those kinds of things and be genuinely inclusive for everybody and promote an inclusive and diverse workforce*" (11 April 2024). A similar sentiment was expressed by Graham Silverthorne, a leadership coach from England, who provided us with the following perspective on what values are most important for British business leaders: "*I think kindness and humanity is the most important value*" (1 May, 2024). However, Villiers (2019) notes that a number of corporate scandals and leadership failures in the UK in recent years were traced back to a lack of compassion and unethical behaviour, which led them to argue that British business leaders need to be more emotionally and socially intelligent in order to navigate the changing business landscape. As noted at the beginning of this section, collaboration has been identified as a key value for British leaders to possess, alongside integrity (Brooks et al., 2022). Generally speaking, British leadership is distinguished by a collaborative style, whereby leaders promote cooperation, communication, and inclusion within their organisations (House et al., 2014). This collaborative ethos was illustrated by one of the CCBS Survey (2024) respondents, who when asked to identify what distinguishes British leaders from their international counterparts, answered that "[British leaders] *strongly believe in the benefits of team culture in team performance*" (CCBS Survey, 2024). This is supported by McCarthy's (2004) research with UK business leaders, insofar as 67% of their survey respondents reported that promoting collaboration standard practice in British organisations. Similarly, when Graham Silverthorne was asked about the most important values British leaders should posses, alongside kindness and humanity, he added: *"Communication is not a value, but the ability to or the commitment to share information is crucial"* (1 May, 2024). Alongside these aforementioned attributes and behaviours, British leadership is also characterised by creative thinking processes and strategic planning, which corresponds with the "visionary leadership" characteristic. More specifically, leaders are supposed to establish a clear vision for the future and motivate their employees to work together towards this shared goal (House et al., 2014). Finally, Brooks et al. (2022) highlight the significance of leaders modelling and driving the embedding of values within British organisations. Indeed, 56% percent of the firms in their research cited the importance of this aspect of leadership, with 37% describing their leaders as value exemplars. Indeed, the significance of role modelling is further evidenced by the fact that some organisations in the UK connect performance appraisal and aspects of compensation to the effectiveness of leaders' role modelling (McCarthy, 2004). This leadership-driven approach includes communication of values, setting the tone from the top, monitoring values in the culture, embedding values in leadership development programs, and using values in goal setting and reviews (Brooks et al., 2022). In conclusion, the top business values in the UK encompass collaboration, integrity, excellence, customer service and creativity, with leaders tasked with embodying these ideals. Ethical behaviour and empathy are also highly prized, whilst a collaborative leadership style, emphasising innovative thinking and strategic planning, is prevalent, which serves to facilitate the integration of these values within organisations.

Survey results and what local respondents say

In the latest iteration of the CCBS Survey, we had the opportunity to gain in-depth insights from C-level professionals across Great Britain. A total of 74 leaders from diverse industries shared their knowledge and experiences of various aspects of leadership within the UK context. This section delves into the most significant of these survey results, revealing significant trends and notable divergences from global leadership norms. One of the core aspects investigated was the decision-making process within British organisations. In this respect, the survey revealed a moderate degree of flexibility in decision-making amongst British managers. This was evidenced by the fact that only 19% of the respondents identified strongly with the trait of sticking rigidly to their decisions once they made them, which is suggestive of a somewhat flexible approach to leadership decisions (CCBS Survey,

2024). The survey also highlighted a significant preference for adhering to meeting deadlines, insofar as 60% of leaders indicated that missing deadlines was akin to failure. This underscores a high-performance culture in which deadlines are treated with utmost seriousness, reflecting a broader trend within UK workplaces that equates timely delivery with success. Whilst, traditionally speaking, British communication is viewed as indirect, interestingly, around half of the respondents reported witnessing a shift towards more direct interactions, especially in multinational settings. As one leader noted, *"Things need to be said in a more indirect approach than direct as this can cause offense. However, in international business, directness is often appreciated and expected"* (CCBS Survey, 2024). Regarding feedback, British leaders seemingly prefer a more indirect approach, insofar as over one-quarter of the respondents stated they prefer to handle criticism and feedback in indirect ways, outside of formal meetings, in order to maintain a respectful and non-confrontational environment. This was illustrated by one participant who stated: *"Better training and education are needed to address challenges indirectly and politely but still firmly"* (CCBS Survey, 2024). In terms of confronting subordinates to achieve desired outcomes, the responses varied: 37% of leaders stated that they engage directly during meetings to ensure targets are met, which suggests a direct but balanced approach to addressing performance issues within teams. One particularly striking finding was the strong emphasis on the well-being of team members, which aligns with the information we gathered in our interview with Graham Silverthorne (1 May 2024). Specifically, an overwhelming 92% of the respondents believe that managers should actively invest time in ensuring the well-being of their employees, indicating a leadership style that values employee welfare as a cornerstone of organisational success (CCBS Survey, 2024). Echoing this perspective, Villiers (2019, p.12) notes a significant transition from an autocratic to a more compassionate, empathetic approach, particularly amongst the new generation *"Survey after survey shows that millennials want to work for companies that place a premium on employee welfare, offer flexible scheduling and, above all, bestow a sense of purpose'.* Similarly, three-quarters of leaders expressed a preference for minimising formal distinctions based on hierarchy within their organisations (CCBS Survey, 2024). Whilst some leaders see encouraging competition as a mechanism to enhance performance, the majority lean towards a more collaborative approach, with only 25% strongly advocating for competition within teams (CCBS survey, 2024). A sone respondent noted: *"Servant leadership is emphasised. Being brash about your achievements can be negative but positive affirmation, recognition and highlighting people's achievements (especially others not your own) is very well received".* Finally, the survey explored how leaders are viewed in terms of office space and transportation benefits reflecting their status. A notable 53% of the respondents indicated that such status symbols are not crucial, thus highlighting a cultural shift towards valuing leaders for their competence and role performance over traditional symbols of power. This sentiment was captured in this statement: *"Status is not important when you work together; what matters is the contribution each person makes"* (CCBS survey, 2024), thus illustrating a shift towards more egalitarian workplace cultures.

Local leadership analysis

Fiona Denney, Professor of Leadership at Brunel Business School

Professor Fiona Denney is a distinguished expert in leadership and coaching, blending theoretical insights with practical applications. She has enriched the educational journeys of a broad spectrum of learners, including undergraduates, postgraduates, and PhD candidates, and has led extensive development programs as the Head of Graduate Development. Her tenure at Brunel University as a director involved spearheading initiatives to cultivate a culture of efficiency and effective leadership. Currently, as a Professor of Leadership and Business Education at Brunel Business School, she continues to shape future leaders and entrepreneurs at one of the UK's leading universities. Additionally, as an associate coach at The Iversen Practice, she focuses on transformative change through executive coaching and systems theory, enhancing leadership resilience. Professor Denney began our interview by addressing the question of hierarchical structures within British organisations (Denney, 11 April, 2024). She noted that there has been a significant shift towards less formal and more flexible working arrangements. As she herself put it: *"Whilst traditional hierarchies still exist, there is a move towards more matrixed environments and project teams, particularly influenced by younger generations who favour egalitarian workplace cultures"* (Denney, 11 April, 2024). She then proceeded to discuss how global trends and the COVID-19 pandemic have accelerated the move away from rigid hierarchical norms within British organisations. In relation to this point, she opined: *"The pandemic, in particular, has hastened the adoption of remote working practices, which in turn has influenced leadership styles and workplace dynamics"* (Denney, 11 April, 2024). In response to a question related to diversity and inclusion within British organisations and British leadership skills and practices, Professor Denney proceeded to underscore the increased importance of these elements in contemporary British leadership. As she herself explained: *"Effective leadership today is fundamentally about inclusivity and compassion, which are crucial for*

121

fostering a supportive and productive organizational culture" (Denney, 11 April, 2024). Towards the end of the interview, as part of a move towards looking forward to the evolution of British business leadership, Professor Denney shared her optimism about the continued evolution of leadership practices, noting that: *"As we see an increasing emphasis on people over hierarchy, British businesses are poised to benefit from more engaged and innovative teams"*(Denney, 11 April, 2024). In conclusion, Professor Fiona Denney's insights offer a valuable perspective on the transformation of leadership within the British business landscape, illustrating a shift towards more inclusive, flexible, and people-focused practices.

Graham Silverthorne: Leadership coach

Graham Silverthorne is a seasoned educational leader, consultant, and author originally from the UK who is known for his transformative and values-based leadership approach. With a twenty-one-year tenure, he led four large schools, including multiple schools in England and the prestigious UWCSEA (East) in Singapore. In 2022, he founded Solutions@, extending his expertise globally as a strategy consultant and workshop leader in multiple countries including France, Malaysia, Singapore, Hong Kong, Japan, and the UK. His leadership is acclaimed for fostering 'happy' educational communities and he has been recognised as 'visionary' by CIS/WASC and 'Outstanding' by OfSTED in the UK. He is also a prolific writer, maintaining a popular leadership blog. Our interview centred on three min topics – British leadership, hierarchy, and empathy (Silverthorne, 1 May 2024). Silverthorne began the interview by explaining how British leadership is profoundly shaped by the class system, noting significant differences in leadership styles and attitudes between leaders from privileged backgrounds and those who are self-made. Leaders from elite educational backgrounds often display an entitled approach, whilst those from working-class backgrounds tend to adopt more entrepreneurial styles. Silverthorne asserts that leaders from elite educational backgrounds, *"where there is an assumption that people are born to lead"*, often display an entitled approach, whilst those from working-class backgrounds tend to adopt more entrepreneurial styles (Silverthorne, 1 May 2024). This distinction has persisted despite various changes and modern influences. Silverthorne then proceeded to address how British leadership has evolved due to globalisation, accessibility of Higher Education, and immigration, which has diversified leadership but not eradicated the traditional traits of the British ruling class. Silverthorne noted that it is common to assume that *"the British way is the right way"* (Silverthorne, 1 May 2024). He elaborated that although he does not agree with this mindset, British people often think that *"somebody from abroad might be a bit flaky, might not be quite at our level, not quite at our standard"* (Silverthorne, 1 May 2024). When asked about hierarchy, Silverthorne explained that British leadership traditionally favours top-down approaches, which may not always be effective in today's dynamic environments. Silverthorne argued that because of the hierarchy *"people do not take collective responsibility for a business or for an enterprise"*, leaving the responsibility to the boss (Silverthorne, 1 May 2024). In response to a question about the top three qualities required of British leaders, Silverthorne responded that the most important values are kindness, humanity and the ability or commitment to share information ensuring the inclusion of employees. According to Silverthorne, effective British leaders are those who can genuinely connect with people at all levels, showing empathy and valuing every team member's contribution, which contrasts with the sometimes distant, formal style associated with traditional British leadership (1 May, 2024). Drawing upon his snow globe metaphor, he explained that leaders should be able to operate within the confines of the snow globe, demonstrating their concern for its internal dynamics. However, they must also possess the capability to rise above the globe, gaining a broader perspective of its trajectory and destination. Silverthorne wrapped up our interview by pointing out that leadership styles vary significantly across different regions of the UK—such as England, Scotland, Wales, and Northern Ireland—due to distinct educational, economic, and cultural developments. This diversity within the UK presents unique challenges and opportunities for leadership. Silverthorne noted that British leadership needs to adapt to technological changes, regulatory environments, and cultural shifts, which requires a departure from traditional methods. Graham Silverthorne's insights offer a comprehensive view of British leadership, revealing a landscape that is both rooted in tradition and dynamically evolving. His perspective underscores the importance of adaptability, empathy, and regional awareness in fostering effective leadership in the modern era.

In-country leadership bestseller

One of the best-selling books about leadership was written by Neil Jurd in 2020 and is called *The leadership book – A step by step guide to excellent leadership*. This book is a comprehensive manual designed to assist current and aspiring British leaders to develop excellent leadership skills through a step-by-step approach. Jurd advocates that leadership is attainable by anyone willing to embrace it, centred on the principles of authenticity, vision, teamwork, and continuous improvement. The core principle is authenticity: leaders thrive in the UK when they remain true to themselves whilst mastering essential skills. The book is split into four accessible chapters that offer insights into understanding

British leadership dynamics and empowering individuals and teams. Jurd emphasises self-awareness as the cornerstone of effective leadership in Britain, advocating for leaders to understand their own motivations and strengths before leading others. This approach fosters personal growth but also enhances one's ability to connect with and empower team members. Jurd recognises that many people who are led aspire to feel empowered, but he also points out that this is difficult for leaders who are used to maintaining strict control. However, he contends that embracing a mission command mentality, where leaders trust and empower their teams, yields greater benefits than risks. By embracing this approach, leaders can maximise their impact by leveraging the diverse talents and perspectives within their teams. Many individuals familiar with leadership development are likely acquainted with Tuckman's 'Form to Perform' model. The model primarily emphasises group dynamics, considering both interpersonal relationships and task accomplishment. It was intended to serve as a framework for analysing evolving groups for the following two decades (Jones, 2019). Jurd's "stagnation to excellence" model builds on Tuckman's stages, acknowledging the inevitability of conflict during change. However, Jurd advises leaders to acknowledge and accept this phase as a natural part of the process. Additionally, he suggests practical steps for navigating through change: fostering a shared sense of purpose amongst team members, promoting open communication, and driving change through trust, support, and empowerment. In closing, Neil Jurd's 2020 book, *"The Leadership Book – A Step by Step Guide to Excellent Leadership,"* provides a comprehensive guide to developing leadership skills through practical, accessible chapters based on authenticity, vision, teamwork, and continuous improvement. Jurd emphasises that effective leadership is achievable for anyone dedicated to personal authenticity and skill mastery (Jurd, 2020).

Local leadership book	
Title	*The leadership book*
Subtitle	A step-by-step guide to excellent leadership
Author	Neil Jurd
Publisher	Mr Gresty
Year	2020
ISBN	9780956928573

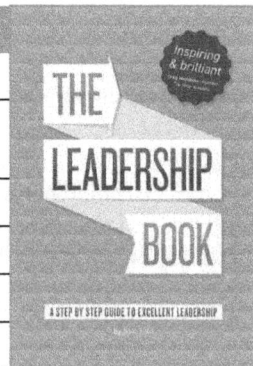

Great Britain leadership YouTube review

In a recent webinar, Dr. Ian Peters and Dr. Edward Brooks (2023) from The Oxford Character Project discussed their latest research titled "*Good Leadership in UK Business*." This report sheds light on varying perceptions of effective leadership across different sectors within the UK, providing a comprehensive view of the essential qualities that define 'good' leadership. This study involved gathering information via surveying 1158 workers across thirty-six companies located throughout the UK. The findings highlight competence, communication, integrity, hardworking and professional as the top attributes required by a good British leader. Another noteworthy finding emerging from their survey is that 52% of the respondents reported that good leadership is based on personal character, 35% reported that it is about interpersonal skills, whilst 13% stated that professional competence was the most important attribute. Conversely, based on their survey findings, the five least appreciated qualities in British leadership are being humorous, humble, creative, charismatic and kind (Peters & Brooks, 2023). The speakers argue that these findings are in contradistinction to the values that have been identified in literature, where humility and kindness are valued as highly significant. Dr. Edward Brooks proposes that this inconsistency could stem from the perception that these traits are inherently human attributes rather than being directly pertinent to leadership. He believes this perspective is a mistake, as supported by literature on the subject (Peters & Brooks, 2023). In another leadership video, Peter Vicary-Smith (2014), CEO of the UK consumer association Which?, emphasises the importance of cultivating leadership skills in the modern British workplace during a discussion with the London Business School. He outlines the critical role of passion and sound judgment in leadership, asserting that the combination of these two elements is important. Passion can sometimes steer you in the wrong direction, and judgment serves as the compass where you discern between what is beneficial and what is not. However, solely relying on one's judgment without passion can render decisions to feel soulless. Furthermore, he advises British leaders to focus intently on a few key success factors and maintain clear, honest communication with their teams. Vicary-Smith then proceeds to advocate for visionary thinking, projecting leadership plans five years into the future. The next video to be summarised involves British leadership consultant, Peter Anderton, who spoke at a TED Talk in Derby. In the video he outlines two fundamental principles of effective leadership in the UK: "*it is NOT about you*" *and "it is ONLY about you*." (Anderton, 2016, 8:20). Echoing Eleanor Roosevelt's insight, Anderton emphasises that whilst good leaders inspire confidence in their employees, great leaders empower individuals to have confidence in themselves. He argues that the best leaders cultivate future leaders rather than followers,

125

recognising the complexity of modern leadership challenges. Further perspectives were shared in interviews conducted by WSP in the UK with their employees. Emily Ellis and Steve Smith (2019), Managing Director of WSP, discuss how visionary leadership involves inspiring others with clarity and passion whilst, simultaneously, empowering employees to take control of their career paths. Above all, they stressed the importance of surrounding oneself with capable individuals and fostering an environment in which everyone understands and fulfils their responsibilities, ensuring accountability within the organisation. This holistic approach to leadership underscores the multifaceted nature of effective leadership practices in the UK. The discussions presented offer a multifaceted view of effective leadership within the UK, emphasising attributes such as integrity, competence, and communication as foundational. By nurturing an environment where empowerment, accountability, and proactive career support are prioritised, leaders can inspire confidence and foster independence amongst team members.

Understanding hierarchy in Great Britain

Status and hierarchy influence decision-making and leadership approaches in British leadership (Schroevers, 2024). To value team contributions in business concerns, collaboration and consultation are essential. This strategy emphasises teamwork and empowers employees to take on shared responsibilities. Direct reporting and a horizontal organisational structure are preferred by British managers. To avoid conflict, managers strike a balance between being approachable and being objective. They assign responsibilities whilst also upholding distinct roles. This kind of teamwork combined with clarity is characteristic of British leadership (Schroevers, 2024). Understanding hierarchy in Great Britain involves recognising differences in empowerment, communication, coaching/mentoring, and improvement practices. According to McCarthy (2005), only 36% of the respondents in their study stated that it is typical practice to encourage employee initiative in the UK, thus suggesting that empowerment is not widely enacted. In light of the general trend towards decentralised forms of decision-making, communication styles vary, with the UK tending to favour informal methods like *"management by walking around."* (McCarthy, 2005). Coaching and mentoring are also prevalent in the UK, as a means through which to encourage personal development. Notwithstanding these discussions, Oshagbemi (2003) states that hierarchy remains important in UK organisations, albeit it can be difficult to discern differences between various levels of management when there are multiple layers. In large British corporations like HSBC or Shell, the hierarchy may consist of numerous management tiers, which blurs the distinctions, especially in complex decision-making processes where multiple layers of approval are required (Oshagbemi, 2003). According to a leadership coach we interviewed, Yvonne Akinmodun (30 April, 2024), hierarchy is especially relevant in SMEs employing ten thousand employees or less as the job functions are more fixed. Similarly, Silverthorne acknowledges that British companies maintain a strong hierarchical structure, with the drawback being that *"hierarchy manifests itself in disempowerment,"* which means that individuals in Britain often shirk collective responsibility, deferring it solely to the higher-ups (1 May, 2024). This "us versus them" mentality is deeply entrenched, largely fuelled by the prevalent union culture, which holds strong sway. Dr. Mohammad RashedKhan (2021) claims that when individuals move to the UK, they often change their leadership style to a democratic leadership style. This stems from the fact that British culture is characterised by low power distance and individualist dimensions. On the other hand, Schroevers (2024) states that vertical leadership remains common in traditional British businesses, but cooperative alternatives are gradually taking their place. British leaders are excellent at consensus-building, cooperation, and emotion management. They promote a culture of shared responsibility by appreciating contributions from all levels. This harmony between hierarchy and cooperation fosters situations in which people flourish and work together to achieve shared objectives (Schroevers, 2024). To conclude, in British leadership, the balance between hierarchy and cooperation is essential, with a strong emphasis on teamwork, shared responsibilities, and valuing contributions from all levels to foster a productive work environment. Despite historical tendencies towards hierarchical structures, contemporary British leadership is shifting towards more democratic and cooperative methods, promoting a culture where consensus-building and emotional intelligence are prioritised to achieve goals.

How Britons achieve leadership empathy

Lambert et al. (2021) emphasise the critical role of emotional empathy in leadership within postgraduate British business programs, noting its capacity to bolster relationships, communication, decision-making, emotional intelligence, as well as support for diversity and inclusion. The increased importance upon empathy within British business leadership was also emphasised by Graham Silverthorne (1 May 2024), who shared with us that the three values a good empathic British leader should have, are kindness, humanity, and inclusion. He proceeded to illustrate this as follows: *"The way I would always have built a rapport with the community is I've already said it. You know, you have to treat people as individuals, but it is not just being nice to the chair of the board and to the senior staff. You have got to stop and talk to the to the security guard. You have got to talk to the cleaners, you have got to sit down in a school. You have got to sit down with the kids and chat to them. You have got to give equal value to every member of the community"* (Silverthorne, 1 May 2024). In addition, Graham Silverthorne developed the metaphor of leadership as managing a dynamically moving snowball, arguing that a leader's role is not to maintain stillness but rather to be able to manage constant turbulence effectively. Shanahan (2023) states that British organisations have implemented important strategies that enhance empathy levels and boost mental health in the workplace, such as empathy training, greater transparency and feedback and a focus on work-life balance. Both executives and employees can benefit from such empathy training, specifically in terms of improving understanding, perspective-taking, and emotional intelligence. The aforementioned prioritisation of flexible work arrangements can also help to support employees' work-life balance and mental health, which is important, because our interviewee stated that: *"In Britain it is much more about lifestyle and about well-being"* (Silverthorne, 1 May 2024). Engler (2016) explores the role of empathy within British business leadership through recourse to Heron's six intervention styles. According to Engler, it is evident in the British context that pull tactics significantly outperform push tactics in terms of leaders motivating employees within organisations. There are three pull mechanisms. Firstly, cathartic/cleansing is when managers engage with employees by asking a series of questions, aiding them in clarifying their thoughts. Secondly, the catalytic pull mechanism is formed by discussing various questions and scenarios, through which managers help employees to catalyse or reach decisions and encourage them to form their own conclusions. Thirdly, the supportive pull mechanism consists of offering praise and constructive feedback to employees, by virtue of which leaders bolster their employees' self-confidence, thus emphasising the employee's accomplishments and actions. This emphasis on empathetic and supportive leadership in British business leadership is corroborated by the results of the CCBS Survey (2024), insofar as 45% of the respondents reported that it is important for British leaders to prioritise the well-being of their team members. This finding is in line with an emergent trend for compassionate leadership within UK organisations (Silverthorne, 1 May 2024). Further evidence for the importance of empathy in British leadership comes from the fact that a servant leadership style has gained traction in the UK in recent years. A servant leadership approach is grounded in fundamental skills, including, most importantly, empathy, compassion, and altruism, with leaders striving to encourage mentally and emotionally healthy workplaces via facilitating greater cohesiveness, collaboration, and relationships with their employees (Jit et al., 2017). Similarly, a study conducted by Wang et al. (2022) suggests that servant leadership in UK organisations positively influences employees' psychological safety as well as their well-being, which, in turn, enhances their creativity. Overall, empathy is beginning to play a greater role in the context of UK business leadership, contributing towards a more positive professional environment, enhanced job satisfaction, and improved well-being amongst employees.

India

Jeffrey de Dood, Renske Hogeboom, Tamara Liefting, Manisha Chand, Isak Douah, & Jiya Anwar

Mahatma Gandhi's timeless adage, *"The best way to find yourself is to lose yourself in the service of others"*, captures the spirit of India's culture beautifully. Indian culture can be classified as vertical-collectivistic, which is to say that people value hierarchical group structures, identify strongly with their in-groups, and work together towards common goals (Bahl et al., 2021). As Clem and Mujtaba (2011) state, India has a relationship-oriented culture; however, it is important to stress here that India is far from a homogeneous culture. On the contrary, it is a rich cultural tapestry with hundreds of cultures, languages and religions. It is the country where Hinduism, Sikhism and Buddhism originated, whilst there is also a sizeable Muslim population today, which makes India tremendously multicultural (Chandra & Mahajan, 2006). This distinct masala blend of culture is distinguished by a high level of tolerance and respect towards the diverse religions and communities (Satpathy, 2015), which is required for it to function as a democracy. Despite its challenges, India's political system is a liberal democracy with high rates of electoral participation from all social strata, distinguishing it from other Asian and African nations (Chandhoke, 2009). It is home to 1.437 billion people which makes it the most populous country and largest democracy in the world. India's impact on the global economy is as fast growing as its population; the World Economic Forum (2024) expects India to have the third biggest economy in five years, which makes understanding India's business culture crucial. Perhaps the key feature of Indian culture is displaying emotion, which is synonymous with active involvement and genuine care, qualities that are pivotal in Indian leadership (Sen, 2005). In essence, India's kaleidoscopic cultural mosaic extends its vibrant influence even into the realm of business. This dynamic fusion of tradition, diversity, and emotional depth not only propels India's economic ascent but also infuses its business ethos with the melodious symphony of emotion, where genuine care and active involvement reign supreme. To navigate the intricate dance of Indian business culture is to embrace its spirit, where every interaction is a heartfelt performance, woven with threads of empathy and resilience.

How the Indians characterise leaders?

Indians traditionally characterised leaders as authoritarian, with individuals within the group anticipating and respecting this behaviour from those in positions of authority. However, there has been a discernible shift towards a more democratic leadership style in India in recent decades, where successful managers are now defined as both task-oriented and relationship-oriented (Vilkinas et al., 2008). This transformation can be attributed to Western influences in the more international industries like IT, for example. This, in turn, has led to many Indians expressing a preference for participative leadership, equity, autonomy, and personal development (Sinha & Parvinder, 2002). This shift is also marked by a move towards a leadership approach that balances task accomplishment with nurturing and considering the needs of individuals within the team (Vilkinas et al., 2008). According to our interviewee, Tripti Chopra (25 April 2024), founder at The PhdCoach, Indian leadership has begun to embrace a transformational style of leadership. House et al. (1999) argue that Indians hold leaders in high esteem when they exhibit power and strength. Thus, leadership is closely associated with traits that convey both confidence and decisiveness. Leaders thus garner respect when they demonstrate a willingness to take risks and manage them effectively (Pal & Kapur, 2011). In navigating these risks, leaders are required to be adaptable to changing circumstances and environments (Naik, 2015). According to the results of the CCBS Survey (2004), just over two-thirds of the Indian managers reported being steadfast in their decisions and refraining from changing them once they had made up their mind. Such steadfastness reflects a commitment to their chosen course of action, even in the face of uncertainty or changing circumstances. Indians also appreciate leaders who exude qualities of authority and assertiveness. However, Indian leaders themselves often downplay the use of power in their relationships with their subordinates, instead opting to lean towards more consultative or participative leadership styles (Singh, 1990). Effective leaders, as noted by Naik (2015), are valued for their modesty, which entails remaining grounded despite their achievements. It is also important that leaders possess self-awareness and understand their strengths and weaknesses. Consequently, Indian leaders are comfortable in dealing with uncertainties in life and work, showing ease in unclear situations (Kumar & Sharma, 2018). Charisma and integrity are highly esteemed qualities amongst the Indian population. Indians admire leaders who are empathetic, motivated, committed, optimistic, and effective communicators. They also value leaders who connect well with diverse groups of people (House et al., 1999). Consequently, the Indian leadership style often aligns with an ethical leadership approach, where leaders prioritise openness and honesty in communication, act with integrity in decision-making, and adhere to ethical principles and high moral standards. In other words, they strive to set a positive example and inspire others to act in an ethical and moral manner (Pal & Kapur, 2011). Moreover, Indians look for leaders who can help them expand their knowledge and skills, providing guidance, support, and inspiration for growth and achievement (Mitra, 2020). This is corroborated by the results of the CCBS Survey (2024) insofar as the vast majority of the respondents reported that employees look up to their leaders on the basis of both their organisational experience and being visionary thinkers. Similarly, a study conducted by Palrecha (2012) also showed that most Indian employees desire support, guidance, and encouragement from their leaders, even when they have sufficient competence to make independent decisions.

Survey results and what local respondents say

In order to gain additional empirical insight into leadership skills and practices in India, we administered the CCBS Survey (2024) to C-Level managers in India, who kindly shared their extensive knowledge and expertise with us. In contradistinction to conventional wisdom, the results of the survey sheds light on a rich tapestry of diverse leadership styles and practices in India. The most significant findings are presented in turn below. The first interesting finding is that Indian leaders are ordinarily willing to change their minds after a decision has already been made, as only a mere 5% of the respondents strongly identified with this statement, which suggests a preference for adaptable leadership styles. This finding was further evidenced by one of our survey respondents, who opined: *"The dynamic nature of the startup industry and ever-increasing competitive environment calls for one to be a situational leader, and we adopt different styles depending on the type of employee we are dealing with. It is basically no one technique fits all, as all members in the team come from different backgrounds, have different aspirations, and have different work dedication too!"* (CCBS Survey, 2024). This finding is in line with the work of Naik (2015), who also argued that Indian leaders must be able to navigate risks and demonstrate adaptability to changing circumstances and environments. The second significant finding emerging from the survey is the prevalence of a direct, yet inclusive and collaborative leadership style amongst Indian leaders. This was indicated by the fact that 35% of leaders reported being willing to confront subordinates during staff meetings in order to achieve the desired results (CCBS Survey, 2024). This approach, described by one respondent as '*accommodative, collaborative, and inclusive*', underscores the assertiveness and teamwork that characterises Indian leadership. The third interesting finding from our survey is that Indian leaders tend to encourage a certain degree of competition amongst team members, which 35% of the leaders deemed to be beneficial for improving performance. One survey respondent wrote that the work environment in India is *"competitive and sometimes political"* (CCBS Survey, 2024). This finding indicates that for leaders in India, fostering a competitive environment is viewed as a tool through which to secure better outcomes from their subordinates. The final significant finding is that 50% of the survey respondents showed no significant inclination towards maintaining personal distance from employees in order to maintain the right level of respect. One survey respondent addressed this point as follows: *"Leadership in India emphasises hierarchy, respect for authority, and inclusive decision-making, often guided by emotional intelligence, adaptability, and a long-term, relationship-oriented approach. These values and a focus on spirituality and ethics distinguish Indian leadership from other countries"* (CCBS Survey, 2024). Therefore, maintaining a more open professional relationship with subordinates can be a distinctive part of leadership in India, through a structured yet empathetic leadership style. These findings from the CCBS Survey (2024) illustrate the sheer diversity of Indian leadership, ranging from adaptability and assertiveness on the one hand to competition and professional relationship distance on the other, all of which shape the dynamic landscape of management and leadership in India.

Local leadership analysis

Dr Tripti Chopra: An Indian leadership scholar

Dr Tripti Chopra, an award-winning writer and founder of ThePhdCoach, was interviewed in order to gain insight into her knowledge and professional experience of Indian leadership skills and practices. Dr Chopra is an award-winning writer and former faculty member at the CH Institute of Management & Commerce. She has both an MBA and a PhD in Management and has extensive knowledge of research and management-related subjects; through this knowledge she helps international students and scholars in her capacity as the founder of ThePhdCoach. At the beginning of the interview, when asked about how she would describe a typical Indian leader, Dr Chopra (25 April 2024) responded: *"We combine two major types of tactics. One is leadership by fear, and one is leadership by empathy."* By this, Dr Chopra meant that leadership works best if it is dynamic. Your employees sometimes must fear you, if that means they listen to you better. However, she proceeded to explain, the relationship works best if your employees can also come to you in an informal way if they have an issue they are facing and can discuss this openly with you (25 April 2024). Next, Dr Chopra proceeded to explain how Indian leadership styles have changed over the course of the last decade. As she herself put it: *"It is a combination of transformational leadership and autocratic leadership, whereas earlier it was primarily democratic leadership"* (25 April 2024). The reason for this change, according to Dr Chopra, is the influx of different cultures in India, which has resulted in the leadership style becoming more hybrid. When asked about what distinguishes Indian leaders from their international counterparts, Dr Chopra stated that is very different, noting that: *"The power distance in India has reduced to a very great extent."* (25 April 2024). She then proceeded to discuss how the power distance in the US is lower, but due to changing leadership styles the power distance in India is now closer to American culture. Conversely, in comparison to Chinese culture, where the power distance is significant, there is a particular decorum that you must follow. As well as considering promotion, you cannot put young people into senior-level positions. With respect to how elderly people are treated, Dr Chopra (25 April 2024) stated: *"Of course elderly people in India are treated with respect as well, but at the same time, we cannot deny the fact that young people these days can be equally experienced."* She proceeded to explain how as a result of having multiple resources and access to artificial intelligence, young people today can be equally as qualified as their older counterparts. Although experience increases with age, we cannot deny that young people are capable of holding good positions in Indian companies. Towards the end of the interview, Dr Chopra moved onto discuss how Indian leaders can build trust and respect with their employees. Dr Chopra stated that one way to do this is to have a good balance between work and personal life. You must get to know your employees, spend time with them, understand where they come from and what their needs are. *"If you personally know your employee, and if you make them feel valued, then this is what I feel is an important aspect towards building trust"* (Chopra, 25 April 2024).

Priya Venkatesan: An Indian cross-cultural trainer

We interviewed Priya Venkatesan, a global executive coach, in order to gain insight into Indian leadership skills and practices. Venkatesan has over twenty-four years of corporate and coaching experience as well as the highest levels of accreditation (MCC) from the International Coach Federation and the European Mentoring and Coaching Council (SP). The interview began with Venkatesan explaining what constitutes a typical Indian business leader. In response he opined: *"An Indian business leader is ambitious. Wants to do cutting edge work and add value. But they are also highly empathetic, they value the humanness of people"* (Venkatesan, 24 April 2024). This is in accordance with other research showing that empathy and personal connections are highly valued in India (House et al., 1999). However, she argued, in larger organisations, there could be some variances, insofar as they are much more hierarchical. Venkatesan (24 April 2024) proceeded to explain *"There is a huge respect for hierarchy* [in India]*."* In larger organisations the hierarchy tends to be more visible: there is a director, a vice president whilst the remainder of the employees are all below here. Respect for seniority is inherent to the familial system in India, where the father is ordinarily the head of the family. Indians are socialised to listen to people who have more life experience than themselves. According to Venkatesan (24 April 2024), this also applies in the business context were: *"Irrespective of accomplishments, experience of life is valued."* Next, she proceeded to discuss what distinguishes Indian leaders from their international counterparts. In response, Venkatesan proceeded to divide typical Indian leadership styles into two extreme poles: on the one hand, a task-based leader and, on the other, an empathetic leader. Task-based leaders want to get things moving, whilst empathetic leaders are more supportive, and tasks come second. As she herself put it, *"In India, you tend to see a lot to the right* [of this binary]*"* (Venkatesan, 24 April 2024). With respect to building trust and respect, Venkatesan (24 April 2024) stated: *"Any leader is only as good as their team."* In this regard, she moved onto explain how understanding is key in this process, namely in terms of understanding who your employees are, what their aspirations are, what their needs are, as well as possessing self-awareness about how you yourself are leading. Finally, when asked about inspiring Indian leaders, Venkatesan explicitly referred to Doctor Abdul Kalam, who was the President of India from 25 July 2002 until 25 July 2007 and a scientist who launched the first rocket for India. Venkatesan (24 April 2024) stated: *"I think he had the right mix of everything. He was task focused, but he was also people focused and brought people together, which perfectly represents the nature of the country and the culture."*

In-country leadership bestseller

"The Leadership Sutra" by Devdutt Pattanaik (2016) explores the nature of power, significance, property, and stability in leadership roles by looking at leadership through the lens of Indian mythology. Devdutt Pattanaik is a mythologist and writer from Mumbai, who wrote over fifty books including seven books about management. He has a degree in medicine and mythology. His book was also referred to on several occasions by the respondents of the CCBS Survey (2024). In the Hindustan times he made the following statement about the relationship between science, humanities and mythologies and society: *"Science uses measurement to understand society, humanities apply scientific methods to*

study society but differ from material sciences in their reliance on measurability, whilst mythology is about reality based on faith; mythology shapes worldviews influencing leadership and economics" (Sinha, 2016). According to Pattanaik, true leadership in India is about empowering people and going above and beyond their primal need for dominance, which is how it is commonly misunderstood. One should think of true leadership as the lion's rule in the jungle, focus on nurturing the self-esteem of one's followers, challenging the often rigid and hierarchical structures typically observed in Indian society and business sector. In the context of discussing how property validates a person's social standing and sense of self-worth, the book puts forward the argument that true leadership should be centred on values that are intrinsic in nature rather than placing too much emphasis on material wealth. This involves understanding and integrating subjective truths of people, recognising those personal beliefs shape business and governance practices. Furthermore, Pattanaik (2016) looks at how important rules are in establishing structured environments that support effective leadership, but he also issues a warning that rules can be a source of self-doubt or be used as a means of consolidating power. The concept of *"lokasamgraha"* (welfare of the people) is central, insofar as it draws attention to leaders' role in maintaining stability and order, whilst, simultaneously, balancing freedom and control. By stressing the philosophical and ethical aspects of leadership over efficiency and results, Pattanaik presents an alternative perspective to Western leadership models. It accomplishes this by using *"sutras,"* or aphorisms, to condense these insights into guidance that is both philosophical and practical in nature (Pattanaik, 2016).

Local leadership book	
Title	*The Leadership Sutra*
Subtitle	An Indian Approach to Power
Author	Devdutt Pattanaik
Publisher	Rupa Publications
Year	2016
ISBN	978-9384067465

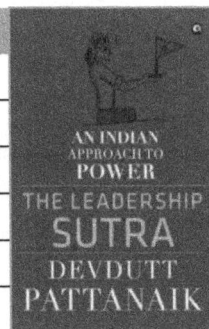

Indian leadership YouTube review

At the prestigious Leadership Summit, Ratan Tata, the iconic figure in Indian business, delivered an electrifying speech on leadership, business strategy, and career advice. With decades of experience at the helm of the Tata Group, Tata's insights are invaluable for anyone aspiring to leadership excellence in India. The discussion delved deep into the core qualities of effective leadership in the country. Above all, Tata emphasised the paramount importance of integrity, vision, and empathy in Indian leadership. Drawing from his own leadership journey, he underscored the significance of integrity as the bedrock of trust and credibility in Indian leadership (Six Sigma, 2022). Next, Tata elucidated on the strategic acumen necessary for success in the competitive business landscape in India. He shared anecdotes and lessons from the Tata Group's strategic decisions, stressing the need for innovation, adaptability, and possessing a long-term vision (Six Sigma, 2022). In terms of career advice, Tata advocated for pursuing passion and purpose in one's leadership journey, urging individuals to embrace challenges and see them as opportunities for growth and learning (Six Sigma, 2022). The next video to be summarised is a compelling YouTube video entitled "Future of Indian Business Leadership: Business & Beyond", where Sapna Rao, a visionary leader in the Indian business landscape, delivers a thought-provoking discourse on the future of Indian business leadership (The conference room, 2014). In the beginning of the video, Sapna Rao advocates for a paradigm shift towards authenticity and empowerment in Indian leadership. In particular, Rao highlights the untapped potential within India's labour force and resources, urging organisations to prioritise the cultivation of authentic leadership identities. By empowering leaders to lead authentically, organisations can foster a culture of innovation, adaptability, and inclusivity. Next in the video, Rao underscores the significance of self-awareness and authenticity in Indian leadership, asserting that true leadership excellence stems from alignment with one's innermost values and aspirations. In this vein, she encourages leaders to lead from a place of integrity, empathy, and purpose, inspiring trust and fostering meaningful connections within their teams (The conference room, 2014). In response to a question about developing future leaders in India, Rao advocates for a holistic approach that goes beyond traditional training methodologies. Whilst technical skills are important, she stresses the importance of other qualities such as emotional intelligence, resilience, and adaptability. Rao encourages Indian leaders to cultivate a growth mindset and seek opportunities for experiential learning, allowing them to unleash their full potential in natural environments (The conference room, 2014).
To close the video, Rao leaves viewers with a powerful call to action: to embrace authenticity and visionary thinking in their pursuit of leadership excellence.

By heeding Rao's insights and fostering a culture of empowerment and inclusivity, organisations can navigate the complexities of the future business landscape with confidence and resilience. Rao's visionary perspective offers a compelling blueprint for the future of Indian business leadership—one that celebrates diversity, fosters inclusion, and empowers leaders to drive sustainable success and impact (The conference room, 2014).

Understanding hierarchy in India

Whilst hierarchy in the West is largely visible in terms of organisational power dynamics, in India, it manifests across the continent via the powerful caste system (Rio & Smedal, 2009). As a result of this system, hierarchy is simply taken for granted in almost every kind of organisation and is largely considered as being essential for avoiding chaos (Chattopadhyay, 1999). Indeed, according to Sinha and Sinha (1990), Indians tend to arrange things, persons, relationships, ideas and almost everything hierarchically. Even the Indian Gods are hierarchised. Dumont (1980) states that hierarchy in India can also be described as 'clear and distinct' and whilst power is dominant over hierarchy in the West, in India hierarchy is dominant over power. In this respect, the assertiveness one observes in superiors' behaviour is not only a characteristic of senior-level management but is also a feature of authority relations across all levels of an organisation. Indians are highly status conscious and find it easier to work in superior-subordinate roles rather than with equals (Kothari, 1970). Once the hierarchy is established, junior members of staff yield to senior-level staff on every possible occasion, both at work and outside of work, by, for example, offering their seat to a senior person in a crowded bus or train, standing up when the senior person walks into the office, opening the door for them, refraining from smoking or drinking in front of them, speaking humbly, not being seen to strongly disagree with them and withdrawing from situations which could lead to a potential confrontation (Roland, 1984; Sinha, 1988). Indeed, research conducted by Cole (2016) showed that individuals within different hierarchical levels of Indian organisations may even go so far as to perceive the entire identity of the organisation differently to one another. With respect to how leaders and employees communicate with one another, the results of the CCBS Survey (2024) revealed that more than half of the respondents reported that they preferred to receive criticism indirectly, often outside of formal staff meetings. This is in line with other research, which demonstrates that anger and hostility against one's superior are generally suppressed and displaced within Indian organisations (Sinha, 1990). Given these discussions, it is perhaps unsurprising that several studies have found that Indian society scores high on power distance (Hofstede, 1980; Mendonca and Kanungo, 1996). The result of this is that senior-level leaders expect loyalty, compliance and total submission from their subordinates. In return, younger employees expect their elders to protect, help and provide them with affection. Sinha (1988) compares the senior-junior relationship to how Hindu's see Lord Krishna. The senior or Lord Krishna for instance, demands abandoning all commendable acts and seeking shelter with him alone. In return, he liberates you from all sins and takes away your worries. In the business context, this results in subordinates seeking out guidance and direction from their superiors, which if they do not receive leaves them feeling dejected. However, a study by Kaur and Sandhu (2019) demonstrates that a worker at the bottom of a large Indian organisation has a much larger superstructure of organisational levels and several leaders above them, which, in turn, results in there being no one leader with absolute influence over their work. Consequently, one's full potential is not realised which might result in psychological withdrawal from work, low job involvement and deteriorating work outcomes (Kaur & Sandhu, 2019). Finally, when attempting to understand hierarchy in India it is also important to know that employees who are personally connected to the leader are often immune from any pressure or disciplinary action even if they engage in forms of organisational misconduct (Sinha, 1988). The reason for this is that they are not where they are in the organisation because they are a hard worker but rather because they are a 'connected' person. This is also the case with the many small and large family-run organisations in India, which are headed by family members who groom their own family to succeed them even if this leads to inefficient outcomes (Sinha, 1988).

How the Indians achieve leadership empathy

In India the heart is king (Roberts, 2003), or, in other words, empathy and personal connections are of critical importance. Achieving empathy in leadership involves prioritising compassionate communication and genuine interactions that build deep connections with team members (Viswanathan, 2023). The fact that in India it is expected that leaders show care for their employees was also something that was noted by one of our interviewees, who opined: *"We value the humanness of people, so that is something that stands out."* (Venkatesan, 24 April 2024). Specific ways in which Indian leaders can exhibit this in their day-to-day practices in organisations is to engage in active listening, be present, foster inclusivity, encourage and support employees' personal development and demonstrate compassion (Srinivasan & Thangaraj, 2021). This was also noted by our other interviewee, who expressed that *"It is common in India to go out for lunch and talk*

139

more about personal achievement and life; this builds trust and empathy" (Chopra, 25 April 2024). Further corroboration for empathy being a defining feature of Indian leadership comes from the results of the CCBS Survey (2024), as evidenced by the fact that the majority of the respondents reported that they actively invest time and effort into ensuring the personal well-being of their team members. This finding underscores the importance placed on employee care within Indian organisational cultures. Roebuck et al. (2016) emphasise that effective listening helps leaders foster an environment of supportiveness and trust, which, in turn, boosts employee motivation and productivity. However, active listening is challenging in some instances due to the high-context nature of Indian communication, where much often remains unsaid. That is to say, Indians often hesitate to call out the elephant in the room and instead hope that it will just vanish (Bakshi, 2018). This makes it harder for non-native leaders to achieve empathy through their communication, insofar as it takes time and a lot of cultural awareness to truly understand what is being said by employees (Bakshi, 2018). The reason why empathy is so important is that Pattanaik (2016) argues that a leader's primary job in India is to provide security to their employees. This aspect of Indian leadership is also supported by the results of the CCBS Survey (2024) insofar as around three-quarters of the respondents either disagreed or strongly disagreed with the statement that *"As a leader, I prefer to retain a personal distance from my employees, in order to maintain the right level of respect"*. By being emotionally and intellectually connected to the workforce Indian leaders show that they care about their security almost like a parental figure. This was illustrated by our interviewee, Mittal (3 March 2024), the CEO of International Tractors Limited, who explained: *"I think Indian leaders are more emotional. You connect to the people more emotionally, so they know you are with them, in the good and the bad."* Roebuck et al. (2016, p. 23) state that this connection is simply what is expected from an Indian leader: *"It is important for an Indian leader to demonstrate to their employees that both they and their work are valued. This fosters a sense of mutual care and respect, ultimately enhancing productivity."*

Nepal

Ayumu Keira, Job Pesch, Artem Liubenko, Cis den Blanken,
Marlon Clijd, Ansa Mohammad & Anna Csillag

The Himalayas constitute a place of exceptional importance in the heart of
Nepalese society, insofar as it serves a cornerstone of their national history,
culture, and economic development. Indeed, the successful summit of Mount
Everest by Tenzing Norgay and Sir Edmund Hillary in 1953 was a pivotal event that
sparked the expansion of Nepal's mountaineering and tourism industries. These
sectors have flourished in the interim, becoming more economically significant
than traditional agriculture and manufacturing, and now stand as a pillar of
Nepal's economy (Altitude Himalaya, 2021). Nepal, which transitioned to a
democracy in 2008, and is a sovereign state in South Asia bordered by India and
China. Publicly known as the Federal Democratic Republic of Nepal, the nation was
previously identified as the Kingdom of Nepal. Its Nepali language is part of the
Indo-Aryan family of languages, sharing commonalities with Hindi and Bengali,
which testifies to the linguistic diversity in the region (Darrah, 2023).
In Nepalese culture, respect for the familial hierarchy is paramount, with
deference accorded to the father or the eldest male in the family. This patriarch
bears responsibility for decision-making, which can include arranging marriages
and finding jobs for relatives (Darrah, 2023). The business culture within Nepal is
also hierarchical in nature, in the sense that decision-making often involves
several layers of approval, and culminates with the patriarch or business leader,
who is known locally as the *Hakim* (boss). This traditional approach can result in
slower decision-making processes (Feller & Mercel-Sanca, 2020). However,
contemporary leaders in Nepal are beginning to blend respect for these traditions
with innovative and practical solutions to address current social and economic
challenges. It is also common practice for leaders within the Nepalese business
community to actively participate in social and community development activities,
thus highlighting their commitment to contributing towards the broader societal
good (Feller & Mercel-Sanca, 2021).

How the Nepalese characterise leaders?

In many ways, the prevailing Nepalese leadership style that one sees in operation within contemporary business is a result of the country's relatively recent change in governmental leadership style. That is to say, the journey from a monarchy to a democracy has profoundly reshaped the way the country is governed. This transition, including the drafting of the new constitution in 2015, reflects the country's commitment to a democratic-led country. It is geographically landlocked between China and India, who both have profound influence over the population of around 30 million people (Feller & Mercel-Sanca, 2021). China and India, the two countries with which Nepal shares their borders, have marked differences with respect to both their cultures and how leaders display their emotions within political and business settings. This, in turn, influences how Nepalese society characterise their political and business leaders. As we turn our attention to business leadership, it is important to first stress that it is difficult to make generalisations about Nepal generally and Nepalese leadership specifically, in terms of preferred, values, traits and behaviours, and so on, as a consequence of the sheer diversity of its communities. However, generally speaking, Nepalese leadership is characterised by an acute awareness of respect, authority and social structures on the one hand, and humane and inclusive activities on the other (Feller & Mercel-Sanca, 2021). As noted by researchers, leadership is an important situational variable within employees' work lives, insofar as it profoundly impacts upon their psychological well-being, motivation and organisational performance (Karki & Maharjan, 2022). Indeed, Nepalese organisations' success is primarily dependent on the particular leadership style that is adopted (Saleem, 2015). Similar to China and India, respect is a key value in Nepalese leadership, which, in reality, serves to creates a stronger top-down hierarchy. It is important to stress here that this is more the case with the older generation of leaders than it is the younger generation in the country. The younger generation of leaders in the new Nepal are practical problem solvers, who combine respect and sensitivity to traditional leadership with solutions to social and economic problems. The younger generation of business leaders also tends to make decisions with the input of their teams, whilst the older generation continues to see decision-making as the sole responsibility of the leader (Feller & Mercel-Sanca, 2021). One of our interviewees, Ms. Pooja Dangol, a professional International Communication Coach and an HR Consultant with more than 10 years of experience in that field, told us that globalisation and modernisation means that both Nepali organisations and Nepali culture, have begun to change, which means that more and more people from different generations, countries and cultures start to work together

(Dangol, 2 May 2024). For modern Nepali leaders, it is crucial to be able to adapt to all the changes in culture and dynamics among people (Dangol, 2 May 2024). A good leader must be able to clearly communicate with any of his employees, clearly explain the vision, goals and strategy if needed (Rimal, 2 May 2024). However, due to the country's relatively recent industrialisation, management techniques are not as developed yet as they are elsewhere, and are still in a state of relative infancy. The principal focus of Nepalese leaders therefore tends to be upon output and fulfilling the organisational goals, with minimal focus on the personal ambitions of their employees (Adhikari, 2022). Another interesting insight into the Nepalese leadership style is that in Chapagain's (2008) survey-based research, they found that senior-level managers agreed with the view that 'to behave in a responsible way is a moral duty of business towards society'. The author attributes this, firstly, to the traditional customs and beliefs they have grown up with, and secondly, to their detailed understanding of business-society interrelationships (Chapagain, 2008). Finally, research has shown that an Asian strategic management style also prevails in Nepal, an approach which is characterised by trust, loyalty, networking, relationship-based and reactive strategic decision- making, which is in marked contrast to the more strategic management practices observed in western contexts (Shrestha & Gnyawali, 2013).

Survey results and what local respondents say

In order to gain insight into Nepalese leadership skills and practices, we administered the CCBS Survey (2024) to business owners, C-level managers and academic scholars from a range of different professions, who shared their knowledge, experience and expertise of living and working in Nepal.
In order to enhance the response rate, the survey was available in both English and Nepalese, with the majority of the respondents opting to complete the survey in English. The most significant findings emerging from the survey are discussed in turn below. The first noteworthy finding is that it very important to respect leaders or managers in Nepalese organisations (CCBS Survey, 2024). That being said, one of the key caveats of respecting leaders is that this respect must be earned rather than simply being given. This respect is earned through knowledge, experience and having worked either in a specific field or for an extended period of time (CCBS Survey, 2024). The importance of respect and hierarchy in Nepalese culture is corroborated by the fact that the respondents stated that it is important for employees to address Nepalese leaders by their titles, rather than by their first names (CCBS Survey, 2024). The next interesting finding is that the respondents reported that men and women have equal opportunity to attain senior-level

positions within Nepalese organisations (CCBS Survey, 2024). Next, it is evident from different results of the survey that it is important for Nepalese leaders to save face in public, as one sees in most Asian countries. For example, on the one hand, the respondents expressed a preference for employees giving indirect criticism outside of official meetings, whilst, on the other hand, the respondents also noted that it is unlikely that leaders will change their mind once a decision has been made (CCBS Survey, 2024). The reason for the lack of direct criticism in Nepalese organisations according to our respondents is that this appears as disloyal (CCBS Survey, 2024). Finally, although as we have seen, respect for rank and status is very important in Nepalese organisations, the results of the CCBS Survey (2024) also demonstrate that it is important for leaders to cultivate bonds with their employees, based on private interests or other non-work-related matters, in order to show interest in their employees' private lives (CCBS Survey, 2024).

Local leadership analysis

Leadership scholar from Kathmandu University

In an effort to gain insight into leadership in Nepal, we conducted an interview with a local Professor from Kathmandu University (3 May 2024). The local scholar, who preferred to remain anonymous for the purposes of this interview, works at the department of general management and human resources. That has an extensive background of more than a decade in teaching management-related subjects. The insights provided by the scholar shed light on the multifaceted challenges leaders face in Nepal. In the beginning of the interview, the professor explained that the transition from an absolute monarchy to a constitutional monarchy represented the starting point with respect to the erosion of leadership values in Nepal. He proceeded to inform us how the erosion of trust in leaders over the last twenty-five years, stemming from the perceived untruthfulness and corruption, is reflective of a broader societal disillusionment, which, in turn, has served to undermine effective governance and progress. The Professor emphasised that this this is not only his observation but that of most people in the country (3 May 2024). Next, in response to a question about shaping the next generation of leaders in Nepal, he stressed that: "*Education plays a vital role in creating the next generation of leaders* (3 May 2024). The preference for young people to gain their education abroad underscores systemic issues within Nepal's educational system, including a perceived lack of relevance, quality, and opportunities for skill development. Specifically, the professor noted:

"1% of the students go abroad to study on a yearly basis" (3 May 2024). Although at first glance, this seems like a small percentage, the professor noted that this is a lot when your population is roughly 30 million. The consequence of this is that you can *"forget about shaping the next generation* [of leaders] *"* (3 May 2024). The conversation then shifted to cultural influences. With respect to this point, the Professor acknowledged that traditional values like honesty, integrity, and compassion were waning in Nepal. As they themselves put it: *"They are no longer present in the urban sector"* (3 May 2024). He attributed this particularly to Western influences and globalisation more broadly. In this respect, they noted, the emphasis on material gain over traditional virtues like honesty and integrity is reflective of broader societal shifts. The effect of this is that it leads to a re-evaluation of leadership paradigms and ethical frameworks. Later in the interview, the professor brought up Nepal's geopolitical positioning between China and India, noting that: *"They are the ones who decide, who is going to rule, and are reliant on the support of these two neighbours"* (3 May 2024). This external influence on leadership selection, according to the professor, underscores the need for domestic resilience and autonomy in decision making. Moreover, they proceeded to explain, Nepal is thus characterised by instability. *"In our country, we can see there is a failure of leadership or there is a lack of leadership which has caused significant impact on the development of the country, and, at the same time, the well-being of the people of Nepal."* (3 May 2024). The discussion then turned to the role of academic institutions in leadership development. Overall, the professor expressed scepticism about their effectiveness, citing low graduation numbers and minimal leadership training programs. In their words: *"I don't think that educational institutions in Nepal have played any significant role in the development of leadership skills amongst students or professors for our University"* (3 May 2024). Overall, addressing these multifaceted challenges requires a holistic approach that involves, amongst other things, educational; reform, cultural revitalisation, and strategic autonomy in geopolitical affairs. By nurturing a new generation of ethical and competent leaders, Nepal can embark on a path of sustainable development and prosperity, guided by principles of integrity and accountability, so that the professor proudly stated: *"our graduates are well received in the market and now we can see that our graduates have demonstrated good leadership abilities which is evidence of their top leadership positions in the corporate sector"* (3 May 2024).

Mr. Jayendra Rimal - Leadership coach/trainer

To gain deeper insight into leadership skills and practices in Nepal, we conducted an interview with Mr. Jayendra Rimal, the Chief Operating Officer at Leadership

Academy Nepal, who has thirty years of experience of working in areas like HRM, HRD, Project Management, Stakeholder Engagement and Organisational Development. At the beginning of the interview, Mr. Rimal in response to a question about what is the most sought-after leadership skill in the Nepali business environment, Rimal emphasised the importance of adaptability and advanced interpersonal communication skills, such as cultural sensitivity and the ability to work in harmony within a diverse team with people from other cultures and different backgrounds (Rimal, 2 May 2024). He then proceeded to discuss how a good leader in Nepal must be able to easily communicate with any of their employees, and clearly articulate their vision, goals and strategy if required (Rimal, 2 May 2024). In addition to this, he noted that in the ambiguous era of modernisation and change, leaders must today be resilient and possess an ability to adapt to the multifaceted challenges they will encounter (Rimal, 2 May 2024). Later in the interview he moved onto discuss the delicate balance between traditional hierarchical systems and a more egalitarian leadership practices in the contemporary Nepali business environment. According to Rimal, due to the cultural background of Nepal, historically it was relatively normal to have a large power distance inside the company (Rimal, 2 May 2024). However, with the passage of time, the ability and willingness to embrace progressive leadership ideas increased. As he himself put it *"I feel that when more and more educated people are getting into organisations, they are starting to look at why differences should be discussed, why sometimes conflict will happen and why conflicts need to be managed"* (Rimal, 2 May 2024). However, Rimal also stated that not all changes can be implemented all at once, noting that: *"...In my personal opinion, most of the leadership styles were written or expounded by authors, scholars and experts who lived in the Western culture...Sometimes I see a problem with that when we try to copy and implement that in Nepali organisations, because sometimes there is this cultural gap..."* (Rimal, 2 May 2024). In other words, there must be an understanding that companies should not simply copy the practices of their Western counterparts, but rather adapt them in a way that *"...respects the traditional styles whilst also maintaining the utilitarian styles..."* (Rimal, 2 May 2024). Interesting insights were also gained with respect to how to handle international business relations. Rimal told us that the opening up of Nepal to foreign companies created yet another complication for the locals, namely, to be able communicate and do business with foreigners. Since the international ways of doing business are different from what Nepali companies were used to, there arose the need for people to build a diverse global mindset and develop their cross-cultural communication skills (Rimal, 2 May 2024). In order to do so, several methods were used, according to Rimal. One of these methods was to establish study tours and exchange programs, which enabled Nepali specialists to explore the different cultures themselves. *"For example, we have an ordinance called OS. It is Japan based...The ordinance provides scholarships to Nepali executives and takes them to Japan for a week-long or two-week long excursion..."* (Rimal, 2 May 2024). Finally, when we asked Mr. Rimal about the main challenges that companies face in contemporary Nepal, he replied that the main challenges that modern leaders face are uncertainty and ambiguity: *"If you look at Nepal maybe twenty years ago, the situation was more stable...But now, I feel that the challenges are changing so fast and the external environment is also throwing up new challenges, new threats and new opportunities for Nepali people"* (Rimal, 2 May 2024).

In-country leadership bestseller

One of the latest best-selling books about leadership in Nepal is written by Basant Chaudhary, an entrepreneur who was born in Kathmandu, Nepal in 1953.
He has been publishing articles and columns in Nepal's most prestigious business magazines. The book was published in 2023, and is entitled *Management 360 Degrees: Making a New Nepal*. In this book, the author addresses management perspectives that are imperative for Nepalese professionals to succeed in an age of volatility, uncertainty, complexity and ambiguity. The objective of the book is to take the existing work culture of Nepal and combine it with best-practices from around the globe. The book covers multiple Nepalese management standards and characteristics, and compares these with different economies across the world to bridge the gap between Nepal and the rest of the world. The most important takeaway lesson from the book is that everybody has their own place in the chain of command, and that this has to be respected. Due to the turbulent history of Nepal, leaders and manager have to be clear in their instructions and orders.

Local leadership book		BASANT CHAUDHARY
Title	*Management 360 Degrees*	
Subtitle	Making a New Nepal	
Author	Basant Chaudhary	
Publisher	Rupa Publications	
Year	2023	
ISBN	9355207603	

Nepal leadership YouTube review

Alongside academic literature and survey and interview data, YouTube also constitutes a valuable resource for gathering insights about leadership skills and practices, including in the Nepalese context. The first video to be discussed here comes from the Nepal Rastra Bank which explains the nature of management. They state that management in Nepal involves a process of planning, decision making, organising, leading, motivating and controlling the human resources, financial, physical, and information resources of an organisation to achieve its goals efficiently and effectively (B&B Class, 2020, 1:45). According to the Nepal Rastra Bank, one of the key principles of Nepalese management is that there should be a unity of direction; that is to say, "a*ll related activities should be put under one group, there should be one plan of action for them, and they should be under the control of one manager"* (B&B class, 2020, 8:22). Discipline is also important in Nepalese leadership, insofar as employees will only obey orders if management plays their part by providing good leadership (B&B class, 2020, 7:53). The next video to be summarised is a business studies class lesson video by Gurubaa, where it is explained that in Nepal leadership refers to someone's ability to influence others, to guide others and to present a clear vision to other people, to other teams and to the entire organisation (Gurubaa, 2022, 2:00). In this regard, effective business leadership can create an environment of confidence in the entire organisation. Through good leadership, one can create a vision and motivate others to make it reality. A successful Nepalese business leader typically exhibits traits such as a strong sense of responsibility, moral integrity, emotional resilience, in addition to a commanding presence. This includes one's outer appearance, physical fitness and confidence level (Gurubaa, 2022, 6:50). Besides physical qualities, there are also the managerial qualities which include having good human relationship skills, organisational ability, technical knowledge of the organisation, communication skills and having good judgement (Gurubaa, 2022, 7:50). By embodying both personal and managerial qualities, effective business leaders can steer their teams towards success, fostering growth and innovation within their organisations.

Understanding hierarchy in Nepal

With a Power Index Score (Hofstede) of 65, Nepal is considered a relatively hierarchical society, which is to say that people accept a hierarchical business structure in which every person has their own place that does not require any justification (Hofstede Insights, n.d). In Nepalese society, social status is regarded as the natural order of things, and it is normal for people to submit to and obey those who are in a higher position, have more status, a better reputation, or are older (Evason, 2017). Nepalese people also tend to avoid conflicts and do not like to criticise, or disagree with people directly (Feller & Mercel-Sanca, 2021). Indeed, even in everyday conversation, it is relatively common to ask about one's life, such as a person's age, profession, and family, in order to determine the amount of respect that this person deserves (Iacob & Dumitrescu, 2012). This respect for hierarchy is also reflected in Nepalese organisations (Schroevers, 2024). In terms of leadership, most decisions are made by senior-level management with little or no input from subordinates (Evason, 2017). Moreover, even the smallest of decisions require being processed along several levels in the chain of command, before, ultimately, the *hakim* (boss) makes the final decision (Shrestha & Gnyawali, 2013). The *hakim's* decision is considered almost to be the law and therefore requires no formal review or consultation (Feller & Mercel-Sanca, 2021). This was supported by the results of the CCBS Survey (2024), insofar as the respondents reported that once a decision has been made by a Nepalese leader, they are unlikely to change it. Employees will usually obey the *hakim's* word unless it is perceived to be harmful and unjust (Feller & Mercel-Sanca, 2021). This rigid hierarchical structure with of power located amongst a few figures in the upper echelons of the organisation makes the entire system less mobile in terms of being able to quickly respond to changing circumstances (Schroevers, 2024). However, this is difficult to change due to its deep roots in the religion, tradition, and social customs of Nepali people (Schroevers, 2024). In Nepal, traditions and religion are closely connected with work life, as relationships and castes drive business, rather than the other way around, as one sees in Western countries (Feller & Mercel-Sanca, 2021). The caste system is based on how closely one follows Hindu norms (Iacob & Dumitrescu, 2012). It is socially accepted for people

149

from higher castes to barely engage in physical contact with lower castes as they believe this would corrupt their caste's purity (Feller & Mercel-Sanca, 2021). Despite the fact that this system was abolished back in 1863, it continues to hold significance within Nepalese society (Iacob & Dumitrescu, 2012). Finally, another important determining factor of the hierarchical nature of Nepalese society and organisations is family. Families in Nepal tend to be larger and more extended than in the West (Feller & Mercel-Sanca, 2021). Every family follows the same hierarchy, as the patriarch - the father or the eldest son or brother-receives the greatest respect. It is their responsibility to arrange younger members' marriages or jobs, and to make all the important decisions for the family (Feller & Mercel-Sanca, 2021).

How the Nepalese achieve leadership empathy

Common administrative norms in the current Nepali business environment include a slow decision-making process, a high level of secrecy and power distance, which does not necessarily bode well for inter-personal relationships between leaders and employees, or the cultivation of empathy amongst Nepalese leaders (Iacob & Dumitrescu, 2012). For example, it is common for senior-level managers to not share offices with their employees, which in itself makes the exchange of information and development of bonds harder than it has to be (Iacob & Dumitrescu, 2012). This aspect of Nepali leadership was highlighted by one of our interviewees, Ms. Pooja Dangol, a professional International Communication Coach and an HR Consultant with more than 10 years of experience in that field, who opined that the consequences of such a system is a reluctance to take feedback from employees, who actually have ideas on how to run things differently, or how to improve the current system of things (Dangol, 2 May 2024). Indeed, research has shown that the overall state of employee-leaders' relations is rather disappointing in Nepalese organisations. One reason for this is the significant problems that Nepalese companies face, such as a lack of a clear and steady communication system, the continued disregarding of the value of delegating authority and responsibility, over-centralisation of power and lack of trust between senior-level management and line managers (Shrestha, 2022). However, with the modernisation of society, the business environment is also beginning to change too, including the relationship between leaders and employees. Whilst still remining loyal to their past, Nepalese people have begun to adjust their leadership style towards more of a mixture between rich traditions and contemporary Western practices (Schroevers, 2024). For example, Shrestha et al. (2023) showed that employees working in the public sector in Nepal are now more involved in the decision-making process than they were in the past. However, they note, there remains a lack of freedom and involvement for those workers who are employed at private companies (Shrestha et al., 2023). Similarly, there are more training programs which take place in Nepal, that teach people intercultural communication (Dangol, 2 May 2024). However, this method is far from ideal. Since the majority of firms are located in Kathmandu, the capital of Nepal, such programs take place only in Kathmandu Valley and only for employees who also work in that region, making the whole process pretty limited (Dangol, 2 May 2024). Of course, these things take time. Leaders and employees have to get accustomed to these new leadership styles and practices and responsibilities. However, there are some signs that even senior-level managers in Nepalese companies have begun to expand their knowledge of strategic-planning, task delegation and the crucial value of communication (Shrestha, 2022). Moreover, leaders are starting to recognise the benefits of a collaborative and diverse work culture, where a range of opinions can be heard and where decisions are made collectively (Schroevers, 2024). However, even though some changes can be discerned, it must be noted that these vary from company to company, and in the majority of cases, Nepalese senior-level management tend to remain distant from their employees (Shrestha, 2022).

Portugal

Emma Dijkstra, Lara da Fonseca, Naomi van der Jagt,
Karen Loth & Douha Moudou

Portugal, or as it otherwise often referred to the *'Land of Explorers'*, played a crucial role in the age of global maritime exploration during the fifteenth and sixteenth centuries, with notable figures like Vasco da Gama and Ferdinand Magellan helping to expand European perspectives and interests across the globe and influence the direction of world history (Subrahmanyam, 1993). The country is located on the southwestern edge of the Iberian Peninsula, bordered by Spain and the northern Atlantic Ocean (Moreira, 2018). Portugal includes the Madeira and Azores islands and is twice as large as the Netherlands, with nearly 11 million inhabitants, who are primarily concentrated along the coastal cities of Lisbon and Porto (Statistics Portugal, n.d.). Interestingly, Portuguese, a major global language, ranks as the second most spoken language on Twitter (Souza et al., 2016). Both the Portuguese language and musical genre of Fado profoundly reflect the country's historical and cultural identity. Fado, characterised by its emotional singing and rich instrumentation, expresses the Portuguese spirit and an integral part of the nation's cultural heritage (Gray, 2013). The famous expression, "*Quem não arrisca, não petisca* (Nothing ventured, nothing gained), testifies to Portugal's ethos of embracing risk to achieve success (Paixão et al., 2016). Portugal's economy is anchored in services, industry, and agriculture. The service sector, including finance, real estate, and tourism, dominates, reflecting the country's shift towards a more modernised economy. The main industries in Portugal are textiles, auto-parts, technology, in addition to being the world's leading cork producer (Redman, 2010). The agricultural sector focuses on quality exports like wine and olive oil. Despite past economic challenges, EU support has facilitated development, modernisation, and improved living standards, mirroring global economic transitions (Pariona, 2018). Business leadership skills and practices in Portugal involves guiding organisations towards achieving their goals through strategic planning, effective communication, and decision-making, which are shaped by cultural, economic, and social factors that are unique to Portugal (Rego & Pina Cunha, 2007).

How the Portuguese characterise leaders?

The *chefe*, Portuguese for leader, is characterised by a focus on improvisation and adaptability (Moreira & Subtil, 2012). This is supported by Ferreira (2007), who states that the ability to learn quickly and effectively respond to new situations is considered crucial for effective leadership in Portugal. Perhaps unsurprisingly, then, decisiveness is also a highly valued trait amongst leaders in the country (Ferreira, 2007). Having said that, that the decision-making process of Portuguese leaders has also been shown to be participative in nature insofar as leaders involve others in this process (GLOBE Project, n.d.). This dichotomy of Portuguese leadership was also supported by one of our interviewees, who noted that although leaders will make the final decision, feedback from their team members is always valued (Cotrim, April 26 2024). This was also found to be the case in the CCBS Survey (2024), where in response to a question about what distinguishes leaders from their international counterparts, one of the respondents stated the following: *"Aproximação da equipa e feedback constante"* ("Team approach and constant feedback". Given the importance of this team approach, it is also unsurprising that one of Portuguese leaders' key attributes is effective communication. Those who can communicate clearly, both verbally and non-verbally, with their team members and other stakeholders, are highly regarded (Ferreira, 2007). Through this communication they can motivate others, inspire them, and articulate a vision that resonates with others. These characteristics are valued in the Portuguese context; indeed, Rego (2004) argues that the most effective leadership style in the country's organisations is motivation and that it is important for leaders to be connected with their employees, which often takes place via informal interactions – a fact which was also supported by the results of the CCBS Survey (2024).They possess the ability to inspire, motivate, and also expect high performance from others based on core values (GLOBE Project, n.d.). Furthermore, Portuguese leaders must be able to empathise with the needs and feelings of their team members and encourage teamwork. This aspect is evident in their ability to assemble effective teams with shared objectives (GLOBE Project, n.d.). This aspect of Portugues leadership was also evidenced by one of our survey respondents, who opined: *"Algo muito português é que essa relação muitas vezes ultrapassa o foro estritamente profissional, criando-se mentores e amigos, numa relação que vai além do escritório"* ("Something very Portuguese is that this relationship often goes beyond the strictly professional forum, creating mentors and friends, in a relationship that goes beyond the office) (CCBS Survey, 2024). One of our interviewees also underscored this as a key aspect of leadership, noting that: *"Leaders may incorporate elements of informality and warmth"*

(Cotrim, April 26 2024), as by incorporating these elements of informality and warmth the leader forms a connection with their team members. Therefore, Portuguese leaders are clearly people-oriented, empathise with their team members as well as needing to possess good communication skills.

Survey results and what local respondents say

In order to gather additional insights into Portuguese leadership styles and practices, professionals occupying C-level positions across various industries in the country were approached to participate in the CCBS Survey (2024), sharing their invaluable professional expertise and extensive local knowledge. The findings reveal several significant characteristics of leadership in Portugal, which will be discussed in turn below. First and foremost, the respondents emphasised the importance of leaders in Portugal fostering closeness with their teams. One of the ways in which Portuguese leaders encourage informal interactions is by allowing their employees to address them by their first names and actively engaging in their team members' personal well-being (CCBS Survey, 2024). One respondent aptly summarised this practice as follows: "*Proximidade com a equipa fora do ambiente de trabalho*" ("proximity with the team outside the work environment"), which illustrates the emphasis on spending time with team members outside of work contexts (CCBS Survey, 2024). The second noteworthy finding is that all of the respondents indicated that charisma and intellect are highly valued traits that employees expect from leaders in the country. The importance of the latter was also supported by one of our interviewees, who informed us that wisdom is an important factor and is a well-respected trait in Portugal (Cotrim, April 26 2024). Effective communication skills were also identified as a cornerstone of Portuguese leadership, with leaders being open to reconsidering decisions based on feedback and criticism received during staff meetings (CCBS Survey, 2024). A third noteworthy finding concerned the fact that the majority of the respondents reported that Portugal has a hierarchical business culture (CCBS survey, 2024). Unlike some cultures where age, appearance, and family background may hold sway, Portuguese professionals prioritise organisational experience and market expertise when looking up to their leaders. This underscores the significance placed on achievements, authority, titles, and status within the Portuguese business context (CCBS Survey, 2024; Lopes, 2010). In summary, the CCBS Survey (2024) sheds light on the distinctive characteristics of leadership in Portugal, emphasising the importance of closeness, charisma, effective communication, and a hierarchical organisational culture.

Local leadership analysis

João Miguel Cotrim: a Portuguese leadership scholar

In order to gain deeper insight into leadership skills and practices in Portugal, we conducted an interview with João Miguel Cotrim, an academic member of the European Academy of Management, associate professor of the Research Group "Impactful entrepreneurship and Innovation" and "Foreign Visiting Professor" of Management and Leadership at Tecnológico de Monterrey. At the beginning of the interview, when asked about what distinguishes Portuguese leaders from their international counterparts, Cotrim explained that there are three key attributes that set Portuguese business leaders apart: their long-term vision, resilience, and cultural sensitivity (26 April, 2024). Firstly, Portuguese leaders possess a remarkable ability to envision the future beyond immediate gains, prioritising sustainable strategies for long-term success (Cotrim, 26 April 2024). Their visionary outlook enables them to navigate complex business environments with foresight and adaptability. Secondly, resilience emerges as a defining trait amongst Portuguese leaders, stemming from the nation's history of overcoming adversity. Cotrim proceeded to explain that their unwavering resolve in the face of challenges inspires confidence and fortitude within their teams, which, in turn, fosters a culture of perseverance and determination (26 April 2024). Thirdly, Cotrim highlighted the cultural sensitivity ingrained within Portuguese leadership practices by saying: *"they are culturally sensitive, meaning they embrace and welcome people regardless of gender, sex, sexuality, colour or religion"* (Cotrim, 26 April 2024). Drawing from Portugal's tradition of embracing diversity, leaders prioritise inclusivity and equality. Next in the interview, Cotrim proceeded to shed light on the nuanced interplay between authority and warmth within Portuguese leadership paradigms. Reverence for hierarchy and tradition remains ingrained in societal norms, Cotrim argued, which is expressed by using *"vôce,"* a respectful way of saying "you" (26 April 2024). Alongside this, Cotrim explained that leaders adeptly infuse their interactions with a sense of informality and congeniality. This delicate balance between deference to authority and genuine warmth facilitates the cultivation of authentic connections and fosters a collaborative ethos within teams. He shared an example of a business leader who shared his dividends with his team, which serves to illustrate the warmth of Portuguese leaders (Cotrim, 26 April 2024). In conclusion, Portuguese leaders are characterised by their long-term vision, resilience, and cultural sensitivity. Grounded in cultural heritage and values, Portuguese leaders exemplify a leadership style that prioritises sustainability, inclusivity, and authentic human connections.

Manuel Pelágio: a Portuguese cross-cultural trainer

To gain a deeper understanding of Portuguese leadership in a cross-cultural context, we conducted an enlightening interview with Manuel Pelágio, an executive with over twenty-five years of experience who now specialises in leadership training and executive coaching. Pelágio, who has transitioned from a high-pressure executive role to focusing on personal and professional development, is passionate about cultivating self-awareness and empathy amongst leaders. At The beginning of the interview, he stated, "*Leadership is much more than being an executive. For me, it is about leading yourself first, changing the way you know yourself, how you control yourself*" (Pelágio, 26 April 2024). Pelágio outlined the characteristics of typical Portuguese business leaders, noting that the leadership styles in Portugal tend to be influenced by regional differences. This is illustrated in the following extract in which Pelágio described Portuguese leadership as more empathetic, focusing on human needs and building connections through understanding and respect. As she himself explained, "*The Portuguese leadership style is more about a feminine way of leading. We care more about people. We are more sensitive*" (Pelágio, 26 April 2024). In response to a question about the evolving landscape of leadership in Portugal, Pelágio replied that the integration of younger generations is bringing new values and expectations to the workplace, which, in turn, necessitates a shift towards more open and flexible management styles. He emphasised, "*Leadership is not about the position you are working; it is more about how you inspire others to work and live in a different way*" (Pelágio, 26 April 2024). Reflecting on the challenges of leadership, Pelágio shared his belief that true leadership is not about asserting power but about fostering an environment in which employees feel valued and heard. He stressed the importance of leaders engaging in continuous learning and cultivating a willingness to adapt and grow alongside their teams. As he proceeded to explain, "*The most difficult part of my work is just to say that leaders need to know that they really do not know themselves. Opening up to this fact allows them to look at life and the company in different ways*" (Pelágio, 26 April 2024). As the Portuguese business landscape continues to evolve with increasing diversity and shifts in cultural values, leaders like Pelágio are at the forefront, advocating for a more humane and empathetic approach to leadership. This interview not only provided insights into the nuances of Portuguese leadership but also underscored the universal themes of respect, empathy, and adaptability that are increasingly relevant in today's globalised business environment.

In-country leadership bestseller

One of the best-selling books on leadership in Portugal was written by Géraldine Correia and Jorge Nascimento Rodrigues in 2004 and is titled "*Mestres Portugueses da Gestão*" ("Portuguese Masters of Management"). Géraldine Correia studied communications and media and worked as an economic journalist and interpreter. Jorge Nascimento Rodrigues is an editor for the portals janelanaweb.com and Gurusonline.tv. He is a contributor to the weekly Expresso and coordinates the Portuguese and Brazilian Journal of Management. Besides co-authoring this book, he has also co-authored other works such as "Masters of Management". The book presents the answers of a collection of interviews with sixteens Portuguese managers, professors, and consultants. From the perspective of these sixteen leading specialists, it becomes evident that the practice of Portuguese management is hybrid in nature, with the influence of North American management being on the rise. However, one aspect of Portuguese leadership requires strengthening above all: strategic and organisational improvisation within complex circumstances. This asset, the authors argue, is underestimated by international consultants (Correia & Rodrigues, 2004). João Vieira da Cunha stresses in his interview that Portuguese leaders prioritise flexibility, creativity, and dynamism in their daily practice, which are regarded as essential traits for success in a rapidly changing world (Rodrigues et al., 2004). He also stresses that the ability to survive in challenging circumstances, by coming up with unexpected solutions, is a distinctive Portuguese skill (Rodrigues et al., 2004). Miguel Pina e Cunha states in his interview that focusing on international experience, continuous improvement and adaptability are key attributes required by Portuguese leadership in a globalised world (Rodrigues et al., 2004). Besides looking at the current generation of leaders, Mário Murteira also refers optimistically to the emergence of a new generation of '*empresariado global*' and managers, who, he argues, have a cosmopolitan vision and international experience, two traits which bode well for the future of Portuguese business (Rodrigues et al., 2004). All the interviewees and experts conclude that Portuguese leadership is distinguished by its adaptability, creativity, and international orientation, all of which are essential for success in the modern global business environment (Rodrigues et al., 2004).

Local leadership book		
Title	Mestres Portugueses da Gestão	
Subtitle	-	
Author	Géraldine Correia and Jorge Nascimento Rodrigues	
Publisher	Edições Centro Atlântico	
Year	2004	
ISBN	978-9728426859	

Portugal leadership YouTube review

In an interview with Alberto Pimenta, posted by the YouTube channel *Portal da Liderança*, he was asked the following question, *"No que mais falha a liderança em Portugal?"* ("What is most lacking in leadership in Portugal?"). In response, he stated that leadership often revolves more around power than relational leadership, which poses significant challenges for many Portuguese organisations. This attitude frequently leads to insufficient collaboration with employees. Alberto Pimenta therefore believes that leadership decisions should be strong and driven, leaving no room for hesitation or doubt. He said the following regarding this point: *"As decisões da liderança têm de ser firmes e obsessivas"* ("Leadership decisions must be firm and obsessive") (Alberto Pimenta, 2015, 1:18). Additionally, leaders often fail to fully utilise the qualities of their employees, which, in turn, results in suboptimal organisational performance (Alberto Pimenta, 2015, 2:19). Furthermore, Alberto Pimenta concludes that younger individuals and those furthest from positions of power can serve as sources of inspiration, harnessing new energies essential for both Portuguese leaders and their companies (Alberto Pimenta, 2015, 3:03). The next video to be summarised is an interview with João Couto, a former Vice President and leader of an advisory firm, with the focal point of the discussion being the following question, *"Como vê a gestão em Portugal e o que poder potenciar a sua qualidade?"* ("How do you see management in Portugal and what can improve its quality?"). He stresses in the video that people in Portugal are very open and flexible and can improvise well, which enables them to effectively engage with employees from diverse cultural backgrounds (João Couto, 2015, 0:54). On the other hand, Portuguese leaders are bad at planning, and leave everything to the last minute (João Couto, 2015, 1:19). João Couto also notes in the interview that the Portuguese have a very pessimistic view of life in general, which means they mainly look at the problem and not enough at the solutions. In his words: *"Temos uma visão muito pessimista sobre a vida e tentamos sempre ver pelo lado do problema e não pelo lado da solução"* ("We have a very pessimistic view of life, and we always try to see it from the problem side and not from the solution side") (João Couto, 2015, 3:04). Drawing from personal experience, he illustrates this with an example, noting that in most meetings, 90% of the time is spent discussing why things went wrong, leaving only 10% for exploring solutions. This should be different; for example, 20% of the time should be spent describing what the problem is, whilst 80% needs to be focused on how to solve it (João Couto, 2015, 3:21).

Understanding hierarchy in Portugal

Understanding how things work in Portuguese organisations requires looking beyond surface-level behaviours (Lopes, 2010). The concept of hierarchy plays a significant role in shaping social interactions and organisational structures. Portugal, along with other countries like Spain, Latin America, Asia, and Africa, is characterised by a high-power distance (Hofstede, 1991). This means that Portuguese people tend to have tremendous respect for their leaders and retain a certain distance from them. Authority, titles, and status are also highly valued in Portugal. The consequence of this is that those in charge expect to be obeyed, whilst those lower down the organisational ladder are expected to be loyal and deferential (Lopes, 2010). As a result, managers often yield considerable power over their teams, and decisions are ordinarily made in a top-down manner. Even in specific sectors like finance, where unions are strong, employees might stick with their jobs even if they are not fully engaged because of the hierarchical nature of the organisational culture (Koles & Kondath, 2015; Aycan et al., 2000). This is suggestive of a more hierarchical dynamic in which managers hold significant power and decision-making authority compared to their employees. This aspect of Portuguese organisational culture was also noted by one of our interviewees, who stressed that professional organisations in Portugal have a strict hierarchy that is very structured. This was explained as something that comes from the past, most likely from the military hierarchy (Pelágio, April 26 2024). They proceeded to explain the difficulties that employees encounter in terms of speaking up beyond their roles, which, in turn, serves to impinge upon their personal growth. However, with the emergence of a younger generation of millennial and Gen Z leaders, there is an observed shift towards more open communication and assistance across all levels of Portuguese organisations (Pelágio, April 26 2024). Our interviewee Manuel Pelágio also stated the following: *"Leadership is not just about the position you are working; it is about how you (as a leader) inspire others to work and live in a different way."* Here, Pelágio is underscoring the fact that leadership is not solely defined by one's position or the power or status one has within the organisation, but rather by one's ability to inspire others. From this perspective, true leadership involves motivating and influencing others to embrace change and strive for their best selves Pelágio, April 26 2024). Another aspect of hierarchy within Portuguese organisations is that gender has a significant impact upon the organisational climate in Portugal (Koles & Kondath, 2015). Women often value teamwork and relationships more than men, whilst older workers tend to think their companies are more forward-thinking than their younger counterparts (Koles & Kondath, 2015). Whilst this hierarchical system in some ways helps to keep everything running smoothly, with clear lines of communication and accountability, it also means that decisions often come from the top down (Figueiredo et al., 2013). Interestingly, however, the results of the CCBS Survey (2024) showed that the majority of leaders disagreed with the statement that they prefer to retain a personal distance from their employees, in order to maintain the right level of respect. This suggests a preference in Portugal for less hierarchical distance between leaders and employees and a greater emphasis on fostering personal interaction in the workplace (CCBS Survey, 2024). In conclusion, the concept of hierarchy in Portuguese culture reflects a deep-seated respect for authority and tradition. Understanding and respecting these hierarchies is crucial for getting along in Portuguese society, affecting everything from how decisions are made to how people communicate.

How the Portuguese achieve leadership empathy

Portuguese leaders are increasingly recognising the importance of empathy in their leadership approach. Empathy allows them to connect with their team members on a deeper level, understand their perspectives, and respond with sensitivity to their emotions and needs (Quintas, 2023). Portuguese culture values strong interpersonal relationships and connections. Leaders must show empathy by building trust with their team members, taking the time to understand their personal backgrounds, and showing genuine interest in their well-being, providing support and encouragement to employees during challenging times (Quintas, 2023). However, our interviewee noted that business leaders in Portugal find it difficult to be vulnerable because they feel that if they open up this will be seen as a sign of weakness rather than strength (Pelágio, April 26 2024). Manuel Pelágio proceeded to explain that this is because *"Society taught us to think, not to feel"* by which he means that modern society places greater emphasis on rationality, logic, and cognitive processes rather than on emotions and empathy. Within Portuguese culture, there is a strong emphasis on education, problem-solving, and critical thinking skills, often at the expense of nurturing emotional intelligence and compassion (Pelágio, April 26 2024). As a result, many people in the country prioritise analytical thinking over understanding and expressing their own emotions or empathising with others. This societal conditioning can in turn lead to a disconnect between individuals and their feelings, as well as a lack of empathy in interpersonal interactions. Therefore, Pelágio informed us that Portuguese leaders must understand that leadership is about the connection you have with employees; it is about having empathy and being more aware of others (April 26, 2024). This is in line with the work of Quintas (2023), who argues that if Portuguese leaders do this then it will help boost morale and create a positive work environment. They can do this by offering their employees words of encouragement, recognition for hard work, and assistance when needed (Quintas, 2023). Another aspect of Portuguese culture with relevance to empathic leadership concerns the importance placed upon generosity, with the exchange of gifts amongst colleagues within a company being a common practice. Therefore, it is a good idea to keep a gift on hand from your company or country since it is seen as a way for leaders to build empathy (Mellão & Mónico, 2013). Indeed, the foundation of business relationships in Portugal rests on personal connections and mutual trust. Viewing a client as a friend is essential; failure to establish this bond can jeopardise the client relationship (Loureiro et al., 2022). This was also corroborated by the results of the CCBS Survey (2024), insofar as the respondents confirmed that Portuguese leaders are clearly people-oriented, empathise with their team members and value good communication skills. Leaders strive to foster a close bond with employees by promoting equality in office spaces and encouraging informal communication. Moreover, the vast majority of the respondents agreed that they encourage their employees to address them by their first names and show genuine interest in their well-being and development. This approach fosters a culture of openness, trust, and mutual respect within the organisation, resulting in a positive work environment in which everyone feels heard, valued, and supported (CCBS Survey, 2024).

Romania

Roksana Beyer, Renata Calvelli Fonseca, Jari Stumeijer, Francisca da Conceicao Boto,
Daan Groot & Obed Bonsu Osei

România (Romania) is located in the heart of south-eastern Europe, and is bordered by Bulgaria, Hungary, Ukraine, and Moldova. Bucharest, the country's capital, is home to 19 million people, which makes it the eighth largest city in the European Union. Whilst the official language is Romanian, there are also regional variations, which is known as the Daco-Romanian dialect. Hungarian is also spoken by over a million people, whilst smaller communities use, amongst other languages, Romany, German, Turkish, and Serbian. Romania is a relational-based culture in which hospitality towards guests is vitally important. *Noroc* is what Romanians say to cheers with their friends and family, preferably with their local plum-based spirit named *Țuică (Muică & Turnock, 2008)*. The currency is the Romanian *lei*, with each *leu* split into 100 *bani*, which refers to both "coins" and "money" (Cret & Pantea, 2008). Due to Bucharest's strategic location, Romania is a pivotal player in regional trade and commerce. Indeed, the city serves as a dynamic hub of economic activity, insofar as it is home to multinational corporations, vibrant start-ups, as well as being a serious entrepreneurial ecosystem (Moise et al., 2017). Romania is attractive to large companies due to its skilled workforce, wages, infrastructure, and cheap materials (Hurduzeu, 2015). This, combined with sizeable foreign investment and local spending, is boosting the country's economy. These aforementioned factors are also resulting in notable shifts in the Romanian business leadership landscape. Whilst, historically, Romanian leaders were domineering and controlling, there is an observed shift towards approaches that are more focused on participative decision-making and inclusivity (Aioanei, 2006). Overall, Romania's mix of culture and evolving leadership is creating new opportunities for businesses, both nationally and internationally (*Huțu, 2010*). The following chapter explores the prevailing leadership skills and practices in Romania by drawing on academic research and primary data collected from surveys and interviews with Romanian professionals and experts.

How Romanians characterise leaders?

In Romania, leadership embodies a fusion of historical, cultural, and organisational factors. According to Aioanei (2006), the prevailing leadership approach in Romania is the autocratic style, which they demonstrated via their survey-based research insofar as approximately 55 percent of the leaders who took part in their study reported that they exhibited authoritarian tendencies in their approach, whilst the remaining adopted a democratic approach. With respect to the specific qualities, traits and behaviours that are valued in Romanian business leader, Noaghea et al. (2017) purport that Romanian leaders are characterised as high potential and as being driven by achieving high levels of organisational performance and staying informed about trends and developments within their industries. According to the authors, there are several behaviours underlying this particular characterisation of Romanian leaders, which we will discuss in turn below. Firstly, Romanian employees place real value upon their leaders being educated and engaging in data-driven decision making, which is reflective of a broader dedication on their behalf to engaging in lifelong learning, and using the best available information (Noaghea et al., 2017). However, other scholars have argued that leaders in Romania also prioritise maintaining strict control and authority over their subordinates, sometimes at the expense of fostering open communication and collaboration within their respective organisations (Ignat, 9 May 2024). From the perspective of one of our interviewees, Smaranda Ignat, an innovation coach, trainer, and business consultant, there is a growing expectation that Romanian leaders must be more receptive towards the ideas of their employees in addition to acknowledging the value of diverse perspectives (9 May 2024). Alongside these aforementioned qualities, traits, and behaviours of Romanian leaders, Crăciun et al. (2015) identified transformational characteristics as being important for leaders in the country to possess, which includes, amongst other qualities, adaptability, cooperation, authority, confidence, and motivation. Moreover, Ignat informed us that: *"most of the entrepreneurs that have lasted in the market more than five years are quite charismatic, [...] reliant on their native skills [...] and their ability to talk themselves out of situations"* (9 May 2024). One of the ways in which Romanian leaders demonstrate adaptability is by being flexible in their approach to challenges, open-minded towards new ideas and changes, willing to modify strategies based on evolving circumstances, and effectively navigating uncertainties. The CCBS survey (2015-202) corroborates the importance of these particular attributes and behaviours in Romanian leaders, insofar as half of the respondents reported that after management has made their decision, it is not impossible to change their minds. Alongside this, Frunza (2022) argues that one of the main components of leadership competence in Romania today is the ability to be a visionary. Visionary leadership is highly valued in Romania due to its ability to provide strategic direction, inspire innovation, and navigate complex organisational challenges (Frunza, 2022). In so doing, visionary leaders in Romania articulate compelling visions that motivate employees and guide strategic decision-making processes. For example, during the transition of state-owned enterprises to market-oriented entities, visionary leaders played a pivotal role in terms of steering these organisations towards modernisation, innovation, and global competitiveness (Catana & Catana, 1996). Our second interviewee, Dr. Laurenţiu Mihai, an Assistant Professor at the University of Craiova in Romania, informed us that Romanian leadership is characterised by a distinct blend between certain Balkans characteristics, such as collectivism, lower risk appetite, high power distance and certain Western types of management practices, especially amongst the younger generation of leaders in the country (9 May 2024). Finally, there is an emergent emphasis upon ethical leadership in the country, namely with integrity and ethical behaviour emerging as key traits associated with effective leadership in Romania in recent years (Agheorghiesei et al., 2015). Ethical leadership in Romania is predicated on specific principles such as transparency, integrity, accountability, respect for others, commitment to the common good, and compliance with laws and regulations. Romanian leaders demonstrate their integrity to those they lead through various strategies like value-based management, empowering employees through consideration of their skills, and fostering open communication. They also exhibit ethical behaviour by focusing on employees' well-being and respecting their rights (Agheorghiesei et al., 2015).

Survey results and what local respondents say

In order to gain comprehensive insight into Romanian leadership skills and practices, we drew upon data from the CCBS Survey which was administered to C-level Romanian executives. In order to strengthen both the generalisability and validity of the findings, we utilised survey data from two periods of data collection, namely 2015 and 2022, in which Romanian executives shared their first-hand knowledge and expertise of leadership skills and practices. This section presents the most significant results emerging from these two data collection points. The first notable finding from the survey data is that the Romanian leadership style is relatively hierarchical in nature. The hierarchical nature of Romanian enterprises was surmised from the fact that 83% of the respondents agreed with the statement 'when a management decision has been made, it will not be changed very easily'. Additional evidence for the hierarchical nature of Romanian organisations stems from the fact that 59% of the respondents reported that 'employees would not bend the rules without asking in order to improve their performance or achieve better results' (CCBS Survey, 2015-2022). Secondly, when asked about what Romanian employees look up to in their leaders, the most commonly selected attributes or qualities were organisational experience, technical competence, and market expertise (CCBS Survey, 2022). Interestingly, despite the seemingly hierarchical nature of Romanian organisations and leadership, 68% of the respondents indicated that is normal for employees to address their leaders by their first names in Romanian organisations (CCBS Survey, 2015-2022), which is suggestive of a more informal relationship between leaders and subordinates. Thirdly, 85% of the C-Level executives who took part in the two iterations of the survey reported that Romanian leaders should actively spend time ensuring the personal well-being of their team members (CCBS Survey, 2015-2020). The final noteworthy observation about leadership in Romania emerging out of the survey was that there is a lack of trust between leaders and their employees, which, in turn, leads to forms of micromanagement as opposed to delegation (CCBS Survey, 2022). Interestingly, one of the respondents opined that the reason for this lack of trust in leadership stemmed from the former communist era in the country (CCBS Survey, 2022), a finding which was also supported by other researchers (Beukers et al., 2022).

Local leadership analysis

Laurențiu Mihai: a Romanian leadership scholar

Dr. Laurențiu Mihai works as a full-time Assistant Professor in the department of Management, Marketing and Business Administration at the University of Craiova in Romania. Dr. Mihai teaches various types of management-related subjects, including, amongst other things, Business Management, Strategy Management, and HR Management. The topic of Romanian business leadership skills and practices has been one of his principal areas of research since he completed his PhD thesis, which focused on exploring the impact of different leadership styles within small and medium enterprises in Romania. We began the interview by asking Mihai about what qualities, traits and behaviours are valued in Romanian leaders, to which he responded: *"the typical Romanian business leader is male between 45 and 55 years old"* (9 May 2024). He proceeded to explain that leaders tend to be more autocratic in nature, but that as a company matures, they tend to transition into a more democratic leadership style. Once Romanian leaders adopt

165

a democratic style, they give their employees greater responsibility, autonomy and freedom over their working life. However, Mihai (9 May 2024) pointed out that the millennial and gen Z generations have different expectations, leadership approaches and mindsets than their older counterparts, which underscores the fact that leadership styles and practices are evolving in the country. Next, when asked a question about what distinguishes Romanian leaders from their international counterparts, Mihai responded that Romanian leadership is characterised by a distinct blend between certain Balkans characteristics, such as collectivism, lower risk appetite, high power distance and certain Western types of management practices, especially amongst the younger generation of leaders in the country (9 May 2024). These Western management models and approaches tend to reduce the level of power distance in Romanian organisations, which, in turn, encourages leaders to engage in more friendly and direct forms of contact with their employees. Later on in the interview, when asked to discuss how hierarchical Romanian organisations are, Dr. Mihai proceeded to inform us that even though the power distance has reduced in recent years, for the reasons he mentioned previously, hierarchical structures nevertheless persist, especially in traditional companies, where leaders are more or less viewed and treated as Kings and, henceforth, engage in almost no form of direct contact with their employees (9 May 2024). Mihai added to this point by proceeding to explain that things are beginning to change somewhat within both smaller and younger companies, but generally speaking, hierarchy remains important in Romania. To illustrate this point, Mihai stated that managers will always have certain power and be of a certain position that makes them stand out from other employees (9 May 2024). As the interview drew to a close, he noted that even though the decision-making process is centralised at the top level, Romanian managers nevertheless always strive to explain to their employees the reasons for their decisions, rather than simply communicating it and demanding that they follow. In this respect, Mihai noted, leaders do seek out feedback and value the opinions of their employees (9 May 2024).

Smaranda Ignat: a Romanian cross-cultural trainer

In order to gain additional insight into Romanian leadership skills and practices from a variety of different perspectives, we conducted an interview with Smaranda Ignat, an innovation coach, trainer, and business consultant. Whilst Smaranda Ignat has been involved in this field throughout her professional life, she is currently working as a "*solopreneur*", which is to say that she assists entrepreneurs who are wishing to expand their products/services globally or develop new products for the global market. To this end, she assists her clients in better understanding their clients or new markets, in addition to connecting them with potential partners, who can help them to further their goals. In the beginning of our interview with her, in response to a question about what distinguishes Romanian leaders from their international counterparts, Ignat replied as follows: *"[Romanians] are very resourceful in solving problems on the spot"* (9 May 2024). However, she proceeded to inform us that in some instances this self-reliance can morph into forms of micromanagement, fuelled by a *"lack of trust"* within the business sector generally in Romania (Ignat, 9 May 2024). Later in the interview, Ignat (2024) explained that leadership styles in Romania are undergoing somewhat of a generational shift. More specifically, she explicated, whilst traditional leaders lean towards more of a paternalistic approach, which resembles the notion of the *"leader is the father,"* the younger generation of leaders in Romania *"want to have nothing to do with the old-school"* (Ignat, 9 May 2024). Moreover, Ignat stated, the upcoming generation of Romanian leaders, *"will be more open-minded and open towards bettering themselves and educating themselves"* (Ignat, 9 May 2024). Whilst acknowledging that, historically speaking, Romanian leaders have been relatively charismatic and reliant on their native skills, Ignat underscored the increased need for Romanian leaders to *"listen to their people* [employees]*"* and display humility towards differing viewpoints in their organisations. In this respect, Ignat believes the future of Romanian leadership appears to be promising, in part, because the challenges faced by Romanian entrepreneurs have forged a generation of resourceful and resilient leaders. Ignat brought our interview to a close by emphasising that: *"this generation and maybe the next generation of leaders and the businesses will be really thriving because they grow and were formed under tough conditions"* (9 May 2024).

In-country leadership bestseller

Published in 2020, *"Către leadership prin management"* (Towards leadership through management) by Radu Nechita explores leadership development within the context of the Romanian business sector. Nechita, who has been an entrepreneur since 1994, boasts a diverse background including capital market brokering (1996-2000) and doctoral studies in diplomacy and international relations (completed in 1998). Since 2004, he has continued his entrepreneurial ventures, whilst, simultaneously, sponsoring over six hundred courses for hundreds of Romanian and international companies. With respect to the quality of leadership skills and practices in Romania, Nechita (2020) underscores the fact that *"Romania has never had a solid management school"*. The consequence of this, he argues, is that Romania lacks a strong management foundation, which promoted the book's focus on improving leadership skills and practices in the country (Nechita, 2020). In this respect, the book not only provides a comprehensive guide for transitioning from intuitive forms of management to more structured and mindful approaches, but also offers insights into Romanian leadership dynamics. Specifically, the book sheds light on the unique challenges and opportunities faced by leaders in Romania, particularly in the context of transitioning family businesses that were founded in the 1990s, that have yet to develop robust management and leadership systems. In relation to this point, the author states, that *"The management system was brought in, copied, tested, practiced, adapted [in Romania]"*. The result of this is that the Romanian business system suffers in terms of innovation. In conclusion, through real-world stories and practical tools, readers can gain an understanding of proactive management approaches that are specifically tailored to Romanian business. Ultimately, the book equips readers as well as current and aspiring Romanian leaders with essential leadership concepts, best practices, and strategies for navigating the intricacies of Romanian leadership, emphasising, above all, the importance of understanding people and fostering effective teamwork in this specific context.

Local leadership book		
Title	*Către leadership prin management*	
Subtitle	Instrumente de management care inspiră	
Author	Radu Nechita	
Publisher	Pim	
Year	2020	
ISBN	9786061356843	

Romanian leadership YouTube review

The first video to be summarised is an episode of MindArchitect featuring Dani Adrian, a professor of Behavioural Psychology and a consultant at Human Synergistics. In this video, the discussion delves into the evolving landscape of business leadership in Romania over the last decade. According to Adrian, effective leadership in Romania is characterised by specific qualities and strategies (MindArchitect, 2023). Firstly, Adrian notes that leaders prioritise creating a sense of psychological safety within their teams, where individuals feel comfortable expressing themselves and can take risks without fearing judgment.

Secondly, trust and reliability amongst team members are emphasised as essential for building strong relationships and a positive organisational culture. Thirdly, Romanian leaders must effectively communicate their vision for the organisation and inspire others to share in that vision, in order to foster alignment and collaboration. Moreover, they also need to strike a balance between addressing organisational objectives and considering the personal concerns and well-being of their team members (MindArchitect, 2023). Adrian then proceeds to discuss that effective Romanian leaders focus on progress and process rather than solely on outcomes, providing positive feedback and support to encourage continual improvement and learning. Next, Dani stresses that traditional leadership paradigms require updating in Romania. Specifically, he underscores the progression in leadership strategies towards more constructive organizational impact (MindArchitect, 2023). This approach, Dani argues, is characterised by a visionary approach to leadership that emphasises future-oriented thinking and long-term performance. Leaders with constructive organizational impact are described as those who operate from a space of complex thought and goal orientation, utilising higher-level cognitive functions to drive organisational success (MindArchitect, 2023). According to Dani, embracing change and continually refining leadership approaches are crucial for achieving organisational success in Romania (MindArchitect, 2023). In the second video to be summarised here, Alexandra Calu, Third Secretary of the Embassy of Romania, talks about personal leadership in Romania from a diplomatic perspective, drawing from her first-hand experiences and observations (Sitchting Soka, 2020). Calu outlines a comprehensive list of essential qualities necessary for effective leadership in demanding environments. She begins by stressing the importance of determination and confidence, which she deems to be essential for successfully executing tasks and projects. Energy is also considered to be important, specifically in terms of motivating teams and driving projects forward, whilst, on the other hand, courage is required for taking calculated risks and learning from mistakes (Sitchting Soka, 2020). The willingness to take responsibility and make difficult decisions is also emphasised by Calu, thus reflecting the importance of accountability in leadership roles. Additionally, good judgment, interpersonal skills, and the ability to foster the best qualities in team members are deemed crucial for successful leadership. Overall, the discourse underscores the multifaceted nature of leadership in Romania, emphasising a blend of personal attributes, professional competence, and effective communication skills. Effective communication and interpersonal skills are noted as indispensable for building relationships and fostering collaboration within teams.

Additionally, she says good leaders need to advocate for a balanced approach to work and life, acknowledging the necessity of enjoying the present moment whilst striving for personal and professional growth (Sitchting Soka, 2020).

Understanding hierarchy in Romania

According to Dalton and Kennedy (2007), the power dynamics in Romanian workplaces tend to lean towards a top-down approach where leaders hold the majority of decision-making power. According to Hofstede, Romania scores high (90) on power distance, thus indicating significant hierarchical structures and an unequal distribution of power. This was also supported by one of our interviewees, Dr. Mihai, a Romanian business scholar, who noted that Romanian leadership is characterised by a distinct blend between certain Balkans characteristics, such as collectivism, lower risk appetite, and high power-distance (9 May 2024). In Romanian organisations, leaders wield significant authority, guiding operations with a firmly established top-down approach that is deeply embedded in the cultural fabric of organisations (Ulrich, 2021). For instance, senior-level executives or owners typically make all the crucial decisions, which are then subsequently implemented by middle managers and frontline employees. This top-down structure also extends to communication channels, where important directives flow from upper management to lower-level staff through written communication such as e-mails and memos (Brandes & Darai, 2014). Moreover, employees generally show strong levels of deference to authority figures, with minimal questioning of their decisions, which, in turn, serves to reproduce the prevailing centralised decision-making process (Malea, 2019). Whilst some limited opportunities for employee input may exist within this structured environment, the overall hierarchical nature of Romanian organisations discussed thus far is in accordance with the observations of the European Commission (2023), who describe a landscape in which clear hierarchies prevail, and power dynamics are distinctly delineated. This depiction underscores the entrenched top-down leadership approach and reinforces the notion of a corporate culture deeply rooted in traditional hierarchical structures (European Commission, 2023). This hierarchical framework often limits employee autonomy and input. The clear delineation of power dynamics and structured hierarchies in Romanian organizations can result in limited opportunities for lower-level employees to shape strategic initiatives (European Commission, 2023). This was supported by one of our interviewees, who told us that there is a lack of trust from leaders towards their employees, and that, in some instances, this can go so far as to result in forms of micromanagement within Romanian organisations

(Ignat, 9 May 2024). However, Ignat (2024) also told us that leadership styles in Romania are undergoing somewhat of a generational shift in that whilst traditional leaders lean towards more of a paternalistic approach, the younger generation *"want to have nothing to do with the old-school"* (Ignat, 9 May 2024). Notwithstanding this point, the results of the CCBS Survey (2015-2022) indicate that, generally speaking, Romanian leaders still tend to prefer maintaining a personal distance from their employees to uphold a perceived level of respect. However, interestingly, the results of the CCBS survey (2015-2022) also show that the vast majority of the respondents disagreed with the proposition that supervisors should be addressed by their title, advocating instead for the use of their first names as a preferred mode of address. This appears to be suggestive of the kind of generational shift identified by Ignat (9 May 2024).

How Romanians achieve leadership empathy

Empathy is a key aspect of emotional intelligence and can represent the changing point between an adequate and an exceptional leader (Deliu, 2019). Aioanei (2006), in his research about leadership in Romania, explored two leadership styles, namely the authoritarian and democratic approaches, and found out that at that time leaders in Romania were more authoritarian in their approach. This preference for an autocratic style was evidenced by their lack of involvement with subordinates, the fact that they frequently made the final decision, and their use of coercive strategies with their employees (Aioanei, 2006). Furthermore, when it comes to Hofstede's cultural dimensions, as aforementioned Romania scores high on Power Distance (90), which makes it even more difficult for leaders to demonstrate empathy towards their subordinates, insofar as they maintain distance from each other. This distance was underscored by one of our interviewees, Dr. Mihai, who told us that in some traditional Romanian organisations, leaders are more or less viewed and treated as Kings and, henceforth, engage in almost no form of direct contact with their employees (9 May 2024). This lack of empathic leadership can be seen as a consequence of the Communist legacy. However, as both Dalton and Kennedy (2007) and Ignat (9 May 2024) conclude, leadership styles and practices in Romania are undergoing a period of profound transition. Specifically, these same authors purport that Romanian leadership is transitioning towards a more decentralised, modernized, and culturally adaptive approach. This shift involves embracing new management practices, integrating external models, and navigating the complexities of Romania's historical and cultural context to drive effective leadership (Dalton and Kennedy, 2007). This shift was also noted by both of our interviewees, who noted that: "the younger generation *"want to have nothing to do with the old-school"* (Ignat, 9 May 2024) and that things are beginning to change somewhat within both smaller and younger companies in Romania (Mihai, 9 May 2024). Such changes amongst the younger generation are also discernible in the fact that a study exploring business students' perspectives on leadership showed that team-oriented leadership and charismatic leadership were the two preferred leadership styles (Alexandru & Catana, 2010). This shift towards more relational and individually tailored forms of leadership in Romania also finds support in the results of the CCBS Survey (2015-2022), insofar as 70% of the respondents reported that it is (very) likely that managers actively spend time ensuring the personal well-being of their team members. Similarly, 68% of the respondents stressed that it was important for Romanian leaders to be good listeners (CCBS Survey, 2015-2022). The change towards more empathic forms of Romanian leadership is also supported by a recent study conducted by Ogarcă et al. (2016) about Romanian leaders, where 57% of the 129 survey respondents considered their superior to be a democratic leader as opposed to an authoritarian leader. This result is important insofar as empathy can more easily be achieved within democratic leadership style, since it encourages participation amongst team members and fosters open communication (Popa, 2012). Finally, the topic of empathetic leadership in Romania was also further addressed by our interviewee, Smaranda Ignat, who told us that even though she does not believe Romanian leaders are particularly empathetic, she thinks this is changing in recent years because they are aware of its importance. As they put it: *"Emotional intelligence is an important concept. Communication is an important tool and leaders were forced to take action and to really start caring, let us say so. It's more and more important. It is more and more present in the boardroom."* (Ignat, 2024). She proceeded to note that Romanian leaders achieve empathy by listening to their employees and by making them feel understood, noting that *"I may not agree with what you are doing or saying, but I understand what drives your beliefs, what is behind what you are saying."* (Ignat, 2024).

Ukraine

Alex Stavitskyi, Erik Oomen, Erin Hoek, Mantej Dhaliwal,
Marit de Zeeuw & Nikki van Pelt

Ukraine (*Україна*), or as it is often referred to '*the breadbasket of the world*', is an Eastern European country with a rich and complex history. It is the 58th largest economy in the world, with a GDP of $161 billion, albeit it has the lowest GDP growth due to the ongoing conflict. The primary economic sectors in Ukraine include, amongst others, wholesale and retail trade, agriculture, and manufacturing (Statista, 2023). These industries, which involve selling goods, farming crops such as, for example, wheat and sunflowers, along with the production of machinery and clothing, are crucial for job creation and economic development. The country has a population of around 43 million people, and its official language is Ukrainian. Its capital city is Kyiv (*Київ*), which has a population of 3 million people. Kyiv is a city with a rich history which spans back almost a thousand years, at which point it was given the title *"мати міст російських"* (*Mother of Russian Cities)* (КИЙАВІА, 2020). The ethnic composition of the country mainly consists of Ukrainians, which comprise more than two-thirds of the population, with Russian being the next largest nationality, which makes up around one-fifth of the population (Statista, 2022). The currency in Ukraine is Hryvnia (UAH ₴). Ukrainian culture is characterised by a strong focus on social values, religion, and family life. Important social values in Ukraine include education, professionalism, and efficiency. The main religion is Orthodox Christianity, which was restored after Ukraine secured its independence in 1990 (Kliuchnikov, 2014). Given the prominence of religion, it is unsurprising that Ukrainian society also has strict rules on drugs, alcohol, and smoking (Migration Policy, n.d.). In terms of leadership, Volodymyr Zelensky is the current President, who has led the country during the ongoing conflict, and received international attention and support (*Wilson Center*, 2020). Ukraine's business culture is deeply formal, and people are acutely aware of their own and others positions within the organisation, as a result of the fact that *ієрархія* (hierarchy) and *статус* (status) are taken very seriously (Gomółka & Flisikowski, 2016). This chapter explores Ukraine's leadership skills and practices in greater detail by drawing upon both primary and secondary research with Ukrainian experts and professionals.

How Ukrainians characterise leaders

Ukrainian business culture can best be defined as authoritarian and demanding, but also charismatic (Kliuchnikov, 2014). In the context of Ukrainian business leadership, *КОНТРОЛЬ* (control) is the operative word. Generally speaking, leaders in the country adopt an authoritarian approach and role, which is to say that they exercise control over their teams as much as they possibly can (Oromanyshyn, 2024). In practice, this manifests in specific measures like micromanagement, exercising strict control over deadlines, and tracking the time it takes for employees to perform tasks. According to Auer et al. (2022), these sorts of behaviours and attributes are simply what is expected of leaders, insofar as it demonstrates to employees that they are competent, possess the requisite knowledge, and take their role seriously. Historically, strong, and authoritarian figures have always been highly valued in the country, so if managers were not to engage in such forms of micromanagement, then Ukrainians would not accord them respect (Auer et al., 2022). Alongside these aforementioned traits and behaviours, Ukrainian leaders are also expected to possess a broad range of knowledge in their respective field and should be able to both answer any questions that their employees have or deal with any problems that may arise (Linville, 2021). In the event that a manager or leader is not able to solve problems or answer questions, they will likely lose respect from their employees (Oromanyshyn, 2024). The importance of these attributes for Ukrainian leaders was also corroborated by the results of the CCBS Survey (2024), insofar as 55% of the respondents reported that employees in Ukrainian organisations look up to their leaders on the basis of their technical competence, in addition to their experience and market expertise. However, according to Hejkrlik (2020), and as aforementioned, strict authoritarianism is not the only characteristic of leadership in Ukrainian companies, charisma is also of the utmost importance. The principal reason for this is that cultivating and maintaining a family-like atmosphere within organisations, allied with being empathetic, humane, and caring, is expected of leaders in Ukrainian companies. The importance of both charisma and these aforementioned behaviours was also identified by our interviewee, Inna Chernyshova, an executive business and life coach, who informed us in our interview that explained that what makes an effective and respected Ukrainian leader has much more to do with competence, empathy, and being able to take risks and shoulder responsibility. Moreover, they proceeded to explain, they must possess the requisite knowledge, be strong decision makers, be strict but yet exhibit compassion towards their teams (Chernyshova, 26 April 2024). Whilst Chernyshova explained to us that the best leaders in Ukraine are balanced in several qualities, in practice there are two different styles of leadership that prevail in Ukrainian businesses to this day. Fuxman (2004) designates these as the enforcement style of leadership, and the encouragement style. The enforcement style, as the name indicates, is based on making clear what the consequences will be if and when standards are not met. By making employees afraid of the negative consequences of failure, their drive to work harder will in turn increase their level of efficiency (Fuxman. 2004). This strategy is often used within Ukrainian companies that are not very stable. Conversely, the encouragement style of leadership in Ukraine utilises motivation to increase employees' efficiency. As one can discern, this is an altogether more positive style of management and is typically observed more within companies that are more economically stable (Fuxman, 2004). To conclude, although Ukrainian leadership in business is primarily strict and authoritarian in nature, at the same time they are expected to be charismatic and to take an interest in the well-being and lives of their employees by cultivating a family-like atmosphere within their organisations.

Survey results and what local respondents say

In order to gain a deeper knowledge and understanding of leadership skills and practices in Ukraine, C-level executives and managers with extensive leadership experience were asked to share their expertise and insights in the CCBS Survey (2024). The survey primarily focuses on leadership approaches, preferred leadership traits, organisational culture and the level of gender (in)equality within organisations in the country. The most important findings that emerged from the 92 survey respondents are summarised in turn below. To strengthen the validity of the findings, we have combined survey data from this year with data from a previous period of data collection. The first interesting outcome of the survey is that the majority of the respondents answered that they do not prefer to retain a personal distance from their employees, because it can help to keep the right atmosphere in the team, release stress and therefore contribute towards better results in the future (CCBS Survey, 2024). This result is in line with previous research, which also showed that Ukrainian society is more relationship-oriented, and that good employer-employee relations facilitate a better chance of success (Muhka, 2018). Secondly, it is interesting to note that the respondents were more or less evenly split with respect to the question of whether Ukrainian leaders prefer to hear criticism in an indirect manner outside of staff meetings (CCBS Survey, 2024). According to the Wilson Centre (2020), one reason for this observed difference may be that old-fashioned leaders, who grew up in and worked during the Soviet Union era may be more inclined to not receive direct criticism, whilst younger leaders are more open-minded due to the increased influence of Western leadership styles and practice sin recent decades. This was corroborated by one of the respondents, Andrii Krylov, a CEO in the infrastructure sector, who stated: *"Currently, I see a big movement to western leadership with getting rid of soviet background, with young people coming to managing positions. They do their work with completely different approach, which make it more productive and innovative."* (CCBS Survey, 2024). The next significant finding is that the vast majority of the C-level managers responded that they are ready to confront subordinates during staff meetings, in order to obtain the desired results (CCBS Survey, 2024). Moreover, the respondents also reported that it is common for Ukrainian leaders to encourage some degree of competition within their teams, in order to achieve better results and ensure that their employees remain highly motivated. This is in accordance with previous research, which argued that Ukrainian business culture is authoritarian and demanding (Kliuchnikov, 2014). The persistence of hierarchy was also noted by one of the respondents, who noted: *"Hierarchy also takes place, representing the fact that lower-level employees are also doing larger amounts of work"* (CCBS Survey, 2024).)

Local leadership analysis

Inna Chernyshova: A Ukrainian Business Coach

Inna Chernyshova is an executive business and life coach with an ACC certification from Ukraine. Inna has been working as a coach in the banking field since September 2008. In 2017, she switched to the manufacturing and production branch. She has been working as a business coach and trainer in this field ever since. Her work as a business coach for the past several years within different sectors, including, amongst others, finance, automotive and even the Armed Forces, has provided her with excellent knowledge and insight into leadership skills and practices within Ukrainian organisations. At the beginning of our interview, Inna Chernyshova (26 April 2024) reflected upon how much leadership in the Ukraine has changed over the last decade. In contemporary Ukraine, leaders have become much more accessible than they were historically. She proceeded to explain that whereas age once played a major factor in terms of both who became leaders and who was accorded respect within Ukrainian companies, in recent years it has become much more a question of whether someone is actually competent and sufficiently skilled to be able to lead an organisation, irrespective of what age they are. Ms. Chernyshova did go onto say that the age of leaders in Ukrainian organisations has shifted towards 27-45, although she emphasised to us that age and gender do not matter as much as they used to in the country (26 April, 2024). In response to a question about the attributes that are valued in Ukrainian leaders, Chernyshova responded that good communication from leaders is absolutely fundamental to the performance of a company. Today, Ukrainian leaders must be able to speak up when things are not going well, in addition to being open and honest with their employees (26 April, 2024). When asked about how hierarchical Ukrainian companies are today, Chernyshova (2024) explained that companies and organisations used to be defined by much more of a top-down mentality, where certain decisions were simply forced upon employees without any input from them. She proceeded to explain that this had changed in recent years, noting that: *"Humanity matters more and more now. It is important for people to feel their involvement, to feel their contribution and, accordingly, to want their work to be valued, to be valued, to be recognised for their merits and to contribute to grow as such"* (Chernyshova, 26 April 2024). She concluded the interview by stating that currently, more and more companies are adopting a more horizontal approach.

Ukrainian social media review

This section expands the analysis to include various social media outlets in order to better comprehend Ukrainian leadership styles and practices. The following will summarise the perspective of both Ukrainian industry leaders and local activists. Firstly, in an interview with Forbes, Victoria Repa, founder and CEO of BetterMe, explored the topic of business leadership styles in Ukrainian organisations. In response to a question about what strategies she utilises to better help her team navigate their roles, Repa explained that a good Ukrainian leader *"provides energy to the team, and takes their fear and stress"* (Repa, 2022, 15:00). The advice that Repa offers for current and aspiring Ukrainian leaders is especially significant considering the recent conflict in the country. At a time where most Ukrainians are living under hostile conditions, business leaders must be capable of providing a sense of calm and stability to their respective teams, whilst, simultaneously, instilling a culture of high energy and motivation. Next, in a podcast series with "Ukraine in English", the key differences of leadership structures between Ukraine and Russia were examined. The guest on the podcast, Deborah Fairlamb, is a founding partner of a venture capital firm in Ukraine and has been living in the country since 2015. In the podcast, Fairlamb plainly states that there are fundamental differences in the leadership styles and structures that make the two countries vastly different. She argues, *"Russia is a vertical society, it is*

177

extremely hierarchical. Ukraine is a horizontal society.... there are incredibly strong powerful networks between people" (Fairlamb, 2024, 7:15). Fairlamb proceeds to make the point that Ukrainians typically do not wait for someone in leadership positions to tell them what to do, but rather take it upon themselves to take the initiative. Next, another video clip from the United Nations Europe, involves an interview with local Ukrainian female leaders who have created a self-help group in an effort to drive local development in Eastern Ukraine. These groups were created to help assist in the development of leadership skills and practices for local women over a span of 18 months. They have also helped empower many of the local women to run for political office and to attain senior-level business positions who previously would never have considered it. For instance, the leader of one of the groups, Lyudmyla Komlyk, expressed that she is planning to run in the next election with the support of these groups. Ukraine has one of the lowest levels of representation of women in parliament, and initiatives like this help uplift women to run at the local political level; ultimately, this helps to pave the way for generations of Ukrainian women to have a greater influence in Ukraine's social, political, and corporate entities. The perspectives offered by these aforementioned leaders aptly captures the essence of Ukrainian leadership styles as observed across different social platforms.

In-country leadership bestseller
A well-known book about leadership in Ukraine is *"Різнобарвний менеджмент. Еволюція мислення, лідерства та керування (2-ге видання, доповнене)"* (*Colorful Management: Evolution of thinking, leadership and management*), which is written by Valery Aleksandrovitsj Pekar. Pekar is an entrepreneur, public figure and Vice President of a major company in the country. He has over twenty years of experience in leadership. In this particular book, he talks about the limitations of a traditional Ukrainian leadership approach and suggests ways to implement a new style of management called 'colourful management' into a company. The book starts off by outlining the limitations of a traditional management approach within Ukraine, such as the strict hierarchical rules and the lack of listening to the input of employees. After presenting these problems, Pekar introduces a more adaptive and inclusive approach to management that embraces diversity and creativity. The benefits of colourful management are shown in the book through the use of case studies and real-world examples. In this respect, there are several lessons that current or aspiring Ukrainian business leaders could learn from reading the book. Firstly, the book explains that every individual has different

paradigms of thinking. Therefore, it is important for leaders in the Ukraine to be aware of this and to understand what role this plays in managing an organisation. Each of the different paradigms of thinking are given a colour along with an accompanying explanation. This book challenges Ukrainian leaders to think about the different types of people in their organisations as well as their different paradigms of thinking. Pekar wants to show that every colour requires a unique approach to learning, goal setting and motivation, rather than thinking the same way about every employee like as was the case in traditional management in Ukraine. Secondly, four types of companies are described, with the author teaching managers how to think about the match between the company culture and the paradigm of thinking from employees' perspectives.

Local leadership book	
Title	*Різнобарвний менеджмент*
Subtitle	Еволюція мислення, лідерства та керування
Author	Валерій Пекар (Valery Pekar)
Publisher	Folio
Year	2023
ISBN	978-9660376205

Ukraine leadership YouTube review

Alongside academic research and interview and survey data, YouTube also constitutes an excellent resource through to gain a different perspective on leadership skills and practices, including within the Ukrainian context. The first video to be summarised is an interview with Oleksandra Alkhimovych with the UCU Business School in Lviv, which explores the topic of transformational leadership during conditions of uncertainty within Ukraine. Throughout this interview, Alkhimovych emphasises key points regarding how Ukrainian business leaders can effectively inspire and galvanise their teams to embrace the changes that are required at this particular juncture. Specifically, Alkhimovich highlights the importance of the core elements of a transformational leadership approach, namely its capacity to generate a collective vision, boost motivation, and spur innovation within organisations in Ukraine. These insights are invaluable for grasping how Ukrainian leaders can apply transformational strategies to successfully manage and prosper during unpredictable circumstances, especially war. Oleksandra states that *"the events of the last months and years have shown that the manifestation of leadership, in principle, is now needed at all stages"* (Alkhimovych, 2023, 2:50). Alkhimovych's ultimate ambition is for small and medium sized businesses in Ukraine, along with managers from large companies, to establish a comprehensive framework on transformational leadership in an organisational structure. The second video to be summarised in this section is another interview, this time with Oleg Khaidakin, CEO of Carlsberg Ukraine. In this video, Khaidakin also discusses the role and importance of effective leadership during times of conflict and unrest. The principal point of Khaidakin's argument is that Ukrainian business leaders at this juncture should be driven by a common goal of rebuilding Ukraine instead of fulfilling their own personal ambitions. He proceeds to explain that this collective approach will help protect Ukraine from future conflicts. As Khaidakin himself puts it: *"It is also about the economy, about helping the country.... you should focus not on achieving your personal goals, you should focus on helping others achieve their goals"* (Khaidakin, 2024, 0:33). In conclusion, Khaidakin argues that a collective approach by Ukrainian business leaders results in stronger organisational structures, which, in turn, will lead to more resilient supply chain systems, during difficult periods.

Understanding hierarchy in Ukraine

In order to gain insight into hierarchy and power distribution in Ukraine, the distribution of the power distance is a good benchmark to look at. The Hofstede Country Comparison indicates that in Ukraine, with a score of 92, power distance plays a major role in the country (Hofstede Insights, 2024). In countries with high levels of power distance a certain level of inequality is generally accepted and those in power tend to exercise a high level of control over others, including within the business culture, as is the case in Ukraine. According to Muhka (2018), the strict corporate culture one sees in Ukrainian organisations is a by-product of the Soviet era. During the highly bureaucratic Soviet period, companies had a strict authoritarian leader, who employees deferred to and followed absolutely. These strict rules are still discernible in Ukrainian organisations to this day, insofar as it is common for Ukrainian companies to still adhere to Soviet-style management practices and processes (Демуз et al., 2019). One of the ways in which the Soviet legacy persists is that companies often operate according to strict hierarchical rules, with management working via a top-down structure in which employees often have little say. This culture is characterised by a high degree of bureaucracy and a low degree of adaption and flexibility (Демуз et al., 2019). One example of these strict rules is that employees in some Ukrainian organisations can only leave the office after the leader has left (Muhka, 2018). Alongside this rule, Ukrainian leaders still also prefer employees to execute their commands rather than allowing them to take the initiative and continue to largely ignore their employees' opinions (Szydło, 2017). The research of Вікторівна (2020) who conducted a survey amongst 50 employees within the company "Interavia llc" about the culture within the company also helps to shed light on how hierarchy functions within Ukraine. Their research revealed that employees believe their managers are strict and demanding. Furthermore, the organisation was largely result-oriented, which is to say that the most important thing was fulfilment of tasks (Вікторівна, 2020). The hierarchical nature of Ukrainian organisations was also corroborated by the results of the CCBS Survey (2024), insofar as in response to the question: "Is there something specific about leadership in Ukraine? One respondent stated: *"Our entire system is built on the principles of the Soviet Union. The more status that someone has, the more trendy someone is."* (CCBS Survey, 2024). However, there is some evidence pointing towards the fact that employees want to reduce the formalism and authoritarian power they encounter. For example, the employees of Interavia llc reported that they wished that *"their managers would set an example as a mentor"* and, moreover, that *"they could be more flexible and creative, to look for new opportunities"* (Вікторівна, 2020). These viewpoints are reflective of a broader shift that is taking place in Ukrainian organisations, which is that the older employees and leaders who grew up in the Soviet era are giving way to a younger generation of employees and leaders who prefer a culture in which there are no strict rules and where they have input in the decision-making process (Bogodistov & Lizneva, 2017). This is also corroborated by Демуз et al. (2019) who argue that that new modern companies within Ukraine are incorporating more Western leadership approaches and practices, which are characterised by flexibility and more horizontal structures. This was also pointed out during our interview with a business coach, who stated that the old hierarchical system is slowly fading and making way for a new leadership style and organisational culture (Chernyshova, 26 April 2024).

How the Ukrainians achieve leadership empathy

Based on a study conducted by Kliuchnikov (2014), there is a correlation between how much freedom Ukrainian employees experience during their time at work, and their motivation/attitude towards the work that they do. More specifically, the study reports that Ukrainian employees who have, relatively speaking, higher levels of freedom in their workspace have greater motivation and are more positive (Kliuchnikov,)2014. The reason for this is because the Ukrainian managers in this case respect their employees' decisions, which, in turn, makes the employees feel heard and understood. One of the ways in which Ukrainian leaders can make their employees' voices heard and make them feel like their opinions matters is by seeking their input in meetings, along with asking them for feedback once a decision has to been made (Kliuchnikov, 2014). The value of this type of approach was also underscored in other research, this time by Hejkrlik (2020), who conducted research in a Ukrainian organisation. The respondents in their research reported feeling positive in their work as a result of the fact, as they put it: *"I believe that my opinion can influence the decision-making processes* [in the company]". Similarly, another respondent stated: *"The leader allows the members to express dissenting point of views"* (Hejkrlik, 2020). According to Kliuchnikov (2014), these types of leaders in Ukraine have better relationships with their subordinates than managers who do everything their own way without seeking any input from their teams. The fact that Ukrainian leaders care about their employees' wellbeing was also confirmed by the results of the CCBS Survey (2024), insofar as over two-thirds of the respondents agreed with the statement that *'Managers should actively spend time ensuring the personal well-being of their team members.'* Furthermore, research has also shown that more empathic leadership approaches can help to reduce stress and anxiety amongst their employees (Singh, 2014). It is important for Ukrainian business leaders to inspire and encourage their subordinates, whilst, simultaneously, being empathetic. Leaders typically do this by speaking to their employees and identifying their individual needs, finding out what makes them enjoy and feel fulfilled by their work, and then seeking to act upon this feedback. In this way, in Ukraine, employees can be both driven, and at peace in their workspace (Singh, 2014). The fact that employees are at ease with their managers is also supported somewhat by the results of the CCBS Survey (2024). Specifically, when asked the question *'In my country, it is important for subordinates to address leaders by their titles or positions within the organization (e.g., director, president) when communicating with them either verbally or in writing,'* most of the respondents answered that employees do not have to address their leaders using their titles or positions (CCBS Survey, 2024). This appears to indicate that their work environments are becoming increasingly informal, as also identified by our interviewee, Chernyshova, who told us that: *"Humanity matters more and more now. It is important for people to feel their involvement, to feel their contribution and, accordingly, to want their work to be valued, to be valued, to be recognised for their merits and to contribute to grow as such"* (26 April 2024).

Bibliography

Bibliography

Вікторівна, Ш. (2020). *Корпоративна культура як складова управління організацією (на прикладі компанії «Інтеравіа»).*

Демуз, И. А., Зленко, А. Н., & Исайкина, Е. Д. (2019). *Формирование корпоративной культуры: мировой опыт и украинские реалии. Экономический Вестник Университета. Сборник Научных Трудов Ученых И Аспирантов, 40.* https://cyberleninka.ru/article/n/formirovanie-korporativnoy-kultury-mirovoy-opyt-i-ukrainskie-realii

Кийавіа. (2020, 30 January). *Київ - столиця України.* https://kiyavia.com/cities/kyiv

Adhikari, R. (2022). Issues of religion in Nepal. *International Research Journal of MMC, 3*(3), 66–72. https://irjmmc.edu.np/index.php/irjmmc/article/view/85/112

Agarwal, R., & Gupta, B. (2021). Innovation and Leadership: A study of organizations based in the United Arab Emirates. *Foundations of Management, 13*(1), 73–84.

Agheorghiesei, D.T., Poroch, V., & Perţea, M. (2015). Ethical leadership in healthcare institutions from romania. An approach from a management perspective. *Revista Romana De Bioetica, 13.*

Ahmad, A. R., Alhammadi, A. H. Y., & Jameel, A. S. (2021). National Culture, leadership Styles and Job Satisfaction: An empirical study in the United Arab Emirates. *Journal of Asian Finance, Economics and Business, 8*(6), 1111–1120.

Aimazrouei, H. (2023). The effect of COVID-19 on managerial leadership style within Australian public sector organisations. *Journal of General Management.*

Aioanei, I. (2006). Leadership in Romania. *Journal of Organizational Change Management, 19*(6), 705-712. https://doi.org/10.1108/09534810610708350

Akad, S. (2022, June). Spotify (D. Revagliatte, Interviewer; season 2, episode 5). Spotify. https://open.spotify.com/episode/0PgMhId6qzv7fDukYbNUmV?si=86c58a0d67c14da8

Akinmodun Y. (2024, April 30). *Leadership in Modern Workplace.* [Personal Interview], Milosteanu V. (Interviewer)

Akroyd, C. (2014). *Egypt.* Simon and Schuster. ISBN: 978-1-4222-1381-0.

Al-Alawi, A., & Alkhodari, H. J. (2016). Cross-cultural differences in managing businesses: applying Hofstede cultural analysis in Germany, Canada, South Korea and Morocco. *Elixir International Business Management, 95*(2016), 40855-40861.

Alberta School of Business. (2021). In Conversation with Don Wheaton - Canadian Business Leader Award. www.youtube.com. https://youtu.be/_XA-bNDpgBk?feature=shared

Alberts, J., Sanderman, R., Eimers, J., & Van Den Heuvel, W. (1997a) *Socioeconomic inequity in health care: A study of services utilization in Curaçao. Social Science & Medicine,* 45(2), 213–220. *https://doi.org/10.1016/s0277-9536(96)00338-3*

Alexandru, C. G., & Catana, D. (2010). Prospective Romanian Leaders' view on leadership dimensions. *Annals of Faculty of Economics, 1*(1), 645–650. https://ideas.repec.org/a/ora/journl/v1y2010i1p645-650.html

Alfaqeeh, K., Hossan, C., & Slade, B. (2019). Influence of Arab culture on managing an innovative work environment: an exploratory study in the United Arab Emirates. *International Journal of Business Innovation and Research, 19*(2), 232.

Ali, M., Jones, A., & Alshamsi, K. (2021). The Relevance of Emotional Intelligence for Leadership – UAE context. *International Journal of Management* (IJM), 12(4), 583–596.

Aliboni, R. (2017). *Egypt's Economic Potential.* Routledge Egypt. ISBN: 9781138108288

Allen, D., McAleer, M., Powell, R. J., & Singh, A.K. (2017). Volatility spillovers from Australia's major trading partners across the GFC. *Direct Science*. Retrieved March 31, 2024, from https://www.sciencedirect.com/science/article/pii/S1059056016302040

Allen, R. (2014). From bondage to national belonging in a Dutch Caribbean context: addressing the Yu di Korsou in post emancipation Curaçao, 1863–1915. In: *Transgressing Neocolonial Boundaries in the Languages and Literatures*.

Allen, R., (2003) Acceptatie of uitsluiting. Enkele belangrijke invalshoeken voor de discussie over beeldvorming over immigranten uit de regio en over de Curaçaoënaars, in: R.M. Allen e.a. (red.): Emancipatie & acceptatie. Curaçao en Curaçaoënaars, beeldvorming en identiteit honderdveertig jaar na de slavernij, SWP, Amsterdam, pp. 79-90

Almeida, F., & Sobral, F. (2005). Emoções, inteligência e negociação: um estudo empírico sobre a percepção dos gerentes portugueses. *RAC: Revista De Administração Contemporânea*, 9(4), 9–30. https://doi.org/10.1590/s1415-65552005000400002

Alnuami, A. (2018). Happiness at Work in the UAE: The Role of Leadership Style and Human Resource Management. Global Development Institute.

Al-Omari, J. (2003). *The Arab Way: How to Work More Effectively with Arab Cultures*. How to Books.

Altitude Himalaya. (2021, 8 June). The Majestic Mount Everest - Beyond its Summit. https://www.altitudehimalaya.com/blog/mount-everest

Altun, T. (2022). *Charismatic Leadership in Egypt Gamal Abdel Nasser* (first edition). The graduate school of social sciences of Middle East technical university.

Anderton, P. [TedX Talks]. (2016, July 25). *Great leadership comes down to only two rules | Peter Anderton | TEDxDerby* [Video]. YouTube. https://youtu.be/oDsMlmfLjd4?si=uOGvJs1lGwd3Z8xP

Aqil, K. (2018). Pearl industry in the UAE region in 1869-1938: Its construction, reproduction, and decline. RUDN *Journal of Sociology*, 18(3), 452-469.

Arafat, W. M. M., Bing, Z. Y., & Al-Mutawakel, O. (2017). Infrastructure developing and economic growth in United Arab Emirates. *Business and Economic Research*, 8(1), 95.

Arbino, D. (2022). "Together we're strong:" Cross-Cultural solidarity in Angie Cruz's Dominicana. *Latin American Literary Review*, 49(99), 30–39. https://doi.org/10.26824/lalr.250

Ashcroft, R.T. & Bevir, M. (2017) Multiculturalism in contemporary Britain: policy, law and theory. *Critical Review of International Social and Political Philosophy*. 21:1, 1-21. https://doi.org/10.1080/13698230.2017.1398443

Ashour, S., & Kleimann, B. (2024). Private higher education: a comparative study of Germany and the United Arab Emirates. *Research Papers in Education*, 1–17.

Asmaa, I. (2019). A Gap Between Theory and Practices: Best Leadership Practices in Multinational Corporations: An Egyptian Case Study. (2019). *Developing Country Studies*. 9(3). https://doi.org/10.717-3-07.

Atty, A., Moustafasoliman, M. and Youssef, A. (2018) The Effect of Board of Directors Characteristics on Firm's Financial Performance: An Empirical Study on the Most Active Firms in the Egyptian Stock Exchange. *Open Access Library Journal*, 5, 1-19. Doi: 10.4236/oalib.1104993.

AUC School of Business. (2022, 4 April). *Leading Change in Challenging Times: Lessons of Disruption and Innovation from Egypt* [Video]. YouTube. https://www.youtube.com/watch?v=NavnloPCkeQ

Auer, M. E., Pachatz, W., & Rüütmann, T. (2023). Learning in the Age of Digital and Green Transition: Proceedings of the 25th International Conference on Interactive Collaborative Learning (ICL2022), Volume 2. Springer Nature.

Aulinger, A., & Schmid, T. (2009). Empathisches Führungsverhalten - Einschätzungen und Beobachtungen aus der Unternehmenspraxis. *ZFO-Zeitschrift Für Führung Und Organisation*, 78, 296–303.

Australian Bureau of Statistics. (2023). Lifestyle and management practices, Australia. Retrieved February 29, 2024, from https://www.abs.gov.au/.

Australian Public Service Commission. (2019). *Australian Public Service Hierarchy and Classification Review.* (No. 978-0-6453376-3–1). https://www.apsc.gov.au/sites/Accessible.pdf

Australian Rural Leadership Foundation (ARLF). (2024, January 10). Leading our regions through disaster. And how it doesn't have to be complicated – with Telstra's Steve Tinker. Spotify. https://open.spotify.com/episode/6EQw66FCp9NRn0Mgsyj55K

Authentic Coaching Academy. (2021, 16 November). *Technology Leadership Stories - Story No. 1 - Ahmed Ibrahim Khalil - Analog Devices Egypt* [Video]. YouTube. https://www.youtube.com/watch?v=WJ89-So7cYg.

B&B Class. (2020, 18 June). Management: Concept, Functions & Principles | Nature of Mangement ब्यबस्थापन English & Nepali [Video]. YouTube. https://www.youtube.com/watch?v=bVApDdEdOpk

Badia, P. P. (2011). *Cross-Cultural Influences on Management Practices: It's Impact on Distribution of Power, Leadership, and Communication. A Comparative Study Between the Dominican Republic and the United States.* Retrieved from [scholarworks.wmich.edu] (https://scholarworks.wmich.edu/honors_theses/739)

Badiane, Mamadou (April 2012). "Négritude, Antillanité et Créolité ou de l'éclatement de l'identité fixe". *The French Review.* 85 (5): 842. doi:10.1353/tfr.2012.0227

Bahl, N. K. H., Nafstad, H. E., Blakar, R. M., & Langvik, E. (2021). Living in the Era of an Ideological Climate of Globalisation: A Study of Psychological Sense of Community Among Young and Older Adults in Two Cultures (India and Norway). Challenges for Community Psychology and the Applied Social Sciences. *Frontiers in Psychology,* 12, 718190–718190. https://doi.org/10.3389/fpsyg.2021.718190

Baird, K., & Harrison, G. (2017). The association between organizational culture and the use of management initiatives in the public sector. *Financial Accountability & Management,* 33(3), 311-329. https://onlinelibrary.wiley.com/doi/10.1111/faam.12125

Bakshi, P. (2018). *Leadership in India: A Need to Keep Pace with India's Growth Story?* Routledge.

Baldini, G., Bressanelli, E., & Massetti, E. (2020). Back to the Westminster model? The Brexit process and the UK political system. International Political Science Review, 43(3), 329–344. https://doi.org/10.1177/0192512120967375

Baroudi, S., & David, S. A. (2020). Nurturing female leadership skills through peer mentoring role: A study among undergraduate students in the United Arab Emirates. *Higher Education Quarterly,* 74(4), 458–474.

Bealer, D., Patel, P., & Bhanugopan, R. (2019). National identity and cross-border business focus of expatriates and host-country managers in the United Arab Emirates. *Academy of International Business (AIB) Annual Meeting.* Newcastle University.

Beattie, A. (2007). Learning from the Germans? History and Memory in German and European Discourses of Integration. *Portal,* 4(2). https://www.proquest.com/docview/sourcetype=Scholarly%20Journals

Beddoes-Jones, F. (2011). Authentic leadership: The 21st century imperative? Business Leadership Review, VIII(II), 1–6

Beekun, R. I., Hamdy, R., Westerman, J. W., & Hassabelnaby, H.R. (2008). An exploration of ethical decision-making processes in the United States and Egypt: JBE. *Journal of Business Ethics,* 82(3), 587-605. Doi: https://doi.org/10.1007/s10551-007-9578-y.

Bekhit, K. (2024) MS Teams interview. 22 April.

Belcourt, M., Bohlander, G. W., Snell, S., Morris, S., & Singh, P. (2017). *Managing human resources* (8th ed., pp. 102–103). Nelson Education.

Benjamin, A. (2002) Jews of the Dutch Caribbean. *Exploring Ethnic Identity on Curaçao.* Routledge.

Bennett, N., & Lemoine, G. J. (2014). What a difference a word makes: Understanding threats to performance in a VUCA world. *Business horizons,* 57(3), 311-317. https://doi.org/10.1016/j.bushor.2014.01.001

Bernardo, S., Anholon, R., Novaski, O., Da Silva, D., & Quelhas, O. L. G. (2017). Main causes that lead strategies to decline at execution phase: an analysis of Brazilian companies. *International Journal of Productivity and Performance Management,* 66(3), 424–440. https://doi.org/10.1108/2015-0126

Beukers et al. (2022). Romania. Cross Cultural Business Skills.

Bogodistov, Y. and Lizneva, A. (2017), "Ideological shift and employees' relationships: evidence from Ukraine", Baltic Journal of Management, Vol. 12 No. 1, pp. 25-45. https://doi.org/10.1108/BJM-11-2015-0220

Bosque, M. M., & Perera, J. B. (2021). Facing challenges: a multidisciplinary overview of Gibraltar through its past, present and post-Brexit future. The Round Table, 110(3), 317–319. https://doi.org/10.1080/00358533.2021.1933084

Bourgon, J. (2024, January 15). CSPS Virtual Café Series - leadership reflections with Jocelyne Bourgon.

Brandao,A. (2024). Microsoft Teams Interview. 12 April

Brandes, L., & Darai, D. (2014). The value of top-down communication for organizational performance. ECON Working Papers 157, Department of Economics - University of Zurich.

Brian, K., & Lewis, D. (2004). Exploring leadership preferences in multicultural workgroups: an Australian Case Study. Leadership & Organisation Development Journal, 25(3), 263–278. https://doi.org/10.1108/01437730410531065

Brodbeck, F., & Frese, M. (2007). Societal Culture and Leadership in Germany. In R. House, J. Chhokar, & F. Brodbeck (Eds.), Culture and leadership across the world: the GLOBE book of in-depth studies of 25 societies (pp. 181–248). Routledge.

Brodbeck, F., Frese, M., & Javidan, M. (2002). Leadership made in Germany: Low on compassion, high on performance. Academy of Management Executive, 16, 16–29. https://doi.org/10.5465/AME.2002.6640111

Broek, A. (2005) 'De buigzame waardering voor cultureel erfgoed: de Nanzivertellingen', Kristòf, jrg. XIII, nr. 2, pp. 1-19

Broek, A. (2017). Down with closed systems: The appropriation of the Caribbean as a borderless enclave. In N. Faraclas, R. Severing, C. Weijer, E. Echteld, W. Rutgers, & 62 Cooper, "What we can learn from Curaçao" R. Dupey (Eds.), Archaeologies of Erasures and Silences (pp. 243–260). Willemstad, Curaçao: University of Curaçao.

Brooks, E. & Peters, I. [Institute of Business Ethics]. (2023, December 12). Good Leadership in UK Business [Video]. YouTube. https://www.youtube.com/watch?v=wB94SXFMLM8

Brooks, E., Park, R., Revell, R., Oxford Character Project, Briggs, M., David, E., Watson, L., Brown, S., Hartland, S., Gosling, J., Hope Hailey, V., Forward Institute, & John Templeton Foundation. (2022). UK Business Values Survey: The Oxford Character Project. https://oxfordcharacter.org/uploads/files/UK-Business-Values-Survey-2022.pdf

Bursens, P., De Landtsheer, C., Braeckmans, L., & Segaert, B. (2016). Political personality and complex decision-making: the psychological profile and leadership style of Angela Merkel, the world's most powerful woman. In Complex Political Decision-Making. Taylor & Francis.

Business School 101. (2022, 4 May). German Business Culture and Etiquette | International Management | From A Business Professor [Video]. YouTube. https://www.youtube.com/watch?v=PwKtEa9p4u4

Camilleri, J. A. (2007). Australia's unique future: Reconciling place, history, and culture. Direct Science. Retrieved March 31, 2024, from https://www.sciencedirect.com/science/article/pii/S0016328706000048

Canuto, O., Cavallari, M., & Reis, J. G. (2013). Brazilian exports: climbing down a competitiveness cliff. ResearchGate. https://www.researchgate.net/publication/234060408_Brazilian_Exports_Climbing_Down_a_Com petitiveness_Cliff

Casado, R. (2018). The "hero-leader": a case of leadership in Brazil. Leadership & Organization Development Journal, 39(4), 495–506. https://doi.org/10.1108/lodj-05-2017-0145

Catana, A., & Catana, D. (1996). Aspects of transformation of corporate cultures in Romania. In Wandel von Untcrnehmenskulturen in Ostdeutschland und Osteuropa (pp. 195–208). Rainer Hampp Verlag.

Cavazotte, F., Hartman, N. S., & Bahiense, E. (2014). Charismatic leadership, citizenship behaviors, and power distance orientation: Comparing Brazilian and US workers. Cross-Cultural Research, 48(1), 3-31.

Cavazotte, F., Moreno, V., & Bernardo, J. (2013). Transformational leaders and work performance: the mediating roles of identification and self-efficacy. Bar. *Brazilian Administration Review*, 10(4), 490–512. https://doi.org/10.1590/s1807-76922013000400007

CCBS Survey. (2015-2020). Worldwide Leadership Survey. In *SurveyMonkey online: Amsterdam University of Applied Sciences.*

CCBS Survey. (2024). Worldwide Leadership Survey. In *Qualtrics online: Amsterdam University of Applied Sciences.*

Chambers, R. (2024, March 5). Dr Richard Chambers on LinkedIn: Really great to spend time chatting recently with Jacob Feenstra.

Chandhoke, N., Priyadarshi, P., & Chandhoke, N. (2009). *Contemporary India: economy, society, politics.* Longman.

Chandra, B., & Mahajan, S. (2006). *Composite Culture in a Multicultural Society*. Pearson.

Chapagain, Bal. (2008). Management Views on Corporate Social Responsibility in Commercial Banks of Nepal. *Socioeconomic Development Panorama*, 1(3), pp. 119-129.

Chattopadhyay, G. P. (1999). A fresh look at authority and organisation: towards a spiritual approach for managing illusion. *Group Relations, Management and Organization*, 112-126.

Chernyshova, I. (2024). Zoom Interview. 26 April.

Cheryl de la Rey. (2005). Gender, Women and Leadership. Agenda: *Empowering Women for Gender Equity*, 65, 4–11. http://www.jstor.org/stable/4066646

Chhokar, J. S., Brodbeck, F. C., & House, R. J. (2007). *Culture and leadership across the world: the GLOBE book of in-depth studies of 25 societies* (pp. 181–248). Routledge.

Chirillo, G. (2019b, September). *Gender Analysis of Ukraine's electoral and political process*. IFES Ukraine. https://ifesukraine.org/wp-content/uploads/2019/10/IFES-Gender-Assessment-Ukraine-v1-2019-09-30-Eng.pdf

Chlap, N., & Brown, R. (2022). Relationships between workplace characteristics, psychological stress, affective distress, burnout and empathy in lawyers. *International Journal of the Legal Profession*, 29(2), 159-180.

Chopra, T. (2024). MS Teams interview. 25 April.

Clark, M. A., Robertson, M. M., & Young, S. (2019). "I feel your pain": A critical review of organizational research on empathy. *Journal of Organizational Behavior*, 40(2), 166-192.

Clem, A. H., & Mujtaba, B. G. (2011). Focus Factors: Exploring Cross-Cultural Business Dynamics Of Making Deals And Building Relationships In India. *Journal of Business Case Studies*, 7(1), 81-. https://doi.org/10.19030/jbcs.v7i1.1585

Cole, M. S., & Bruch, H. (2006). Organizational identity strength, identification, and commitment and their relationships to turnover intention: does organizational hierarchy matter? *Journal Of Organizational Behavior*, 27(5), 585–605. https://doi.org/10.1002/job.378

Collante, A. J., & Flores, M. V. (2018). Los estilos de liderazgo y su influencia en la organización: Estudio de casos en el Campo de Gibraltar. Gestión Joven, 18, 13. https://dialnet.unirioja.es/servlet/articulo?codigo=6448202

Conger, J.A., Kanungo, R.N. and Menon, S.T. (2000), Charismatic leadership and follower effects. *Journal of Organizational Behavior*, 21: 747-767.

Correia, G., & Rodrigues, J. N. (2004, April 1). *Mestres Portugueses da Gestão*. Wook. https://www.wook.pt/livro/mestres-portugueses-da-gestao-geraldine-correia/108824

Cotrim, J.M. (2024). MS Teams interview. 26 April

Country comparison tool. (n.d.). https://www.hofstede-insights.com/country-comparison-tool?countries=brazil%2Cjapan%2Cnetherlands

Couros, G. [@gcouros]. (20 April 2022) From today's post at georgecourois.ca: "want to be a fantastic leader? Lift others. Make them better. [Photo] Instagram. https://www.instagram.com/gcouros/

Couros, G. [@George Couros]. (April 2024) "Don't wait for someone to recognize your strength and passion. Show them. Tell them. [Photo] LinkedIn. https://www.linkedin.com/in/georgecourosim/

Crăciun, L., Năstase, M., Stamule, T., & Vizitiu, C. (2015). Leadership in Romanian small to medium enterprises. *Sustainability*, 7(4), 4183–4198. https://doi.org/10.3390/su7044183

Crawley-Low, J. (2013). The Impact of Leadership Development on the Organizational Culture of a Canadian

Cret, V., & Pantea, D. M. (2008). The Currency and the Money. AGORA *International Journal of Juridical Science.*, 2, 99.

Croes, R. R., Semrad, K. J., & Rivera, M. A. (n.d.). *Curacao: Building on the Power of the Past.* STARS. https://stars.library.ucf.edu/dickpope-pubs/38/

Da Rocha Weishaupt Proni, T. T., & Proni, M. W. (2018). Discriminação de gênero em grandes empresas no Brasil. *Revista Estudos Feministas*, 26(1). https://doi.org/10.1590/1806-9584.2018v26n141780

Da Silva, A. D. S. (2016). Liderança transacional e transformacional: *um estudo de caso em uma instituição pública no interior do Paraná.* RIUT. https://riut.utfpr.edu.br/jspui/handle/1/21274

Da Silva, V. L., Uller, C. M., Santos, J. D. D., & Rezende, F. A. (2017). ANÁLISE DA MOTIVAÇÃO DE PESSOAS: *um estudo baseado em princípios da Hierarquia de Necessidades de Maslow.* Foco, 10(2), 148. https://doi.org/10.28950/1981-223x_revistafocoadm/2017.v10i2.365

Dajani, M. (2015). The Impact of Employee Engagement on Job Performance and Organisational Commitment in the Egyptian Banking Sector. Journal of Business and Management Sciences, 3(5) 138-147.doi: 10.12691/jbms-3-5-1.

Dalhuisen, L., & Donk, R. (2019). *Geschiedenis van de Antillen.* Walburg Pers.

Dalton, K., & Kennedy, L. (2007). Management culture in Romania: Patterns of change and resistance. *Journal of East European Management Studies*, 12(3), 232–259. http://www.jstor.org/stable/23280974

Dan, P., & Elena, T. C. (2014). The Employees' Opinion About Top Management at the Berlin Ltd. Distribution. *Social Science Research Network.* https://doi.org/10.2139/ssrn.2433500

Dana, L. P. (2002). Entrepreneurship and public policy in Gibraltar. International Journal Of Entrepreneurship And Innovation Management, 2(1), 38. https://doi.org/10.1504/ijeim.2002.000473

Dantzer, M. R. (2000). *Leadership requirements in the 21st century: The perceptions of Canadian public sector*

Darrah, P. (2023, 22 April). What is the language of Nepal? GVI. https://www.gvi.co.uk/blog/smb-what-is-the-language-of-nepal/

Das Neves, J. G. (2001). *Clima Organizacional, Cultura Organizacional e Gestão de Recursos Humanos* (2nd ed.). Editora RH. https://www.editorarh.pt/clima-organizacional-cultura-organizacional-e-gestao-de-recursos-humanos

Dastmalchian, A., Lee, S., & Ng, I. (2000). The interplay between organizational and national cultures: a comparison of organizational practices in Canada and South Korea using the Competing Values Framework. *International Journal of Human Resource Management*, 11(2), 388-412.

Davis, P. J., Frolova, Y., & Callahan, W. (2016). Workplace diversity management in Australia: What do managers think and what are organisations doing? *Equality, Diversity and Inclusion: An International Journal*, 35(2), 81-98.

De Bruin, A., & Johnson, L. (2021). *Strategic Management in the Caribbean.* Elsevier.

De Haas, F. (2011, July 8). Makamba!: Heden en verleden van een omstreden 'Antilliaans' begrip. https://werkgroepcaraibischeletteren.nl/makamba/

De La Sota Riva Echánove, M., & Zainos García Cano, E. (2018). *Liderazgo basado en el personalismo: una propuesta de investigación.* Revista Empresa Y Humanismo, 21(2), 91-122. https://doi.org/10.15581/015.XXI.2.91-122

De Los Santos, A. (2023). *"¿Sabias que El liderazgo de Artigas fue fundamental para la Revolución en la BandaOriental en 1811? Mirá este material..."* [Post]. Linkedin. https://www.linkedin.com/posts/antoniodelossantos_antonio-de-los-santo-on-twitter-activity-7076766481115471872-oQxa?utm_source=share&utm_medium=member_desktop

189

De Oliveira Fonseca, A. M., Porto, J. B., & Barroso, A. C. (2012). *O efeito de valores pessoais nas atitudes perante estilos de liderança. RAM. Revista De Administração Mackenzie*, 13(3), 122–149. https://doi.org/10.1590/s1678-69712012000300007

De Souza Pires, J. C., & Macêdo, K. B. (2006b). Cultura organizacional em organizações públicas no Brasil. *Revista De Administração Pública*, 40(1), 81–104. https://doi.org/10.1590/s0034-76122006000100005

De Souza, M. J. C., & Dourado, D. C. P. (2016). ESTILO DE LIDERANÇA: o CASO DE UMA EMPRESA DE SERVIÇOS. *Revista Eletrônica Do Mestrado Profissional Em Administração Da UnP*, 8(2), 34–47. https://doi.org/10.21714/raunp.v8i2.1108

De Souza, V. A. (2021). Setor bancário no Brasil - *impactos do perfil de liderança nos resultados dos liderados. https://repositorio.faculdadearidesa.edu.br/handle/hs826/147*

Deliu, D. (2019). Empathetic Leadership – Key Element for Inspiring Strategic Management and a Visionary Effective Corporate Governance. *Journal of Emerging Trends in Marketing and Management*, 1(1), 280-292.

Deng, L., & Gibson, P. (2008). A qualitative evaluation on the role of cultural intelligence in cross-cultural leadership effectiveness. *International Journal of Leadership Studies*, 3(2), 181-197.

Dias, M. A., & Borges, R. (2015). Estilos de liderança e desempenho de equipes no setor público. *REAd*, 21(1), 200–221. https://doi.org/10.1590/1413-2311.0542014.53468

Diaz, P. P. B. (2011). *Cross-Cultural influences on management practices: It's impact on distribution of power, leadership, and communication. A comparative study between the Dominican Republic and the United States.* ScholarWorks at WMU. https://scholarworks.wmich.edu/honors_theses/739/

Dumont, L. (1980). *Homo hierarchicus: The caste system and its implications* (Revised ed.). University of Chicago Press.

Eakin, M. C. (1997). Brazil: the once and future country. https://ci.nii.ac.jp/ncid/BA50061747

Ebert-Steinhübel, A. (2024). Microsoft Teams Interview. 26 April.

Egyptian Banking Institute (EBI). (2024, 14 March). *Panel 3 - Human Centered Leadership in HR and L&D* [Video]. YouTube. https://www.youtube.com/watch?v=EZ6JC9nWQSk

El Dia RD. (2023, May 29). *#ElDia / Entrevista a Raúl Burgos, Conferencista, empresario y experto en liderazgo / 29 mayo 2023* [Video]. YouTube. https://www.youtube.com/watch?v=ICx31E_hhA8

El Sokary, R. (2024) MS Teams interview. 25 April.

El-Fekhi, I. (2011). *The Magic of Leadership.* Sama For Publishing & Distribution. ISBN 9789776451155

ElKelish, W. W., & Hassan, M. K. (2014). Organizational culture and corporate risk disclosure. *International Journal of Commerce and Management*, 24(4), 279–299.

El-Kot, G., & Burke, R. J. (2014). The Islamic work ethic among employees in Egypt. *International Journal of Islamic and Middle Eastern Finance and Management*, 7(2), 228-235. Doi: https://doi.org/10.1108/IMEFM-09-2013-0103.

El-Kot, G., & Leat, M. (2008). Employees' perceptions of supervisory facets: An investigation within an Egyptian context. *International Journal of Islamic and Middle Eastern Finance and Management*, 1(2), 149-165. Doi: https://doi.org/10.1108/17538390810880991.

Ellis, E. & Smith, S. [WSP in the UK]. (2019, June 17). *What is the future of leadership?* [Video]. YouTube. https://youtu.be/Owqt8mh1YE8?si=NNpuOBKEZw7Huhwg

El-Nahas, T., Abd-El-Salam, E. M., & Shawky, A. Y. (2013). The impact of leadership behaviour and organisational culture on job satisfaction and its relationship among organisational commitment and turnover intentions. A case study on an Egyptian company. Journal of Business and Retail Management Research, 7(2).

El-Zayaty, N. (2018). An Exploration of Leadership Styles and Motivation in Egyptian Business Organizations. International Journal of Business and Applied Social Science, 4(2) SRN: https://ssrn.com/abstract=3130641.

Entrada. (2023, March 29). The People of the Dominican Republic: Celebrating diversity and rich cultural heritage - Welcome to the Entrada Local Stays. Welcome to the Entrada Local Stays.

Erika Linhares. (2020, March 23). #SEGUNDOU: Ep 45 - Por que temos poucas mulheres em cargos de Liderança? | Erika Linhares [Video]. YouTube. https://www.youtube.com/watch?v=ScCIONd3uAo

Esta Noche Mariasela. (2023, July 25). Dominicana se Transforma, una iniciativa de Raul Burgos y la fundación de Liderazgo John C. Maxwell [Video]. https://www.youtube.com/watch?v=Ap0eu2UgH0c

Evason, N., (2017). Nepalese Culture. The Cultural Atlas. https://culturalatlas.sbs.com.au/nepalese-culture

Feetham KC, N., Llamas, N., Akad, S., & Matthews, D. (2023, September 29). Gibraltar Business Winter / Spring 2023 - Gibraltar Business. Gibraltar Business Magazine, pp. 30–32.

Feliz, P. M., & Contreras, J. J. (2021). Impacto de la inteligencia emocional en el liderazgo durante la pandemia covid-19 en supervisores de la empresa grupo laugama, periodo abril-julio 2021, distrito nacional, república dominicana. [thesis, universidad nacional pedro henríquez ureña].

Feller, T., & Mercel-Sanca, A. (2021). Nepal - Culture smart!: The Essential Guide to Customs & Culture. Kuperard.

Fernando. (2024, March 26). Sobre "Las 12 preguntas" GESTION. https://gestion.com.do/

Ferreira, J. A. A. (2007). Concepções de Liderança Excepcional em Portugal: Um Estudo Exploratório. Proquest. https://www.proquest.com/openview/2867ed6980be9edc249e595105c190d8/1?cbl=2026366&dis s=y&pq-origsite=gscholar

Figueiredo, S., Costa, J. A., & Castanheira, P. (2013). Liderança Educacional em Portugal: metanálise sobre produção científica. https://repositorio.ual.pt/handle/11144/3495

Fiona D. (2024, April 11). Leadership and Hierarchy in UK [Personal Interview]. V. Milosteanu (interviewer).

Flores, E. R., & Flores, M. V. (2016). La Gestión de la diversidad en las organizaciones: Estudio de casos en el Campo de Gibraltar, 15, 10.https://dialnet.unirioja.es/servlet/articulo?codigo=6433766

Forbes Middle East (2022) She's Next: Spotlighting Women Entrepreneurs in the Middle East https://www.facebook.com/forbes.ME.page/videos/?rdid=AW2RUw9m5cdF34QR

Forbes Ukraine. (2024, January 9). Як зварити лідерство як пиво? Олег Хайдакін [Video]. Youtube. https://www.youtube.com/watch?v=Zn3-x9PzQdc&ab_channel=ForbesUkraine

Forbes. (2022, June 11). Entrepreneurship During Wartime: Building A Business In Ukraine [Video]. Youtube. https://www.youtube.com/watch?v=HxC1WhHLtFA&ab_channel=Forbes

Frances, H. (2002). Canada's contribution to the "management" of ethno-cultural diversity [CIRCLE-CCRN round table 2000]. Canadian Journal of Communication, 27(2), 231-242. doi:https://doi.org/10.22230/cjc.2002v27n2a1297

Franken, E., Plimmer, G., & Malinen, S. (2019). Paradoxical leadership in public sector organisations: Its role in fostering employee resilience. Australian Journal of Public Administration, 79(1), 93–110. https://doi.org/10.1111/1467-8500.12396

Frunza, G. (2022). Exercitarea leadershipului eficient în entitatea sportivă. Sport. Olimpism. Sănătate: Congresul Ştiinţific Internaţional. https://doi.org/10.52449/soh22.17

Führung auf den Punkt gebracht mit Bernd Geropp. (2024, January 28). fpg319 – Neues in 2024: Backstage Geropp Leadership GmbH [Video]. YouTube. https://www.youtube.com/watch?v=BgdnGoKG2_g

Fuxman, L. (2004). Emerging trends in Ukrainian management styles and the challenge of managerial talent shortage. International Journal Of Commerce And Management, 14(1), 28–43. https://doi.org/10.1108/10569210480000172

Gahan, P. (2016, June 1). Survey of Australian Business Reveals Failure in Leadership - Peter Gahan [Video file]. YouTube. https://www.youtube.com/watch?v=pj3HLTchZG0

Gahan, P., Adamovic, M., Bevitt, A., Harley, B., Healy, J., Olsen, J. E., & Theilacker, M. (2016). Leadership at Work: Do Australian leaders have what it takes. Centre for Workplace Leadership, The University of Melbourne

García, E., & Van Der Voort, H. (2020). *Multilingualism and Effective Communication in the Caribbean*. Kingston: University Press.

Garcia, M. (2021). Building community resilience through leadership empathy: Lessons from Gibraltar. Community Development Journal, 18(4), 567-582.

Gerety Awards. (2024). *Gerety Talks: UAE Creative Leaders 2024* [Video]. YouTube. https://www.youtube.com/watch?v=UYsRfsXQROg

Gibraltar Government. (2023). Annual Report: Promoting transparency and community engagement.

Givens, R. J. (2008). Transformational leadership: the impact on organizational and personal outcomes. In Emerging Leadership Journeys (Vols. 1–1, pp. 4–24). School of Global Leadership

Global Australia. (n.d.). Why Australia - Global connections. *Global Australia*. Retrieved March 1, 2024, from https://www.globalaustralia.gov.au/why-australia/global-connections

Global Leadership Network Canada [@GLNCanada]. (2024, May 8). https://twitter.com/GLNCanada/

Global Leadership Network Canada. (n.d.). Global Leadership Network. Retrieved May 13, 2024, from https://globalleadershipnetwork.ca/

Goede, M. (2004). *Leiderschap op Curacao 2004*. ResearchGate. Goede, M. (2005). Groei en fragmentatie van de overheid op de Nederlandse Antillen en Curaçao. ResearchGate. https://www.researchgate.net/publication/241885611_Groei_en_fragmentatie_van_de_overheid_op_de_Nederlandse_Antillen_en_Curacao

Goede, M. (2009). Can curaçao become a creative economy? A case study.*International Journal of Social Economics*, 36(1), 47-69. doi: https://doi.org/10.1108/03068290910921181

Goede, M. (2011). The dynamics of organizational change in small developing islands: the case of curaçao. *Caribbean Studies*, 39(1/2), 139–167.

Goede, M. (2015). Small and Medium Enterprises in Curaçao: What is the policy? *Journal of Business and Economics*, 6(7), 1306—1312. https://doi.org/10.15341/jbe(2155-7950)/07.06.2015/008

Goede, M. (2022). Liever vergiffenis schenken dan op excuses wachten.

Goede, M. (2022, May 31). *30 mei 1969 – 30 mei 2022*. https://www.linkedin.com/pulse/30-mei-1969-2022-miguel-goede/

Goede, M. (2024) MS Teams interview. 26 April.

Gomółka, K., & Flisikowski, K. (2016). Economic Annals-XXI. Ekonomìčnij časopis-XXI. https://doi.org/10.21003/ea

Gonzaga, A. R., & Monteiro, J. K. (2011). Emotional intelligence and quality of life in brazilian managers. *Avaliação Psicológica*, 10(2), 117-127.

González, C. E. (2018). The emergence of Papiamentu: A case of language contact in the Portuguese Atlantic. Amsterdam: John Benjamins Publishing Company.Van der Maas, A. A. (?). Strategy Implementation in a Small Island Community: An Integrative Framework. [?], page 73-84

Gonzalez, L. E. (2014). *Management, Leadership and Entrepreneurship in Latin America.: The New Land of Opportunity - the Real Leaders in the Global Economy*. Author House.

Government of Canada, S. C. (2017, November 15). *Illustrated Glossary - Province or territory*. www150.Statcan.gc.ca. https://www150.statcan.gc.ca/geo/prov/prov-eng.htm

Government of Canada. (2019, November 26). Statistics on official languages in Canada.

Gray, L. E. (2013). *Fado resounding: affective politics and urban life*. Duke University Press.

Greer, I. (2008). Organised industrial relations in the information economy: the German automotive sector as a test case. *New Technology, Work and Employment*, 23(3), 181–196. https://doi.org/10.1111/j.1468-005x.2008.00212.x

Gurubaa. (2022, 6 June). Leading || Chapter 5 || Business Studies Class 12 in Nepali || NEB - Gurubaa [Video]. YouTube. https://www.youtube.com/watch?v=NSzV6Nbihoc

Hamid Yaryura. (2023, April 10). *EP#131: Las 12 Preguntas ft. Ney Diaz* [Video]. YouTube. https://www.youtube.com/watch?v=1TyRjAMIP3s

Hartney, E., Melis, E., Taylor, D., Dickson, G., Tholl, B., Grimes, K., Chan, M.-K., Van Aerde, J., & Horsley, T. (2022). Leading through the first wave of COVID: a Canadian action research study. *Leadership in Health Services* (2007), 35(1), 30–45. https://doi.org/10.1108/LHS-05-2021-0042

Hawass, H.H. (2015). Ethical leadership and job insecurity: Exploring interrelationships in the Egyptian public sector. *International Journal of Commerce and Management, 25*(4), 557-581. Doi: https://doi.org/10.1108/IJCoMA-02-2013-0015.

Hawass, H.H. (2017). Employee feedback orientation: A paternalistic leadership perspective: *MRN. Management Research Review*, 40(12), 1238-1260. https://www.proquest.com/scholarly-journals/employee-feedback-orientation-paternalistic/docview/1968401291/se-2.

Hease, M. (2023, December 23) Martin Haese, Serial Entrepreneur on Mastering Leadership and Entrepreneurship [Video file]. *YouTube.* https://www.youtube.com/watch?v=Czp351LPExI

Heijes, C. (2010). Cross-cultural perception and power dynamics across changing organizational and national contexts: Curaçao and the Netherlands. *Human Relations*, 64(5), 653–674. doi:10.1177/0018726710386394

Heinrichs, K., & Sonnabend, H. (2022). Leaky pipeline or glass ceiling? Empirical evidence from the German academic career ladder. *Applied Economics Letters*, 30(9), 1189–1193. https://doi.org/10.1080/13504851.2022.2041168

Heiß, M., Stoeckl, S., & Hausknotz, C. (2004). The bottom-up/top-down pattern: an organizational pattern for a balanced management system. 2004 IEEE International Engineering Management Conference. https://doi.org/10.1109/iemc.2004.1407127

Hejkrlík, J., Chaloupková, P., & Sokolska, T. (2021). The role of transformational leadership and leaders' skills for new agricultural cooperatives in post-soviet countries. Annals Of Public And Co-operative Economy, 94(1), 109–129. https://doi.org/10.1111/apce.12353

Helgesen, S. (2005). The web of inclusion: Architecture for building great organizations. Beard Books.

Helms, L., Van Esch, F., & Crawford, B. (2018). Merkel III: From Committed Pragmatist to "Conviction Leader"? *German Politics*, 28(3), 350–370. https://doi.org/10.1080/09644008.2018.1462340

Henein, A., & Morissette, F. (2007). *Made in Canada leadership wisdom from the nation's best and brightest on leadership practice and development* (1st ed.). Jossey-Bass.

Herzog-Stein, A., Lindner, F., Sturn, S., & Till van Treeck. (2010). Vom Krisenherd zum Wunderwerk? Der deutsche Arbeitsmarkt im Wandel. *EconPapers*, 56(2010).

Heussinger, W. H., Görner, H., Wilk, R.-D., & Quandt, H.-P. (2020). *Freimaurer in Deutschland zwischen den Weltkriegen*. FinanzBuch Verlag.

Hill, C. E., Loch, K. D., Straub, D. W., & El-Sheshai, K. (1998). A qualitative assessment of Arab culture and information technology transfer. *Journal of Global Information Management*, 6(3), 29–38.

Hofstede Insights (2024). Country comparison tool. https://www.hofstede-insights.com/

Hofstede, G. (1985). The interaction between national and organizational value systems. *Journal of Management Studies*, 22(4), 347–357.

Hofstede, G., Hofstede, G. J., & Minkov, M. (2010). *Cultures and Organizations, Software of the mind. Intercultural Cooperation and Its Importance for survival*.

Holst, E., & Kirsch, A. (2014). Executive board and supervisory board members in Germany's large corporations remain predominantly male. In German Institute for Economic Research (DIW Berlin), *DIW Economic Bulletin* (pp. 35–47): https://www.econstor.eu/bitstream/10419/106808/1/81713512X.pdf

House, R. J. (2004). *Culture, leadership, and organizations: the GLOBE study of 62 societies*. Sage Publications.

House, R. J., Dorfman, P. W., Javidan, M., Hanges, P. J., & De Luque, M. F. S. (2014). *Strategic Leadership across Cultures: The GLOBE Study of CEO Leadership Behavior and Effectiveness in 24 Countries*. https://doi.org/10.4135/9781506374581

Hughes, M., Patterson, L., & Terrell, J. (2005) *Emotional Intelligence in Action: Training and Coaching Activities for Leaders and Managers*. USA: John Wiley & Sons.

Hurduzeu, R.E. (2015). Culture And Leadership: The Case Of Romania. *The Romanian Economic Journal*, 124-131.

Huţu, C. A. (2010). Leading the change for quality enhancement: a Romanian cultural perspective. *International Journal of Leadership Studies*, 5(3), 305-316.

Iacob, D., & Dumitrescu, V. M. (2012). Cultural awareness, sensitivity, and competence: basic requirements for business success in Nepal and South Africa. *Synergy, 8*.

Ignat, S. (2024). Microsoft Teams Interview. 9 May.

Impulsa Tu Liderazgo RD [@impulsa.rd]. (2024, May 2). *"En el viaje del liderazgo, hay una elección fundamental: ¿quieres acumular seguidores o prefieres sembrar semillas de liderazgo en…"*. Instagram.

Jacobs, B. (2012). *Origins of a Creole: The History of Papiamentu and Its African Ties*. de Gruyter.

Jallad, R. (2024). *Visionary leadership: Harnessing opportunities in the UAE'S dynamic economic environment*. LinkedIn: https://www.linkedin.com/pulse/visionary-leadership-harnessing-opportunities-uaes-dynamic-economic-qqtbf/

James, G. (2011). *Introduction to Dominican Republic*. Gilad James Mystery School.

Javidan, M., & Carl, D. E. (2005). Leadership Across Cultures: A Study of Canadian and Taiwanese Executives. *MIR: Management International Review*, 45(1), 23–44. http://www.jstor.org/stable/40836038

Javidan, M., Dorfman, P. W., De Luque, M. S., & House, R. J. (2016). In the eye of the beholder: Cross-cultural lessons in leadership from Project GLOBE. In *Readings and cases in international human resource management* (pp. 119-154). Routledge.

Jit, R., Sharma, C. S., & Kawatra, M. (2017). Healing a broken spirit: Role of servant leadership. Journal for Decision Makers, 42(2), 80-94.

Johnson, B. (2024, May 6). Brad Johnson on LinkedIn: 53% of women say they're lonely at work and it only gets worse the higher. . . |. https://www.linkedin.com/posts/wbradjohnson_53-of-women-say-theyre-lonely-at-work-and-activity-7193285998800183297-I873?utm_source=share&utm_medium=member_desktop

Jones, A. (2019). The Tuckman's model implementation, effect, and analysis & the new development of Jones LSI model on a small group. *Journal of management*, 6(4), 23-28. ssrn.com/abstract=3525281

Jones, R. (2020). Inclusive decision-making: Strategies for leadership. Leadership Quarterly, 12(3), 221-237.

Jurd, N. (2020). The leadership book: A step by step guide to excellent leadership. Mr. Gresty. Kingston University London. (2022). UK culture: lifestyle, higher education, food and traditions. https://www.kingstonisc.com/blog/uk-culture

Kamel, A. (2017). *Impact of leadership styles on employees' job satisfaction and employees' intention to quit in not-for-profit organizations in Egypt*. [Master's Thesis, the American University in Cairo]. *AUC Knowledge Fountain*. https://fount.aucegypt.edu/etds/649

Kampf, R., Hitka, M., & Ližbětinová, L. (2018). Direction of the Corporate Culture in Slovak and German Transport Companies from a Top Managers' Perspective. *Periodica Polytechnica Transportation Engineering*, 47(3), 213–219. https://doi.org/10.3311/pptr.11166

Karki, A., & Maharjan, P. (2022). Factors Influencing Transactional Leadership in Commercial Banks of Nepal. *Journal Of Business And Social Sciences Research*, 7(1), 73–81. https://doi.org/10.3126/jbssr.v7i1.47685

Kaur, N., & Sandhu, A. (2019). The Effect of Organizational Hierarchy on Fulfilment of Employee Needs in an Indian Organization. *Int J Res Eng IT Soc Sci*, 9(4), 278-285.

Kavalchuck, A. (2024). Microsoft Teams interview. 12 April.

Kemp, L. J., Madsen, S. R., & El-Saidi, M. (2013). The current state of female leadership in the United Arab Emirates. *Journal of Global Responsibility*, 4(1), 99–112.

Keneally, T., & Petty, B. (2023, January 4). Federation. *National Museum of Australia*. Retrieved February 29, 2024, from https://www.nma.gov.au/defining-moments/resources/federation

Kenneth Castiel. (n.d.). http://www.kennethcastiel.com/

Keogh, A. (2023, December 8). Allan Keogh on LinkedIn: Wonderful to see our CEO making a difference as a Champion and a Mentor.

Kernaghan, D. (2024) Zoom Interview. 15 April.

Kliuchnikov, A. (2014). A Cross-Cultural Study of Effective Leadership Attributes in Ukraine and Russia. In ProQuest (Nr. 978-1-321-16957–7). ProQuest. https://www.proquest.com/dissertations-theses/cross-cultural-study-effective-leadership/docview/1562749233/se-2?accountid=130632

Koles, B., Kondath, B. (2015). Organizational climate in Hungary, Portugal, and India: a cultural perspective. *AI & Society* 30, 251–259 (2015). https://doi.org/10.1007/s00146-013-0507-6

Koot, W., and Ringeling, A. (1984). *De Antilleanen (the Antilleans)*. Muiderberg

Korpodeko. (2022a, August 12). *What's Up Business - Ep. 10 'Small Business, Big Leadership with Carla Hueck Martina* [Video]. YouTube. https://www.youtube.com/watch?v=9u8iXcnZHIM

Korpodeko. (2022b, June 22). *What's Up Business - Ep. 7 'Personal Growth is Business Growth' with Narayana "Naya" Camelia* [Video]. YouTube. https://www.youtube.com/watch?v=XPOKPb_YCUU

Kothari, R. (1970). *Caste in Indian politics*. Orient Longman.

Kukah, A.S., Akomea-Frimpong, I., Jin, X. and Osei-Kyei, R. (2021), "Emotional intelligence (EI) research in the construction industry: a review and future directions". *Engineering, Construction and Architectural Management*, 29, 4267–4286.

Kumar, V., & Sharma, R. (2018). Leadership styles and their relationship with TQM focus for Indian firms. The International Journal of Productivity And Performance Management, *International Journal Of Productivity And Performance* Management, 67(6), 1063–1088. https://doi.org/10.1108/ijppm-03-2017-0071

Lambert, S., Dimitriadis, N., Taylor, M., & Venerucci, M. (2021). Understanding emotional empathy at postgraduate business programs: What does the use of EEG reveal for future leaders? *Higher Education, Skills and Work-Based Learning*, 11(5), 1180-1191. https://doi.org/10.1108/HESWBL-09-2020-0218

Larsen, B. (2003). German organization and leadership theory—stable trends and flexible adaptation. *Scandinavian Journal Of Management*, 19(1), 103–133. https://doi.org/10.1016/s0956-5221(01)00034-3

Las 12 Preguntas. (n.d.). Cuesta Libros. https://www.cuestalibros.com/5056250940

LATAM Republic. (2024, 23 January). Juan Luis Bosch Gutiérrez: A Leader's Journey in Regional Growth. https://www.latamrepublic.com/juan-luis-bosch-gutierrez-a-leaders-journey-in-regional-growht/

Lawani, K., Abad, L. a. A., Craig, N., Hare, B., & Cameron, I. (2022). Exploring emotional intelligence and conflict management styles in Dominican Republic construction industry. *Journal of Engineering, Design and Technology*. https://doi.org/10.1108/jedt-09-2021-0485

leaders. ProQuest Dissertations Publishing.

LeadershipSurvey2015-2020 (Cross Cultural Business Skills [CCBS]). (not published). [Dataset].

Lebrón Rolón, A. (2008). Cultural Impact on Management Styles: A cross-cultural study between Puerto Rico and Dominican Republic [Turabo University]. https://fae.uprrp.edu/quest/wp-content/uploads/sites/15/2018/09/070305.pdf

Linville, M., & Kliuchnikov, A. (2021). A Model for Understanding and Changing the Practice of Leadership in Ukraine. Business Ethics And Leadership, 5(4), 17–31. https://doi.org/10.21272/bel.5(4).17-31.2021

Lituchy, T.R., Galperin B.L. & Punnett, B.J. (2017). *Lead: Leadership effectiveness in Africa and the African Diaspora*. Springer. https://doi.org/10.1057/978-1-137-59121-0

Loh, J., Thorsteinsson, E., & Loi, N. M. (2019). Workplace incivility and work outcomes: cross-cultural comparison between Australian and Singaporean employees. *Asia Pacific Journal of Human Resources*, 59(2), 305–329. https://doi.org/10.1111/1744-7941.12233

Lopes, A. (2010). A cultura organizacional em Portugal: de dimensão oculta a principal activo intangível. *GestãO E Desenvolvimento (Viseu), 17–18*, 3–26. https://doi.org/10.7559/gestaoedesenvolvimento.2010.127

Loureiro, P., Nunes, P., Araújo, Â., & Polytechnic Institute of Cávado and Ave, Barcelos, Portugal. (2022). Emotional intelligence and performance in social economy Organisations: the Portuguese experience. *In Proceedings of the 18th European Conference on Management Leadership and Governance, ECMLG 2022* (p. 561).

Lutz Von Rosenstiel, Regnet, E., Domsch, M. E., & Fachverlag Für Wirtschafts- Und Steuerrecht Schäffer. (2020). Führung von Mitarbeitern: Handbuch für erfolgreiches Personalmanagement. Stuttgart Schäffer-Poeschel.

Malea, L. (2019). Romania's National Culture in Hofstede's dimensions through the Eurobarometer Standard 90 (2018). *Journal of Global Politics and Current Diplomacy, 7*(1), 5-20.

Maris, C(2013), *On the right to cultural identity in Curaçao*, Proceedings of the ECICC-conference St. Thomas 2012. - Vol. 1, pp 73-91. Willemstad, Curaçao: FPI, Fundashon pa Planifikashon di Idioma.

Martin, S. (2021, June 13). Sterling Martin on LinkedIn: #leadership #people #success #success #people #culture #like #socialmedia. . .. https://www.linkedin.com/posts/sterling-martin-55a99197

Martin, S. (2021, June 14). Sterling Martin on LinkedIn: #leadership #leadershipdevelopment #leaders #success #leader. . .. https://www.linkedin.com/posts/sterling-martin-55a99197_leadership-

Martinez, P. (2018). "Participative Leadership and Organizational Culture in the Caribbean." *Caribbean Journal of Management, 34*(1), 24-37.

Martz, D., & Semple, R. K. (1985). Hierarchical corporate decision-making structure within the Canadian urban system: the case of banking. *Urban Geography, 6*(4), 316–330. https://doi.org/0272-3638.6.4.316

Matira, K. M., & Awolusi, O. D. (2020). Leaders and Managers Styles towards Employee Centricity: A Study of Hospitality Industry in United Arab Emirates. *Information Management and Business Review, 12*(1(I)), 1–21.

Mayer, J.D. and Salovey, P. (1997), "What is emotional intelligence?", in Salovey, P. and Sluyter, D. (Eds), *Emotional Development and Emotional Intelligence: Educational Implications*, 1st ed., Basic Books (pp. 3-31).

McAdam, R., Keogh, W., Tigani, A. a. E., & Gardiner, P. (2013). An exploratory study of business excellence implementation in the United Arab Emirates (UAE) public sector. *International Journal of Quality and Reliability Management/International Journal of Quality Management, 30*(4), 426–445.

McCarthy, G. (2005). Leadership practices in German and UK organisations. *Journal of European Industrial Training, 29*(3), 217-234. https://doi.org/10.1108/03090590510591094

Meade, T. (2002). A brief history of Brazil. https://ci.nii.ac.jp/ncid/BB13237397

Mellão, N., & Mónico, L. D. S. M. (2013). The relation between emotional intelligence and psychological capital of employees. *International Journal of Developmental and Educational Psychology*, 545–550.

Mendonca, M. and Kanungo, R.N. (1996), "Impact of culture on performance management in developing countries". *International Journal of Manpower, 17*(4/5), pp. 65-75

Metcalfe, B., & Mimouni, F. (2011). *Leadership development in the Middle East*. Edward Elgar Publishing.

Meyer, E. (2020). *The Country Mapping Tool*. https://www.erinmeyer.com/tools/culture-map-premium.

Mifsud, N (2024). Microsoft Teams interview. 30 April

Mihai, L. (2024). Microsoft Teams interview. 9 May.

MindArchitect. (2023, Febuary 8). Cum s-a transformat leadershipul în România și ce inspiră liderii în 2022 în contrast cu 2011 [Video]. https://www.youtube.com/watch?_channel=MindArchitect

Mitra, D. (2020). An Analytical Study on Public Leadership Styles Influencing Organizational Effectiveness of Indian Public Sector Banks: Today and Tomorrow. *Journal Of Leadership Studies, 14*(1), 80–88. https://doi.org/10.1002/jls.21689

Mittal, D. (2024). Video Interview. 3 March.

Mohamed Kamal, A. (2023). *The effect of spiritual leadership on innovative behaviour: an applied study on employees of telecommunication companies in Egypt.* Mansoura University, Egypt: Raya Higher institute of management and foreign trade in new Damietta.

Mohammed, H., Abdulla, A., Albert, F. I., Mohamad, I., & Geraldine, D. M. (2023). The impact of leadership styles among UAE municipalities employees. *Global Business and Finance Review, 28*(4), 115–131.

Moise, A.-C., Arjona, R., Vankalck, S., Senczyszyn, Andrez, P., Tataj, D., Dalle, J.- M., & Romanainen, J. (2017). European Commission. *Start-ups, Scale-ups And Entrepreneurship in Romania.*

Molinaro, V. (2011, September 30). Workplace leadership. YouTube. https://www.youtube.com/watch?v=z0P1Dizm-80&ab_channel=CanadianHRReporter

Moll, J., & Kretzschmar, L. (2017). An investigation of the suitability of a Servant Leadership model for academic Group Leaders at German universities. *Journal Of Leadership Education, 16*(2), 166–182. https://doi.org/10.12806/v16/i2/t1

Montesino, M. U. (2002). *A descriptive study of some organizational-behavior dimensions at work in the Dominican Republic: implications for management development and training.* Human Resource Development International, 5(4), 393-409. DOI: 10.1080/13678860110059366. Retrieved from [tandfonline.com] (https://www.tandfonline.com/doi/abs/10.1080/13678860110059366)

Montesino, M. U. (2003). Leadership/Followership Similarities Between People in a Developed and a Developing Country: The Case of Dominicans in NYC and Dominicans on the Island. *Journal of Leadership & Organizational Studies, 10*(1), 82-92.

Moore, M. & Ramsay, G. (2021). United Kingdom: Economic challenges, market consolidation and increasing professional insecurity. In J. Trappel, & T. Tomaz (Eds.), *The Media for Democracy Monitor 2021: How leading news media survive digital transformation* (Vol. 1) (pp. 455–520). Nordicom, University of Gothenburg. https://doi.org/10.48335/9789188855404-10

Moreira, C. T., & Subtil, R. C. (2012). *Liderança em Portugal: Contributo para a identificação de traços distintivos.*

Moreira, C.O. (2018, November 28). Portugal as a tourism destination. *Mediterranée.* 130. https://doi.org/10.4000/mediterranee.10402

Moya Pons, F. (n.d.). Historia de la República Dominicana (2nd ed., Vols. 978-84-00-09240–5). https://books.google.fr/books?hl=nl&lr=&id=Wor3UqsHkToC&oi=fnd&pg=PA9&dq=la+rep%C3%BAblica+dominicana&ots=wkpWrDAlKV&sig=4ii7ZXEkVSZPb9CiXD1DEXuczLU&redir_esc=y#v=onepage&q=la%20rep%C3%BAblica%20dominicana&f=false

Muhka, S. (2018). Modern Ukrainian Corporate Culture. Biznes Inform, 12(491), 413–417. https://doaj.org/article/d93e22b6541548a393d597a5c0a158d7

Muică, C., & Turnock, D. (2008). 'Ţuică'in romania: the historical geography of rural distilling. *Review of Historical Geography & Toponomastics*, 3(5-6), 77-114.

Naik, S. D. (2015). Leadership Styles in India- An empirical Study of Indian Entrepreneurs/Leaders. USHUS *Journal of Business Management*, 14(2), 37–52. https://doi.org/10.12725/ujbm.31.3

Nataly Grace. (2022). Business Etiquette & Culture for Women in UAE. https://www.facebook.com/attynatalygarcia/videos/455914429643916/?rdid=zXiXEPIfkS2IOGPR

Nechita, R. (2020). Către leadership prin management: instrumente de management care inspiră.

Noaghea, C. I., Bălan, M., Marinas, C., & Igreţ, R. Ş. (2017). How Romanian leaders take charge and develop their teams. *Proceedings of the International Management Conference*, 11(1), 794–801. https://ideas.repec.org/a/rom/mancon/v11y2017i1p794-801.html

Nsu. (n.d.). An analysis of global leadership competencies in action in the Dominican Republic. NSU. https://www.nova.edu/academic-affairs/faculty-research-grant/winners1415/analysis-of-global-leadership-dominican-republic.html

O'Leary, K. [@kevinolearytv]. (2023, December 30th). The definition of leadership is that you have to find great people and ask them to do extraordinary things. I've been doing that my whole life. [Tweet]. X. https://twitter.com/kevinolearytv/status/1741084221446189337

197

Odengo, R., & Kiiru, D. (2019). Work Life Balance Practices and Organisational Performance: Theoritical and Empirical review and a critique. *Journal of Human Resource and Leadership 4(2)*, 2519–9099.

Ogarcă, R. F., Crăciun, L., & Mihai, L. (2016). Leadership styles in smes: an exploratory study in Romania. *Directory of Open Access Journals*. https://doaj.org/article/7e9ea4d1cbf14d788bf57de83c5acff1

Oromanyshyn. (2024, March 30). What Leadership Lessons Can Business Learn from Ukraine's War? - Center for Leadership. Center For Leadership. https://uculeadership.com.ua/en/news/yakyh-urokiv-liderstva-biznes-mozhe-navchytysya-v-ukrayinskoyi-vijny/

Oshagbemi, T., & Gill, R. (2004). Differences in leadership styles and behaviour across *hierarchical levels in UK organisations. Leadership & Organization Development Journal*, 25(1), 93–106. https://doi.org/10.1108/01437730410512796

Oudshoorn-Tinga, D., & Kool-Blokland, H. (2023). Ketenen van het verleden. *Justitiele Verkenningen*, 49(2).

Page, N. & Wilkinson, E. (2019). Crafting the future of ethical leadership: Can the event of making itself create empathic leaders who are capable of building socially responsible supply chains? *Making Futures: 2020 International Research Conference*. 19-20. https://drive.google.com/file/d/1adSxdr58W3eEYr37iqgB59Ct77u-8sWa/view

Paixão, R. B., Bruni, A. L., & Júnior, C. V. C. O. (2016). Quem Não Arrisca Não Petisca? Uma Análise Empírica da Associação entre Empreendedorismo e Tolerância ao Risco. *Journal of Entrepreneurship*, 1–3. https://www.researchgate.net/

Pal, S. K., & Kapur, V. (2011, 1 December). Exploring unique corporate leadership styles in India. Semantic Scholar.

Palrecha, R., Spangler, W.D., & Yammarino, F. J. (2012). A comparative study of three leadership approaches in India. *The Leadership Quarterly*, 23(1), 146–162. https://doi.org/10.1016/j.leaqua.2011.11.012

Panayi, P. (2010). *Spicing up Britain: the multicultural history of British food*. Reaktion Books.

Pang, K. (2024, April 10). Great Wall of China: Length, history, map, why & when built it. China Highlights. https://www.chinahighlights.com/greatwall/

Parker, C. (2016, January 20). *Leadership lessons from Canada's Prime Minister Justin Trudeau*. World Economic Forum. https://www.weforum.org/agenda/2016/01/leadership-lessons-from-canada-s-prime-minister-justin-trudeau/

Parrish, D. R. (2015). The relevance of emotional intelligence for leadership in a higher education context. *Studies in Higher Education*, 40(5), 821–837. https://doi.org/10.1080/03075079.2013.842225

Pattanaik, D. (2016). *The leadership sutra: An Indian approach to power*. Aleph Book Company.

Pattanaik, D. (March 28, 2019). Leaders and Leadership by Devdutt Pattanaik [video file]. https://www.youtube.com/watch?v=MGPz3fyK3ZM&t=1s

Pelágio, M. (2024). MS Teams interview. 26 April.

Peroumal, M. (2019, August 27). Why people don't want you to succeed | Infinity Effect Podcast | Episode 15 [Video file]. *YouTube*. https://www.youtube.com/watch?v=ILLm5JJO8m8

Peter Bering, CEO of AADS (D. Revagliatte, Interviewer). (2022b, October 24). Spotify. S3. E2. https://open.spotify.com/episode/1WFYpvN3w19I9TavpvYbua

Pinnow, D. F. (2015). *Führen*. Springer-Verlag.

Pinto, M. M. R. A. (2005). *Cultura organizacional e características da liderança em empresas de Uberlândia e região*. Federal University of Uberlândia.

PNUD Rep. Dominicana, [@PNUDRD]. (2020, March 8). *"La participación de las mujeres en puestos de liderazgo ha demostrado que el poder no solo es cosa de hombres..."* [Tweet]. Twitter

Pooler, J. (2017). *Hierarchical Organization in Society*. Routledge.

Popa, R. I. (2012). An experimental perspective over personality and leadership styles inside Romanian organizations. *Procedia - Social and Behavioral Sciences*, 33, 488-492. https://doi.org/10.1016/j.sbspro

Portal da Liderança. (2015, January 20). *Alberto Pimenta: No que mais falha a liderança em Portugal?* [Video]. YouTube. https://www.youtube.com/watch?v=c_JoAE5kuFU

Portal da Liderança. (2015b, July 7). *João Couto: Como vê a gestão em Portugal e o que poder potenciar a sua qualidade?* [Video]. YouTube. https://www.youtube.com/watch?v=1OkGjVDKZgU

Portugal results - GLOBE Project. (n.d.). https://globeproject.com/results/countries/PRT%3Fmenu=list.html#list

Punnett, B. J., & Greenidge, D. (2009). Cultural mythology and global leadership in the Caribbean islands (pp. 65-78). Edward Elgar Publishing.

Quintas, C. (2023, December 1). *Competências de liderança e trabalho em equipa.* https://comum.rcaap.pt/handle/10400.26/48521

Radtke, F.-O. (2003). Multiculturalism in Germany: Local Management of Immigrants' Social Inclusion, pp. 55-74). https://unesdoc.unesco.org/ark:/48223/pf0000138796

Raihan, A., Ibrahim, S., & Muhtasim, D. A. (2023). Dynamic impacts of economic growth, energy use, tourism, and agricultural productivity on carbon dioxide emissions in Egypt. *World development sustainability, 2,* 100059.

Ramírez, H. (2021, December 17). *Las 12 Preguntas de Ney Díaz encontrarán respuesta en el mercado anglo -Revista Contacto.* Revista Contacto. https://revistacontactord.com/las-12-preguntas-de-ney-diaz-encontraran-respuesta-en-el-mercado-anglo/

RashedKhan, M. (2021). Individual's leadership style changes due to different culture in the UK. *International Journal of Trend in Scientific Research and Development, 5*(3), 1136-1143. https://www.ijtsrd.com/papers/ijtsrd41114.pdf

Redman, C. (2010). A new twist. *Time International* (South Pacific Edition), 176(19), 41-42.

Rego, A. (2004). Uma visão peculiar sobre a cultura nacional: a "tourada portuguesa" como metáfora. *GestãO E Desenvolvimento, 12,* 105-121. https://doi.org/10.7559/gestaoedesenvolvimento.2004.107

Rego, A., & Pina E Cunha, M. (2007). *A Essência da Liderança: Mudança x Resultados x Integridade* (3rd ed.). Editora RH.

Richardson, J., Millage, P., Millage, J., & Lane, S. (2014). The effects of culture on leadership styles in China, Germany and Russia. *Journal Of Technology Management in China, 9*(3), 263-273. https://doi.org/10.1108/jtmc-08-2014-0047

Rio, K., & Smedal, O. H. (2009). *Hierarchy: persistence and transformation in social formations.* Berghahn Books. https://ci.nii.ac.jp/ncid/BA88782661

Robbins, S. J., & Judge, T. (2019). Organizational Behavior, Updated 18e, Global Edition

Roberts, G. D. (2003). Shantaram. St. Martin's Press.

Rodrigues, I. D. G. S. M. (2017, October). *Liderança Transformacional e Transacional: Um Estudo de Caso na Caixa Geral de Depósitos.*

Rodrigues, J. N., Correia, G., Amândio Vaz Velho, Carlos Melo Brito, Carlos Zorrinho, Daniel Bessa, Francisco Lopes dos Santos, João Caraça, João César das Neves, João Vieira da Cunha, Jorge Vasconcellos e Sá, José Crespo de Carvalho, José Paulo Esperança, Luís Reto, Mário Murteira, Miguel Pina e Cunha, Pedro Dionísio, & Pedro Saraiva. (2004). *Mestres Portugueses da Gestão.* https://www.centroatl.pt/titulos/desafios/imagens/excerto-e-book-ca-mestres-pt-gestao.pdf

Rodriguez, M. (2011). Joining the Dark Side: Women in Management in the Dominican Republic. *Gender, Work & Organization,* 20(1), 13-19.

Rodriguez, Y. (2021). *Dominican Identity and the Experience of Interpersonal Conflict.* Seton Hall University Dissertations and Theses (ETDs). 2909. https://scholarship.shu.edu/dissertations/2909

Roe. (2016). The sound of silence: Ideology of national identity and racial inequality in contemporary Curaçao.

Roebuck, D. B., Bell, R. L., Raina, R., & Lee, C. E. (Catherine). (2016). Comparing Perceived Listening Behavior Differences Between Managers and Nonmanagers Living in the United States, India, and Malaysia. *International Journal of Business Communication* (Thousand Oaks, Calif.), 53(4), 485 518. https://doi.org/10.1177/2329488415572789

Roland, A. (1984). *The self in India and America: Toward a psychoanalysis of social and cultural contexts*. International Universities Press.

Römer, N. (2008) *Kòrsou Nobo i su Hende*. Keynote-speech presented for the Man Political Party.

Römer, R. (1981) *Samenleven op een Caribisch Eiland: Een Sociologische Verkenning*. Curaçao: Van Dorp Eddine.

Roseman, M. (1988). World War II and Social Change in Germany. *Total War and Social Change*, 58–78. https://doi.org/10.1007/978-1-349-19574-9_5

Ruhl, S., & J. Ennker. (2012). Empathische Führung. *Zeitschrift Für Herz-,Thorax- Und Gefäßchirurgie*, 26(2), 123–128. https://doi.org/10.1007/s00398-011-0890-6

Sala, M. (2010). Romanian. *Revue belge de philologie et d'histoire*, 88(3), 841-872.

Salari, M., & Nastiezaie, N. (2020). The Relationship between Transformational Leadership and Organizational Intimacy with Mediating Role of Organizational Empathy. *International Journal of Psychology and Educational Studies*, 7(1), 51-60. https://doi.org/10.17220/ijpes.2020.01.005

Saleem, H. (2015). The impact of leadership styles on job satisfaction and mediating role of perceived organizational politics. *Procedia-Social and Behavioural Sciences*.

Samad, A. (2015). Towards an understanding of the effect of leadership on employee wellbeing and organizational outcomes in Australian universities. *The Journal of Developing Areas*, 49(6), 441-448.

Sánchez, A. B. B., & Lozano, W. (2012). *Clientelistic Stability and Institutional Fragility: The Political System in the Dominican Republic (1978-2010)*. Latin American Perspectives, 39(6), 198-211. https://doi.org/10.1177/0094582X12458770

Santos, Dib, G. G., De Oliveira, V. H. L., Gomes Queiroz, J. G., De Souza Barbosa, A., Ramalho, A. A., & Da Silva-Nnes, M. (2023). Fatores associados à preferência de brasileiros por determinados estilos musicais. *Revista De Casos E Consultoria*, 14(1), e31388. https://periodicos.ufrn.br/casoseconsultoria/article/view/31388/16922

Sarros, J. C., Gray, J., & Densten, I. L. (2002). Leadership and its impact on organisational culture. *International Journal of Business Studies, 10(2)*, 1. https://www.researchgate.net/profile/Iain-Densten/publication/288676741_Leadership_and_its_impact_on_organizational_culture/links/5e9022df4585150839cebf0b/Leadership-and-its-impact-on-organizational-culture.pdf

Satpathy, B. B. (2015). *Indian culture and heritage*. Directorate of Distance and Continuing Education, Utkal University. https://ddceutkal.ac.in/Syllabus/MA_history/paper-8-N.pdf

Scarato, L. (2019). The portuguese language in Brazil: multiple peoples, multiple forms. *Revista Diadorim/Diadorim, 21(Esp)*, 200–226. https://doi.org/10.35520/diadorim.2019.v21nespa27338

Schrank, A. (2003). Luring, learning, and lobbying: The limits to capital mobility in the Dominican Republic. *Studies in Comparative International Development*, 37, 89-116.

Schroevers, S. M. (2024). *Hierarchy and Status: Mapping cross-cultural differences in leadership practices*. CCBS Press.

Sen, A. (2005). *The Argumentative Indian: Writings on Indian History, Culture and Identity*. Penguin books.

Senosiain, M. (2012). Managing in Brazil: a guide for American managers. https://stars.library.ucf.edu/honorstheses1990-2015/1302

Shadab, S., & Alam, F. (2024). High-Technology Exports, Foreign Direct Investment, Renewable Energy Consumption and Economic Growth: Evidence from the United Arab Emirates. *International Journal of Energy Economics and Policy*, 14(2), 394–401.

Shahin, A.I. and Wright, P.L. (2004), "Leadership in the context of culture: An Egyptian perspective", *Leadership & Organization Development Journal*, Vol. 25 No. 6, pp. 499-511. https://doi.org/10.1108/01437730410556743

Shanahan, J. (2023). BusinessOlver's eighth annual report [Report].

Shrestha, B., & Gnyawali, D. R. (2013). Insights on strategic management practices in Nepal. *South Asian Journal Of Global Business Research,* 2(2), 191–210. https://doi.org/10.1108/sajgbr-03-2012-0025

Shrestha, P. (2022). Human resource management practices in Nepalese organizations: Some observations. *NCC Journal*, 7(1), 33–40. https://doi.org/10.3126/nccj.v7i1.58617

Shrestha, R. K., Dahal, A. K., & Acharya, G. (2023). Employee participation in decision-making: a comparative study on perception of employees and employers in Nepalese enterprises. *International Journal of Business Management and Economic Review*, 06(01), 170–180. https://doi.org/10.35409/ijbmer.2023.3468

Shurden, M., Shurden, S., & Cagwin, D. (2008). A Comparative Study of Ethical Values of Business Students: American vs. Middle Eastern Cultures. *Journal of College Teaching & Learning/Journal of College Teaching and Learning*, 5(8).

Silverthorne, G. (2024, May 1). *Leadership and Hierarchy in UK* [Personal Interview]. E. Radeva & D. Jansen (interviewers).

Singh, J. P. (1990). Managerial Culture and Work-related Values in India. *Organization Studies*, 11(1), 075–101. https://doi.org/10.1177/017084069001100106

Singh, P. (2014). Employees use of empathy to improve their job behaviour. *International Business & Economics Research Journal*, 13(3), 559-610

Sinha, B. P. J., & Parvinder, G. (2002, 1 January). *Preferred leadership styles and influence tactics*. Sage Journals.

Sinha, J. B. P., & Sinha, D. (1990). Role of social values in Indian organizations. *International Journal of Psychology*, 25(3–6), 705–714. https://doi.org/10.1080/00207599008247922

Sinha, J.B.P. (1988). *Work culture in Indian organizations*. ICSSR Report

Sinha, N. (2016, July 4). No society can exist without myth, says Devdutt Pattanaik. Hindustan Times. https://www.hindustantimes.com/books/no-society-can-exist-without-myth-says-devdutt-pattanaik/story-PG1v4iB17j07dV5Vyv86QN.html

Six sigma, (May 15, 2022). Ratan Tata's Motivational Speech | Inspiring Video Subtitled In English | Six Sigma Films [Video file]. https://www.youtube.com/watch?v=8njHZefA0HU&t=1s

Skelly, T. (2017). Leadership is not a position, it's a behaviour. https://www.linkedin.com/pulse/leadership-position-its-behaviour-tim-skelly/

Smith, J. (2018). Cultural sensitivity in leadership: Understanding diverse perspectives. Journal of Leadership Studies, 5(2), 45-58.

Smith, K. (2017). *Adaptability in Caribbean Business Leaders*. Caribbean Business Press.

Sobrinho, F. R., & Porto, J. B. (2012). Bem-estar no trabalho: um estudo sobre suas relações com clima social, coping e variáveis demográficas. *RAC. Revista De Administração Contemporânea*, 16(2), 253–270. https://doi.org/10.1590/s1415-65552012000200006

Somenzari, M. S., 1, Ramos, A. C. D. C., & Neto, M. S. (2017). Estilos de liderança e cultura organizacional: estudo comparativo de uma organização pública vis-à-vis uma empresa privada. HOME Revista ESPACIOS, 38(53), 22–22.

Sommerlad A, Huntley J, Livingston G, Rankin KP, Fancourt D (2021). *Empathy and its associations with age and sociodemographic characteristics in a large UK population sample*. PLoS ONE 16(9): e0257557.https://doi.org/10.1371/journal.pone.0257557

Sorge, A. (2017). *Management in Germany, the Dynamo of Europe*. In Palgrave Macmillan UK eBooks (pp. 69–113). https://doi.org/10.1057/978-1-137-50929-1_3

Souza, E., Castro, D., Vitório, D., Teles, I., Oliveira, A. L. I., & Gusmão, C. (2016). Characterizing User-Generated Text Content Mining: A Systematic Mapping study of the Portuguese language. *In Advances in intelligent systems and computing (Internet)* (pp. 1015–1024). https://doi.org/10.1007/978-3-319-31232-3_96

Srinivasan, S., & Thangaraj, R. (2021). Essential employable skill sets in management graduates for finance job roles in india. [Essential employable skills for finance jobs] *Higher Education, Skills and Work – Based Learning*, 11(5), 1224-1235. doi: https://doi-org.rps.hva.nl/10.1108/HESWBL-05-2020-0093

Startup Grind Gibraltar. (2018, October 4). SGG Female Leaders Month w/ Girls in Tech [Video]. YouTube. https://www.youtube.com/watch?v=Tu2nUJzxWm8

Statistics Portugal - Web portal. (n.d.). Retrieved March 28, 2024, from https://www.ine.pt/xportal/xmain?xpgid=ine_main&xpid=INE

Stichting Soka. (2020, March 17). Personal leadership in diplomacy | by Alexandra Calu, Third secretary of the Embassy of Romania. YouTube. https://www.youtube.com/watchv=vXjE1_280iM&ab_channel=StichtingSoka

Straub, D. W., Loch, K. D., & Hill, C. E. (2002). Transfer of information technology to the Arab World. In *IGI Global eBooks* (pp. 92–134).

Subrahmanyam, S. (1993). *The Portuguese Empire in Asia, 1500-1700: A Political and Economic History (2nd ed.).* Wiley-Blackwell.

Super7fm. (2023, May 19). *"Domina el arte del liderazgo: Aprende cómo convertirte en un líder exitoso"* con *Raúl Burgos* [Video]. YouTube. https://www.youtube.com/watch?v=Le8G3nftC8Y

Suriel, A. J. y Escalante, J. L. (2023). Competencias emocionales y su relación con el liderazgo efectivo: un acercamiento desde las directoras educativas de la República Dominicana. Cuaderno de Pedagogía Universitaria, 21 (41), 52-63.

Szydło, J. (2017). *The influence of national culture on management culture on the example of polish and ukrainian institutions. DOAJ (DOAJ: Directory Of Open Access Journals).* https://doi.org/10.19253/reme.2017.03.018

Taher Alav, S., Rabah, S., & Jones, A. (2021). Studying transactional and transformational leader and leadership in government and private organizations in UAE. *International Journal of Management (IJM)*, 12(4). *Task Force Interamericano sobre Liderazgo de las Mujeres* (n.d.). https://www.oas.org/en/taskforcewomenleadership/initiatives/past-dialogues.asp

Tatomir, R. (2020). Sappho and Ma'at. Religious and philosophical ideas and societal realities of the sixth and fifth centuries B.C.E. *Pharaonic Egypt as reflected in Sappho's poetry.* Awrāq Kilāsīkiyyaṫ/Awrāq Kilāsīkiyyaṫ, 12(1), 1–42. https://doi.org/10.21608/acl.2020.89509

Tco international - accelerating global agility. (2015b, October 5). *Working in Brazil: Communication & relationship styles* [Video]. YouTube. https://www.youtube.com/watch?v=YFB2aZrH2bU

Tco international - accelerating global agility. (2015b, October 5). *Working in Brazil: building trust* [Video]. YouTube. https://www.youtube.com/watch?v=OlMci_pM6H8

TEDx Talks. (2016, April 25). *Mettaliderazgo, creando líderes de alto desempeño | Roberto Mourey | TEDxBarriodelEncino* [Video]. YouTube. https://www.youtube.com/watch?v=PZuSrV0hsnA

TEDx Talks. (2022, September 13). *Por que devemos ousar liderar? | Felipe Barreiro | TEDxBeloHorizonte* [Video]. YouTube. https://www.youtube.com/watch?v=tP0-VOsQosc

The Dominican Republic management style. (n.d.). https://www.commisceo-global.com/resources/management-guides/dominican-republic-management-guide

 Țiclău, T., & Hințea, C. (2016). Public Sector Leadership. A review of Romanian research done in the field between 2007-2016. *Directory of Open Access Journals*, 92-100.

Tribunal Superior Electoral – TSE. (n.d.). https://tse.do/el-tribunal-superior-electoral-fortalece-habilidades-de-liderazgo-en-areas-directivas/

TurismoRD. (2020, January 31). *República Dominicana mantiene liderazgo de crecimiento del PIB en la región | @MTurismoRD* [Video]. YouTube. https://www.youtube.com/watch?v=k6Wp8njGUo8

Turnbull, B., Graham, M., & Taket, A. (2020). Hierarchical Femininities and Masculinities in Australia Based on Parenting and Employment: A Multidimensional, Multilevel, Relational and Intersectional Perspective. *Journal of Research in Gender Studies 10(2)*: 9–62. doi:10.22381/JRGS10220201

UCU Business School. (2023, October 3). Трансформаційне лідерство в умовах невизначеності. Q&A з Олександрою Альхімович [Video]. Youtube. https://www.youtube.com/watch?v=vruWRLdkWQ4&ab_channel=UCUBusinessSchool

Ukraine in English. (2024, March 21). Ukraine Through the Eyes of Deborah Fairlamb [Video]. Youtube. https://www.youtube.com/watch?v=gYzimu4Qxdg&ab_channel=UkraineerinEnglish

Ulrich, K., Rodríguez-García, M., Gallego-Nicholls, J. F., & Pagán-Castaño, E. (2021). Family Council From A Cultural Approach: the case of eastern european countries. KnE Social Sciences., pp.116-125. https://doi.org/10.18502/kss.v5i9.9889

UN Women Ukraine. (2018, June 27). Women Leaders of Self-Help Group Drive Local Development in Eastern Ukraine [Video]. YouTube. https://ukraine.unwomen.org/en/digital-library/videos/139531

Urbaez, N. (2018). Identificacion de competencias de liderazgo en jovenes dominicanos. Interamerican Journal of Psychology, 52(3), 283-293. https://www.journal.sipsych.org/index.php/IJP/article/download/129/936

Ureña-Espaillat, H. J. (2024). Microsoft Teams interview. 24 April

Ureña-Espaillat, H. J., Peñalver, A. J. B., Conesa, J. a. B., & Córdoba-Pachón, J. (2022). Knowledge and innovation management in agribusiness: A study in the Dominican Republic. Business Strategy and the Environment, 32(4), 2008–2021. https://doi.org/10.1002/bse.3233

Valenta, M., Knowlton, K., Jakobsen, J., Awad, M. A., & Strabac, Z. (2019). Migration system and long–term residence strategies in the United Arab Emirates. International Migration, 58(1), 182–197.

Van der Maas, A. (2008, May 9). Strategy Implementation in a Small Island Community (No. EPS-2008-127-LIS). ERIM Ph.D. Series Research in Management. Retrieved from

Van Marrewijk, A. (2004). The management of strategic alliances: cultural resistance. Comparing the cases of a Dutch telecom operator in the Netherlands Antilles and Indonesia. Culture and Organization, 10(4), 303–314. doi:10.1080/1475955042000313740

Venkatesan, P. (2024). MS Teams interview. 24 April.

Verton, P. (2024) MS Teams interview. 27 April.

Vicary-Smith, P. [London Business School]. (2014, 10 February). Leadership tips from Which? CEO | London Business School [Video]. YouTube. https://youtu.be/bn4Kt1-8psw?si=FvkgxiWrDJm76faW

Vilkinas, T., Monga, M., Mehta, S., & Cartan, G. (2008). Predictors of Leadership Effectiveness for Indian Managers. Anzam.

Villiers, C. (2019). Boardroom Culture: An Argument for Compassionate Leadership. European Business Law Review, 30(2), 253-278. https://doi.org/10.54648/eulr2019012

Viswanathan, K. (2023). Empathetic Leadership In Workplace: Navigating Change And Fostering Success. In Business world (India). Athena Information Solutions Pvt. Ltd.

Voegtlin, C., Frisch, C., Walther, A., & Schwab, P. (2019). Theoretical development and empirical examination of a three-roles model of responsible leadership. Journal of Business Ethics, 1-21.

Vollers, K. (2011). The Modern Egyptian Dialect of Arabic: A grammar with exercises, reading lessons and glossaries. Cambridge University Press. ISBN: 9780521232975.

Vordev. (2024, May 14). Building a sustainable future: the imperative for a balanced and diverse tourism economy in Curaçao. Curaçao Chronicle. https://www.curacaochronicle.com/post/opinion/building-a-sustainable-future-the-imperative-for-a-balanced-and-diverse-tourism-economy-in-curacao/

Vrolijk, C. (2009). Scenario's voor de West en de betekenis daarvan voor de Nederlandse Defensie.

Wang W, Kang S-W and Choi SB. (2022). Servant Leadership and Creativity: A Study of the Sequential Mediating Roles of Psychological Safety and Employee Well-Being. Frontiers in Psychology. 12:807070. Doi: 10.3389/fpsyg.2021.807070

Weir, T. (2015). Leadership Dubai style: The Habits to Achieve Remarkable Success. Emarat Books.

White, C., & Boucke, L. (2024). The Undutchables: an observation of the Netherlands, its culture, and its inhabitants (9th ed.). Xpat Scriptum Publishers.

Wiedel, A. (2019). Zuhören ist ein Geschenk. Kösel-Verlag.

Wilson Center (2020). Ukraine's presidents, power elites, and the country's evolution. https://www.wilsoncenter.org/blog-post/ukraines-presidents-power-elites-and-countrys-evolution

Wilson, P. (2016). A different lesson from German history: OPINION. Financial Times Ltd. https://www.proquest.com/docview/1766983356/&sourcetype=Newspapers

Wipulanusat, W., Panuwatwanich, K., & Stewart, R. A. (2017). Exploring leadership styles for innovation: An exploratory factor analysis. *Engineering Management in Production and Services*, 9(1), 7–17. https://doi.org/10.1515/emj-2017-0001

World Economic Forum. (2024). How India can seize its moment to become the world's third-largest economy. World economic forum. https://www.weforum.org/agenda/2024/01/how-india-can-seize-its-moment-to-become-the-world-s-third-largest-economy/

Yao, X., & Collins, P. (2019). Developments in Australian, British, and American English Grammar from 1931 to 2006: An Aggregate, Comparative Approach to Dialectal Variation and Change. *Journal of English Linguistics, 47(2)*, 120-149. https://journals.sagepub.com/doi/10.1177/0075424219837337

Yarram, S. R., & Adapa, S. (2021). Board gender diversity and corporate social responsibility: Is there a case for critical mass? *Journal of Cleaner Production*, 278, 123319. https://doi.org/10.1016/j.jclepro.2020.123319

Your Gibraltar TV. (2020, December 23). Business Matters Edition: 55 - Katherine Grant [Video]. YouTube. https://www.youtube.com/watch?v=OK8z7fl_7ug

Zovorich, M. (2024). Microsoft Teams Interview. 16 April.

9 789079 646586